A HISTORY OF MODERN IRAN

In a radical reappraisal of Iran's modern history, Ervand Abrahamian traces its traumatic journey across the twentieth century, through the discovery of oil, imperial interventions, the rule of the Pahlavis, and, in 1979, revolution and the birth of the Islamic Republic. In the intervening years, Iran has experienced a bitter war with Iraq, the transformation of society under the rule of the clergy, and, more recently, the expansion of the state and the struggle for power between the old elites, the intelligentsia, and the commercial middle class. The author, who is one of the most distinguished historians writing on Iran today, is a compassionate expositor. While he adroitly negotiates the twists and turns of the country's regional and international politics, at the heart of his book are the people of Iran, who have endured and survived a century of war and revolution. It is to them and their resilience that this book is dedicated, as Iran emerges at the beginning of the twenty-first century as one of the most powerful states in the Middle East.

ERVAND ABRAHAMIAN is Distinguished Professor of History at Baruch College and Graduate Center, City University of New York. His previous publications include *The Iranian Mojahedin* (1989), *Khomeinism* (1993), and *Tortured Confessions* (1999).

A HISTORY OF MODERN IRAN

ERVAND ABRAHAMIAN

City University of New York

CAMBRIDGE
UNIVERSITY PRESS

CAMBRIDGE UNIVERSITY PRESS
Cambridge, New York, Melbourne, Madrid, Cape Town, Singapore, São Paulo,
Delhi, Mexico City

Cambridge University Press
The Edinburgh Building, Cambridge CB2 8RU, UK

Published in the United States of America by Cambridge University Press, New York

www.cambridge.org
Information on this title: www.cambridge.org/9780521528917

First published 2008
5th printing 2013

Printed in the United States of America by Edwards Brothers Inc., Ann Arbor, MI

A catalogue record for this publication is available from the British Library

Library of Congress Cataloguing in Publication Data
Abrahamian, Ervand, 1940–
A history of modern Iran / Ervand Abrahamian.
p.   cm.
Includes bibliographical references and index.
ISBN 978-0-521-82139-1
1. Iran – History – 20th century.   I. Title.
DS316.3.A27   2008
955.05–dc22
2008005641

ISBN 978-0-521-82139-1 Hardback
ISBN 978-0-521-52891-7 Paperback

In memory of the more than three hundred political prisoners hanged
in 1988 for refusing to feign belief in the supernatural

Contents

Maps

Illustrations

Tables

Figures

Chronology

1901	D'Arcy Concession
1905 December	Bastinadoing of merchants
1906 July	Protest in British legation
1906 August	Royal promise of constitution
1906 October	First Majles opens
1907 August	Anglo-Russian Convention
1908	First oil well
1908 June	*Coup d'état*
1909	Anglo-Persian Oil Company formed
1909 July	Revolutionaries capture Tehran
1909 November	Second Majles opens
1911	Russian ultimatum
1912	British Navy converts from coal to oil
1919 August	Anglo-Persian Agreement
1921 February	*Coup d'état*
1925	Constituent Assembly terminates the Qajar dynasty
1926	Coronation of Reza Shah
1927	Abolition of capitulations
1928	New dress code
1933	Cancellation of D'Arcy Concession
1934	Official name change of Persia to Iran
1941 August	Anglo-Soviet invasion
1951	Oil nationalization
1953	CIA coup
1963	White Revolution
1974	Quadrupling of oil prices
1975	Creation of Resurgence Party
1979 February	Islamic Revolution

1979 November	Students take the US embassy
December	Referendum for the Islamic constitution
1980 January	Bani-Sadr elected president
1980 September	Iraq invades Iran
1981 June	Mojahedin uprising; Bani-Sadr dismissed; Khamenei elected President
1983	Iran invades Iraq
1988	Iran–Iraq War ends
1989	Khomeini dies; Khamenei elected Supreme Leader; Rafsanjani elected president
1997	Khatemi elected president
2001	Khatemi reelected president
2005	Ahmadinejad elected president

Glossary

akhund	derogatory term for cleric (*rouhani*)
arbab	landlord
ashraf	aristocrat
a'yan	notable
ayatollah	high-ranking cleric (lit. "sign of god")
basej	support volunteer fighters (lit. "mobilized")
chadour	long-covering for women (lit. "tent")
dowlat	government, state
faqeh	expert on *feqh* (religious law)
fatwa	religious pronouncement
fedayi	fighter; self-sacrificer
hakim	lieutenant-governor
hojjat al-islam	middle-ranking cleric (lit. "proof of Islam")
husseinieh	religious center
kadkhuda	headman
keshvar	country, kingdom, state
komiteh	committee
mahalleh	district, town ward
majles	meeting, parliament
maraj-e taqled	most senior authorities of the law (singular *marja-e taqled*)
mehan	nation, country, homeland, fatherland/motherland
mellat	nation, people
melli	national
mojahed	fighter; crusader
mojtahed	high-ranking cleric
mostazafen	the meek, oppressed, exploited, wretched of the earth
mostowfi	accountant
mullah	derogatory term for cleric (*rouhani*)

pasdar	guards
qanat	underground canal
qazi	judge
rouhani	cleric
rousari	headscarf
rowshanfekr	intelligentsia, intellectual
sayyed	male descendant of the Prophet
shahed	martyr
shari'a	religious law
takiyeh	religious theater
taziyeh	passion play
tuyul	fief
ulama	clergy
'urf	state or customary law
vali	governor
vaqf	religious endowment (plural *awqaf*)
vatan	homeland, place of birth
velayat-e faqeh	guardianship of the jurist
vezir	minister

A political who's who of modern Iran

AHMAD SHAH (1896–1929) The last Qajar monarch. He ascended the throne in 1909 while still a minor and did not come of age until 1914. Lacking real power and fearful for his life, he left the country soon after the 1921 coup. He died in Paris and was buried in Karbala.

AHMADINEJAD, MAHMUD (1956–) The conservative president elected in 2005. Son of a blacksmith and veteran of the Iraqi war, he won the presidential election campaigning on populist themes. He promised to distribute the oil wealth to the people, revive the revolutionary ideals of Khomeini, and deliver a final blow to the "one thousand families" who have supposedly ruled the country for centuries. He was supported by some of the most conservative ulama.

ALAM, ASSADALLAH (1919–78) The main confidant of Muhammad Reza Shah. From a long line of notables in Sistan and Baluchestan known as the "Lords of the Marches," he joined the court in 1946 and served as an advisor to the shah until his death at the beginning of the revolution. Some speculate that his absence explains the shah's vacillations in 1977–78 and thus the eventual revolution. His posthumously published memoirs, however, support the view that he was very much part of the larger problem.

AL-E AHMAD, JALAL (1923–69) The initiator of the "back to roots" movement. He began his career as a Marxist in the Tudeh Party and remained to his last days an intellectual skeptic, but increasingly in the 1960s searched for the cultural roots of Iran in Shi'ism. His best-known work is *Gharbzadegi* which literally means 'Struck by the West' but whose argument is that Iran is being destroyed by a "plague coming from the West." He was one of the few intellectuals openly praised by Khomeini.

ARANI, TAQI (1902–40) The father of Marxism in Iran. Educated in Germany in 1922–30, he returned home to launch the journal *Donya* (The World) and form an intellectual circle whose members later founded the Tudeh Party. Sentenced to ten years' imprisonment for advocating "socialism" and "atheism," he died in prison.

ASHRAF, PRINCESS (1919–) The shah's twin sister. A forceful personality, she played an important role behind the scenes and helped many young Western-educated technocrats attain wealth and high office, especially cabinet posts. Some feel that she epitomized the worst features of the regime. Others claim this is a misogynist's view.

BAHAR, MUHAMMAD TAQI (MALEK AL-SHU'ARA) (1885–1952) Poet laureate of classical Persian literature. He began his political life as an active member of the constitutional movement and died as the president of the pro-Tudeh Peace Partisans. In addition to his prolific poetry, he wrote a well-known work entitled *Short History of Political Parties in Iran*.

BANI-SADR, SAYYED ABUL-HASSAN (1933–) Iran's first president. Although son of an ayatollah who had supported the 1953 coup, Bani-Sadr sided with Mossadeq and spent much of his adult life in Paris active in the National Front and the Liberation Movement. He returned with Khomeini in 1979 and briefly served as his president before accusing the clergy of scheming to establish a "dictatorship of the mullahtariat." He had to escape back to Paris.

BAZARGAN, MEHDI (1907–95) Khomeini's first prime minister. A deputy minister under Mossadeq, he was much more religious than most of his National Front colleagues. In 1961, he founded the Liberation Movement, committed to the ideals of Iranian nationalism, Western liberalism, and Shi'i Islam. Secularists deemed him too religious; the religious deemed him too secularist. He resigned his premiership to protest the students taking over the US embassy in 1979.

BEHBEHANI, SAYYED ABDALLAH (1844–1910) One of the two ayatollahs prominent in the Constitutional Revolution. In the subsequent fights between secular Democrats and the religious Moderates, he was assassinated. His son, Ayatollah Muhammad Behbehani, actively supported the 1953 coup. The money spent in the bazaar for the coup was known as "Behbehani dollars."

BOROUJERDI, AYATOLLAH AQA HAJJ AQA HUSSEIN TABATABAI (1875–1961) The last paramount Shi'i leader. After a long seminary career in Najaf and Boroujerd, in 1944 he moved to Qom where he soon gained the reputation of being the supreme *marja-e taqled*. Although he frowned on clerics participating in politics, he turned a blind eye to those who helped the 1953 coup. His death prompted younger grand ayatollahs to compete for his paramount position. It also prompted the shah to launch the White Revolution.

BOZORG, ALAVI (1904–95) A leading figure in modern Persian literature. Educated in Germany, he returned home in the 1930s, co-edited *Donya*, was imprisoned for belonging to Arani's circle, and, on his release in 1941, helped found the Tudeh Party. Among his works are his prison memoirs, *The Fifty-Three*. He was influenced by Kafka, Freud, and Hemingway as well as by Marx. He was a close friend of Sadeq Hedayat, another literary luminary.

CURZON, LORD GEORGE (1859–1925) The British foreign minister so enamored of Iran that he tried to incorporate it into his empire. As a graduate student he traveled to Iran and published his classic *Persia and the Persian Question*. His Anglo-Persian Agreement of 1919 created a nationalist backlash in Iran.

DEHKHODA, ALI AKBAR (1879–1956) A leading intellectual in modern Iran. A biting satirist during the Constitutional Revolution, he aroused much opposition, especially from the clergy and the landed class. He withdrew from politics and devoted his life to compiling his famous *Loqatnameh* (Lexicon). In the chaotic days of August 1953, when the shah fled the country, some radical nationalists offered him the presidency of their prospective republic.

EBADI, SHIREN (1947–) Iran's sole Nobel Prize Winner. A young judge in the last years of the old regime, she, together with all women, was purged from the judiciary. She opened her own law firm specializing in human rights, especially cases involving women or children. She was awarded the Nobel Peace Prize in 2003.

FARMANFARMA, FIRUZ (NOWSRAT AL-DOWLEH) (1889–1937) Prominent notable. A scion of the famous Farmanfarma family and descendant of Fath Ali Shah, he headed numerous ministries after World War I and was one of the triumvirate that helped Reza Shah establish a strong centralized state. The latter eventually imprisoned and then murdered him. In prison, he translated Oscar Wilde's *De Profundis*.

FATEMI, SAYYED HUSSEIN (1919–54) Mossadeq's right-hand man executed by the shah. A French-educated journalist, he was a vocal and early supporter of the campaign to nationalize the oil industry. He served Mossadeq in a number of capacities, including foreign minister. After the coup, he was arrested and executed for "insulting the royal family" and plotting to establish a republic. He is regarded as a hero of the nationalist movement. He is one of the few National Front leaders to have a street named after him by the Islamic Republic.

FAZLOLLAH NURI, SHEIKH (1843–1909) Leading cleric opposed to the Constitutional Revolution. A prominent theologian in Tehran, he initially supported attempts to limit royal power, but, growing fearful of the secularists, ended up siding with the royalists. He issued *fatwas* accusing reformers of being secret Babis, atheists, and freethinkers. Some were killed and executed in the Civil War. After the war, he was hanged for issuing such lethal *fatwas*. The modern Islamist movement regards him as one of their very first "martyrs."

HOVEIDA, ABBAS (1919–79) The shah's longest-lasting premier. A career public servant, he was raised in a Bahai family – although he himself was not a practicing Bahai – and was appointed premier in 1965, when his patron, the previous premier, was assassinated by religious fanatics. He remained in that post until 1977, when the shah, in an attempt to mollify the opposition, first dismissed him and then had him arrested. He was one of the first to be executed by the revolutionary regime.

ISKANDARI, MIRZA SULAYMAN (1862–1944) Qajar prince prominent in the socialist movement for half a century. Opponent of royal despotism, he participated in the Constitutional Revolution – his elder brother fell victim to the Civil War; helped lead the Democrat Party, 1909–21; was imprisoned by the British in World War I; headed the Socialist Party in 1921–26; and returned to politics in 1941 to chair the Tudeh Party.

KASHANI, AYATOLLAH SAYYED ABUL-QASSEM (1885–1961) The main cleric who first supported and then opposed Mossadeq. A refugee from Iraq where his father had been killed fighting Britain after World War I, he was arrested by the British in World War II. He threw his weight behind Mossadeq when the campaign for the nationalization of the oil industry began. He broke with Mossadeq in 1953 avowedly because the latter did not implement the shari'a. His supporters vehemently deny that he actively supported the 1953 coup.

KASRAVI, SAYYED AHMAD (1890–1946) Leading historian of modern Iran, especially of the Constitutional Revolution. A staunch advocate of national solidarity, he persistently denounced all forms of communalism and sectarianism, including Shi'ism. His most controversial work is *Shi'igari* (Shi'i-Mongering). Denounced as an "unbeliever," he was assassinated. Khomeini, however, continued to keep on his shelves Kasravi's *History of the Iranian Constitution*.

KHAMENEI, AYATOLLAH SAYYED ALI (1939–) Khomeini's successor as Supreme Leader. From a minor clerical family in Azerbaijan, he studied theology first in Mashed and then in Qom with Khomeini. He did not attain prominence until after the revolution when he held a series of high positions including briefly the presidency. Immediately after Khomeini's death, the regime elevated him to the rank of ayatollah and hailed him as the new Supreme Leader. He inherited Khomeini's powers but not his charisma.

KHATEMI, HOJJAT AL-ISLAM SAYYED MUHAMMAD (1944–) Liberal president. Son of an ayatollah who was a close friend of Khomeini, Khatemi studied theology in Qom and philosophy in Isfahan University, in the process learning some English and German. At the beginning of the revolution, he was administering the Shi'i mosque in Hamburg. After the revolution, he headed the government publishing house, sat in the Majles, and as culture minister aroused conservative anger by relaxing the censorship on books and films. Resigning from the ministry, he headed the national library and taught political philosophy at Tehran University. Running on a reform platform, he won the presidency twice – in 1997 and 2001 – both with landslide victories.

KHOMEINI, AYATOLLAH SAYYED RUHOLLAH (1902–89) Charismatic leader of the Islamic Revolution. Born into a clerical family, he spent his early life in seminaries in Qom and Najaf. He entered politics in 1963, when he denounced the shah for granting "capitulations" to American military advisors. Deported, he spent the next sixteen years in Najaf developing a new interpretation of Shi'i Islam. He drastically expanded the traditional Shi'i concept of *velayat-e faqeh* – from clerical jurisdiction over orphans, widows, and the mentally feeble to clerical supervision over all citizens. He also combined clerical conservatism with radical populism. Returning triumphant in 1979, he was hailed by the new constitution as Commander of the Revolution, Founder of the Islamic Republic, Supreme Leader of the Islamic Republic, and, most potent of all, Imam of the Muslim World – a title Shi'is in the past had reserved for the Twelve Sacred Infallible Imams.

MODARRES, SAYYED HASSAN (1870–1937) The main ayatollah opposed to Reza Shah. A member of the Majles since 1914, he was known chiefly as a parliamentary politician. He participated in the national government that opposed the Allies in 1914–18, was a vocal opponent of the 1919 Anglo-Iranian Agreement, and tried to stem the rise of Reza Shah. Banished to the provinces, he was eventually murdered there. Modern Islamists view him as one of their forerunners.

MOSSADEQ, MUHAMMAD (MOSSADEQ AL-SALTANEH) (1881–1967) The icon of Iranian nationalism. From a long line of notables, he studied in Europe and had a successful career in government service until forced into retirement by Reza Shah. Returning to politics in 1941, he gained fame first as an "incorruptible" deputy, and then as leader of the National Front campaigning for the nationalization of the British-owned oil company. Elected prime minister in 1951, he promptly nationalized the oil industry and thus sparked off a major international crisis with Britain. He was overthrown by the military coup organized by the CIA in August 1953. Islamists distrusted him because of his deep commitment to secular nationalism.

MUHAMMAD REZA SHAH PAHLAVI (1919–80) Monarch overthrown by the Islamic Revolution. He was raised by his father to be first and foremost commander-in-chief of the armed forces. Ascending the throne in 1941, he successfully warded off generals and notables who tried to gain control of the armed forces. Consolidating power after the 1953 CIA coup, he ruled much like his father, using oil revenues to expand drastically the state as well as the armed forces. He died soon after the revolution – from cancer which he had kept secret even from his own family so as not to endanger his regime. He has been described as a "majestic failure."

NAVAB-SAFAVI, SAYYED MOJTABA MIR-LOWHI (1922–56) Founder of Fedayan-e Islam – one of the first truly fundamentalist organizations in Iran. The group carried out a number of high-profile assassinations between 1944 and 1952. It also made an attempt on Mossadeq's main advisor and plotted to kill Mossadeq himself. It denied, however, having taken part in the 1953 coup. Safavi was executed in 1956 after an assassination attempt on the then prime minister. The far rightists among Khomeini's followers deem Safavi as one of their forerunners.

QAVAM, AHMAD (QAVAM AL-SALTANEH) (1877–1955) Most notable of the old notables. A court-supporter of the 1906 revolution – the royal proclamation granting the country a constitution is reputed to have been written in his calligraphic writing – he gained the aura of a highly successful wheeler and dealer both in the Majles and in the government. He headed four cabinets in the years before Reza Shah and six after him. He had little regard for the young shah. Some credit him – rather than Truman – with keeping Iran intact by persuading Stalin to withdraw the Red Army from Azerbaijan. He died with his reputation much tarnished, since in 1952 he had offered to replace Mossadeq as prime minister.

RAFSANJANI, HOJJAT AL-ISLAM ALI-AKBAR HASHEMI (1934–) Reputed to be the *éminence grise* of the Islamic Republic. Born into a prosperous agricultural family, he studied with Khomeini in Qom, and was in and out of prison during the 1960s. He wrote a book in praise of a nineteenth-century minister who had tried to industrialize the country. After the revolution, he occupied numerous high positions including the presidency and the chairmanship of the Expediency Council. He is considered to be the most important person after the Supreme Leader.

REZA SHAH PAHLAVI (1878–1944) Founder of Iran's centralized state. Born into a military family, he rose through the ranks to the Cossack Brigade – the country's main fighting force at the time. He led a military coup in 1921, and five years later crowned himself shah, replacing the Qajar dynasty with his own Pahlavi family. He ruled with an iron fist until 1941 when the British and Soviet armies invaded and forced him to abdicate. He died three years later in South Africa. He left to his son not only the crown but also a huge private fortune – considered at the time to be one of the largest in the Middle East.

SARDAR AS'AD BAKHTIYARI, JAFAR QULI KHAN (1882–1934) Crucial figure in the Civil War. He and fellow Bakhtiyari chiefs led tribal contingents into Tehran, providing the constitutionalists with a decisive victory. They turned some of the ministries into family fiefdoms until ousted by Reza Shah. Sardar As'ad was murdered in prison.

SAYYED ZIYA (AL-DIN TABATABAI) (1889–1969) Pro-British politician closely associated with the 1921 coup. An openly pro-British journalist, he was appointed prime minister by Reza Khan in 1921 only to be ousted a few months later. Returning to Iran in World War II after twenty years in exile, he made numerous attempts to become prime minister again – often with British support but invariably with Soviet and American opposition. He had regular private audiences with the shah until his death.

SEPAHDAR, MUHAMMAD VALI KHAN (SEPAHSALAR AL-AZ'AM) (1847–1926) Crucial figure in the Civil War. A major landlord in Mazanderan and the nominal commander of the royal army, he defected to the constitutionalists and thus helped seal the fate of the monarchists. He headed eight different cabinets between 1910 and 1919. In anticipation of being incarcerated by Reza Shah, he committed suicide.

SHARIATI, ALI (1933–77) Considered the "real ideologue" of the Islamic Revolution. Studying in France in the 1960s, he was strongly influenced by theorists of Third World revolutions – especially by Franz Fanon. His prolific lectures – totaling some thirty-six volumes – aimed to transform Shi'ism from a conservative apolitical religion into a highly revolutionary political ideology competing with Leninism and Maoism. His writings influenced many of the activists who took part in the revolution. He died in exile on the eve of the revolution.

TABATABAI, SAYYED MUHAMMAD SADEQ (1841–1918) One of the two ayatollahs prominent in the Constitutional Revolution. A secret freemason, he played a leading role throughout the revolution and had to flee the country after the 1909 coup. His son and namesake was to become a major powerbroker in the Majles in the 1940s.

TALEQANI, AYATOLLAH SAYYED MAHMUD (1919–79) The most popular cleric in Tehran during the revolution. A consistent supporter of Mossadeq and a founding member of the Liberation Movement, Taleqani enjoyed good rapport with all segments of the opposition – with the National Front, the Mojahedin, and even Marxist groups. He organized the mass rallies of 1978. If he had not died soon after the revolution, he might have provided a liberal counterweight to Khomeini.

TAQIZADEH, SAYYED HASSAN (1874–1970) A leading intellectual-politician of the Constitutional Revolution. As a firebrand deputy in the First Majles, he spoke on behalf of the Democrat Party and aroused the wrath of the conservative ulama who issued fatwas against him. He lived in exile from 1909 until 1924, returning home to take up a ministerial position under Reza Shah. He also served as a senator under Muhammad Reza Shah. Some see him as typifying the generation of young radicals coopted into the Pahlavi regime.

VOSSUQ, MIRZA HASSAN KHAN (VOSSUQ AL-DOWLEH) (1865–1951) Signatory to the notorious Anglo-Iranian Agreement of

1919. A prominent notable, he served in numerous administrations between 1909 and 1926. He was Qavam's older brother.

YEPREM KHAN (DAVITIAN) (1868–1912) Leader of the Caucasian fighters in the Civil War. Member of the Armenian nationalist Dashnak Party in Russia, he had been sent to Siberia from where he had escaped to Iran. With the outbreak of the Civil War, he led volunteers from the Caucasus fighting on behalf of the constitutionalists under the slogan "The Love of Freedom has No Fatherland." Immediately after the Civil War, he was appointed police chief of Tehran and was killed fighting insurgents.

ZAHEDI, GENERAL FAZLOLLAH (1897–1963) Nominal head of the 1953 CIA coup. A career officer from the Cossack Brigade, he was in and out of favor with both Reza Shah and Muhammad Reza Shah. He was imprisoned by the British in 1942 for having contacts with the Third Reich. Appointed prime minister in 1953, he was eased out by the shah in 1955. He moved into exile and died in his luxury mansion in Switzerland.

Preface

We view the past, and achieve our understanding of the past, only through the eyes of the present.

E. H. Carr

This book is an introduction written primarily for general readers perplexed by the sound and fury of modern Iran. It tries to explain why Iran is often in the news; why it often conjures up images of "Alice in Wonderland"; why it has experienced two major revolutions in one century – one of them in our own lifetime; and, most important of all, why it is now an Islamic Republic. The book subscribes to E. H. Carr's premise that we historians inevitably perceive the past through our own times and attempt to explain how and why the past has led to the present. This premise can have an obvious pitfall – as Carr himself would have readily admitted. If, by the time this book is published, the regime and even the whole state has disappeared into the "dustbin of history" because of a major external onslaught, then the whole trajectory of the book will appear to have been misconceived. Despite this danger, I take the calculated risk and work on the premise that if no ten-ton gorilla barges on to the scene, the Islamic Republic will continue into the foreseeable future. Of course, in the long run all states die. The period I cover is Iran's long twentieth century – starting from the origins of the Constitutional Revolution in the late 1890s and ending with the consolidation of the Islamic Republic in the early 2000s.

Since this book is not a work of primary research intended for the professional historian, I have dispensed with the heavy apparatus of academic publications. I have used endnotes sparingly to cite direct quotations, support controversial statements, or elaborate further on needed points. For readers interested in exploring specific topics, I have compiled a bibliography at the end listing the more important, more recent, and more available – mostly English-language – books. For transliteration, I have modified the system developed by the *International Journal of Middle East*

Studies, dispensing with diacritical marks, and, where possible, adopting the spelling used in the mainstream media. Consequently, I have Tehran instead of Teheran, Hussein instead of Husayn, Nasser instead of Nasir, Mashed instead of Mashhad, Khomeini instead of Khom'ayni, and Khamenei instead of Khamenehi.

I would like to thank Baruch College, especially the History Department, for giving me the time to write this book. I would also like to thank Marigold Acland for inviting me to undertake the task and for guiding the manuscript through the whole process from inception to publication. Thanks also go to Amy Hackett for editorial work and to Helen Waterhouse for helping out in the publication process. Of course, I am fully responsible for errors and views found in the book.

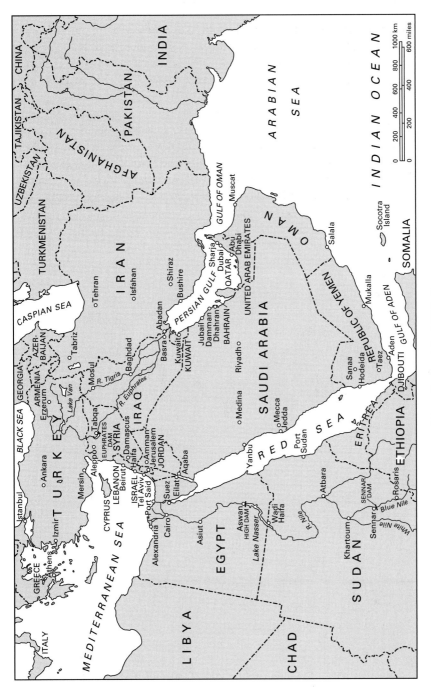

Map 1 Iran and the Middle East

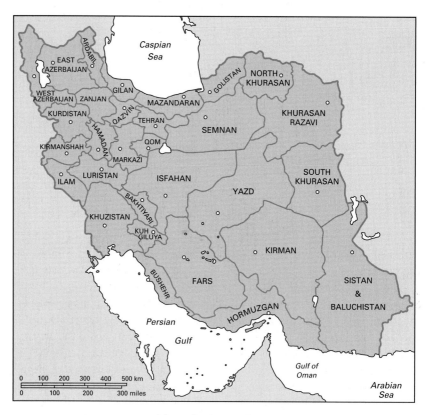

Map 2 Iranian provinces

Introduction

"The past is a foreign country."

David Lowenthal

Iran entered the twentieth century with oxen and wooden plough. It exited with steel mills, one of the world's highest automobile accident rates, and, to the consternation of many, a nuclear program. This book narrates the dramatic transformation that has taken place in twentieth-century Iran. Since the main engine of this transformation has been the central government, the book focuses on the state, on how it was created and expanded, and how its expansion has had profound repercussions not only on the polity and economy, but also on the environment, culture, and, most important of all, wider society. Some repercussions were intended; others, especially protest movements and political revolutions, were not. This book may appear somewhat quaint and even insidious to those convinced that the state is inherently a part of the problem rather than solution of contemporary dilemmas. But since this book is about major transformations, and these transformations in Iran have been initiated invariably by the central government, it will focus on the latter hopefully without falling into the Hegelian–Rankean pitfalls of glorifying the state.

Through all the changes, Iran's geography and identity have remained remarkably constant. Present-day Iranians live more or less within the same borders as their great-grandparents. The region – three times the size of France and six times that of the United Kingdom – is demarcated in the south by the Persian Gulf; in the east by the deserts and mountains of Khurasan, Sistan, and Baluchestan; in the west by the Shatt al-Arab, the Iraqi marshes, and the Kurdish mountains; and in the north by the Aras River flowing from Mount Ararat to the Caspian Sea, and by the Atrak River stretching from the Caspian Sea into Central Asia. Three-fifths of the country, especially the central plateau, lacks the rainfall to sustain permanent agriculture. Farming is confined to rain-fed Azerbaijan, Kurdestan,

I

and the Caspian coast, to irrigated villages and oases scattered throughout the county, especially at the foot of the mountain ranges.

Like all national identities, Iran's is fluid and contested. Nonetheless, Iran's attachment to *Iran Zamen* (Land of Iran) and *Iran Shahr* (Country of Iran) has remained remarkably constant. Iranians identify with both Shi'i Islam and their pre-Islamic history, especially the Sassanids, Achaemenids, and Parthians. Names parents choose for their children are living proof of this: from Shi'ism come Ali, Mehdi, Reza, Hussein, Hassan, and Fatemeh; from ancient Iran, via the poet Ferdowsi and his epic *Shahnameh* (Book of Kings), come Isfandiyar, Iskandar, Rostam, Sohrab, Ardashir, Kaveh, Bahram, and Atossa. This tenth-century epic continues to be widely read into the modern age. Although national identity is often deemed to be a modern invention, the *Shahnameh* refers to Iran by name more than one thousand times, and the whole epic can be read as a mythical history of the Iranian nation. Among Iranians – as among some other Middle Eastern peoples – national awareness seems to have long preceded the modern era. Of course, how it was expressed and who articulated it has not always remained constant.

Despite continuities, the twentieth century brought profound changes in almost all aspects of Iranian life. At the beginning of the century, the total population was fewer than 12 million – 60 percent villagers, 25–30 percent nomads, and less than 15 percent urban residents.[1] Tehran was a medium-sized town of 200,000. Life expectancy at birth was probably less than thirty years, and infant mortality as high as 500 per 1,000 births. By the end of the century, the population totaled 69 million. The nomadic population had shrunk to less than 3 percent, and the urban sector had grown to more than 66 percent. Tehran was a mega-metropolis of more than 6.5 million. Life expectancy reached seventy years; and infant mortality had fallen to 28 per 1,000. At the start of the century, the literacy rate was around 5 percent – confined to graduates of seminaries, Koranic schools, and missionary establishments. Less than 50 percent of the population understood Persian – others spoke Kurdish, Arabic, Gilaki, Mazanderani, Baluchi, Luri, and Turkic dialects such as Azeri, Turkman, and Qashqa'i. Public entertainment came in the form of athletic shows in local *zurkhanehs* (gymnasiums); *Shahnameh* recitations in tea- and coffee-houses; royal pageants in the streets; occasional executions in public squares; and, most important of all, flagellation processions, passion plays, and bonfire celebrations during the high Shi'i holy month of Muharram. By the end of the century, however, the literacy rate had reached 84 percent; some 1.6 million were enrolled in institutions of higher learning, and another 19 million attended

primary and secondary schools. More than 85 percent of the population
could now communicate in Persian although some 50 percent continued to
speak their "mother tongue" at home. Public entertainment now comes in
the form of soccer matches, films, radio, newspapers, and, most important
of all, videos, DVDs, and television – almost every urban and three-quarters
of rural households have television sets.

In the early twentieth century modern modes of travel were just making
their debut – paved roads and railways totaled fewer than 340 kilometers.
According to one foreign diplomat, mules and camels were the normal
means of transport since there were almost "no wheeled vehicles."[2] The
shah was the proud owner of the only motorcar in all of Iran. Under
favorable conditions, travelers needed at least 17 days to cross the 350
miles from Tehran to Tabriz, 14 days, the 558 miles to Mashed, and 37
days, the 700 miles to Bushire. Gas lights, electricity, and telephones were
luxuries restricted to a few in Tehran. One English visitor wrote nostalgi-
cally: "There are no cities in Persia, and likewise no slums; no steam driven
industries, and therefore none of the mechanical tyranny that deadens the
brain, starves the heart, wearies bodies and mind with its monotony. There
are no gas and no electricity, but is not the glow of oil-lamps pleasanter?"[3]
By the end of the century, the country was integrated into the national
economy through roads, the electrical system, and the gas grid. Many
homes – even family farms – had running water, electricity, and refrigerators. The country now has 10,000 kilometers of railways, 59,000 kilometers of paved roads, and 2.9 million motor vehicles – most of them
assembled within the country. Travelers from Tehran can now reach the
provincial capitals within hours by car or train – not to mention by plane.

The century has brought equally profound changes in everyday fears. At
the beginning of the period, the perennial dangers haunting the average
person were highway robbers and tribal bandits; wild animals, *jinns*, the evil
eye, and black cats crossing one's path; famine, pestilence, and disease,
especially malaria, diphtheria, dysentery, tuberculosis, smallpox, cholera,
syphilis, and influenza. By the end of the century, these fears had been
replaced by such modern concerns as unemployment, pensions, housing,
old-age infirmities, pollution, car accidents and air crashes, crowded
schools, and competition to get into college. Iran has truly entered the
modern world. An Iranian Rip Van Winkle gone to sleep in 1900 would
hardly have recognized his environment if woken up in 2000.

The most notable change, however, has come in the structure of the state.
At the beginning of the twentieth century, the state, if it could be called
that, consisted merely of the shah and his small personal entourage – his

ministers, his family, and his patrimonial household. He ruled the country not through a bureaucracy and standing army – both of which were sorely lacking – but through local notables such as tribal chiefs, landlords, senior clerics, and wealthy merchants. By the end of the century, the state permeated every layer and region of the country. Twenty gigantic ministries employed more than 850,000 civil servants and controlled as much as 60 percent of the national economy; semi-governmental foundations controlled another 20 percent. Equally important, the state now wields a military force of more than half a million men. Of the notables who had helped govern the provinces for centuries, only the clerics have survived. The state has so expanded that some call it "totalitarian." But whether totalitarian or not, the state has grown by such leaps and bounds that it now controls the means of organized violence as well as the machinery for collecting taxes, administering justice, and distributing social services. Such a state had never existed in Iran. For centuries, the word *dowlat* had meant royal government. It now means the state in the full modern sense.

Similar linguistic changes can be seen in other arenas. In the late nineteenth century, Nasser al-Din Shah reigned as *Shah-in-Shah* (King of Kings), *Padshah* (Guardian Shah), *Khaqan* (Khan of Khans), and *Zillallah* (Shadow of God). Courtiers hailed him Justice Dispenser, Supreme Arbiter, Commander of the Faithful, Guardian of the Flock, and Pivot of the Universe. The state was merely an extension of his royal person; the royal person, like traditional rulers the world over, was sovereign. By the later twentieth century, Ayatollah Ruhollah Khomeini ruled with such innovative titles as *Rahbar-e Enqelab* (Leader of the Revolution), *Rahbar-e Mostazafen* (Leader of the Dispossessed), and *Bonyadgar-e Jomhuri-ye Islam* (Founder of the Islamic Republic). His "republic" claimed to speak on behalf not only of Iran and Shi'ism but also of the "revolutionary masses" and the "wretched of the world" – terms inconceivable in earlier centuries.

The political language has changed in many other ways. At the start of the century, the key words in the political lexicon had been *estabdad* (autocracy), *saltanat* (kingdom), *ashraf* (noble), *a'yan* (notable), *arbab* (landlord), *ri'yat* (subject), and *tireh* (clan) – a term now as unfamiliar to contemporary urban Iranians as "clan" would have been to a Scotsman living in Victorian London. By the end of the century, the key terms were *demokrasi, pluralism, moderniyat, hoquq-e beshar* (human rights), *jam'eh-e madani* (civil society), *mostarak* (public participation), and a new word: *shahrvandi* (citizenship). In other words, average Iranians now consider themselves no longer mere subjects of the ruler but full citizens, irrespective of gender, with the inalienable right to participate in national politics. Not surprisingly, in

the 1990s more than 70 percent of the adult population regularly participated in national elections.

The century also transformed the meanings of both Iranism and Shi'ism –
the two intertwining threads that have helped create national consciousness.
For centuries, conventional wisdom had seen the *Shahnameh* as legitimizing
the monarchy, linking the crown to the Persian language, and praising epic
achievements not only of Iran but also of ancient Persian dynasties. The
Shahnameh, in other words, was an epic proof that the identity of Iran was
inseparable from that of the institution of kingship; no shah, no Iran. But by
the time we come to the 1979 revolution, many argued that the epic had
been written not in praise of shahs, but in their condemnation since the
heroes came from outside the ranks of the royalty and most of the monarchs
were portrayed as corrupt, tyrannical, and evil. One writer even argued that
the Books of Kings should have been named the Book of Revolt.[4] After all,
he argued, its main hero was Kaveh the Blacksmith who raised the banner of
revolt against a tyrannical shah.

Changes in Shi'ism were even more dramatic. In the past, Shi'ism had
espoused doctrines which on the whole were conservative, quietist, and
apolitical. It had taken interest less in affairs of this world than in the
afterlife, in the soul, and in matters of personal behavior and ethics. The
most sacred event in the holy calendar – Ashura in the month of Muharram –
was commemorated to mark the day in AD 680 when Imam Hussein had
knowingly and willingly gone to his martyrdom in the battle of Karbala in
order to fulfill God's predetermined will. Shi'is memorialized Karbala,
Ashura, and Muharram much in the same way as traditional Catholics
commemorate Christ's Easter Passion at Mount Calvary. What is more,
ever since 1501, when the Safavids established Shi'ism as the official religion
of Iran, they and their successors, including the Qajar dynasty, had systematically patronized Muharram to bridge the gap between themselves and
their subjects, and to cement the bond between their subjects against the
outside Sunni world – against the Ottomans in the west, the Uzbeks in the
north, and the Pashtus in the east.

But by the outbreak of the 1979 revolution, Shi'ism had been drastically
transformed into a highly politicized doctrine which was more like a radical
ideology than a pious and conservative religion. The central message of
Muharram was now interpreted to be that of fighting for social justice and
political revolution. Slogans declared: "Make Every Month Muharram,
Every Day Ashura, and Every Place Karbala."[5] It was now argued that
Imam Hussein had gone to Karbala not because of predetermined destiny,
but because he had come to the rational conclusion that the "objective

Table 1 *Vital statistics*

	1900–06	2000–06
Total population	12 million	69 million
Urban population (% of total)	20%	66%
Nomadic population (% of total)	25–30%	3%
Tehran	200,000	6.5 million
Life expectancy at birth	30	70
Infant mortality per 1,000	500	30
Literacy (above 6 years)	5%	84%
Government ministries	4 (9)	25 (21)
Provinces	8	30
Government expenditures	$8.2 million	$40 billion
Civil servants		850,000
Armed forces	7,000	508,000
Enrolled in state schools	2,000	19 million
Enrolled in universities	0	1.7 million
Miles of paved roads	325 km	94,100 km
Motor vehicles	1	2.9 million
Miles of railroads	12 km	10,000 km
Electrical production	0	129 billion kwh
Telephones	0	15 million
Radios	N/A	18 million
Televisions	N/A	5 million
Public cinemas	N/A	311
Internet users	N/A	4.3 million
Daily newspaper circulation	10,000	2 million
New book titles		23,300
Public libraries	3	1,502

situation" provided him with a good opportunity to carry out a successful revolution.[6] Some even described him as an early-day Che Guevara.[7] Conservatives have difficulty recognizing such ideas. Although Shi'ism – like Iranism – continues to be the language of identity, its real contents have drastically changed.

This book provides a broad sweep of twentieth-century Iran. It tries to explain how we have got to the present from the nineteenth century. It describes, on the one hand, how the formation of the centralized state has placed pressures on the society below; and, on the other hand, how social pressures from below have altered the state – especially in two dramatic revolutions. While the state has gained increasing power over society, it has itself become more differentiated, with various political groups having special links with particular social groups. The book also looks at the intimate and complex dynamics between economic and social change, between social and cultural change, and between cultural and political change – as reflected in the official ideology of the state as well as in the political culture of the larger society. In the Weberian sense, this book is a narrative of how patrimonial rule has been replaced by a bureaucratic state – one where the center dominates the periphery. Household rule has given way first to royal autocracy and then to modern bureaucracy, where paradoxically the citizen claims inalienable rights. In the Tönnies' sense, it describes the transition from *Gemeinschaft* into *Gesellschaft* – from small face-to-face communities ruled by tradition, custom, and kinship into a large nation-state dominated by the impersonal forces of the bureaucracy, market, and industrial production. In the Marxist sense, it traces the transition from feudalism into state capitalism – from a loosely knit geographical region dotted with isolated villages and tribal clans to an urbanized and integrated economy where classes jockey for power within the state. The state is no longer a separate entity unto itself hovering over society, but a large entity deeply enmeshed in society. In the Braudelian sense, it explores the deep-seated and slow-moving shifts that have occurred in popular *mentalités* as well as the sparks, the "fireworks," that light up the surface layer of political events. In the Foucaultian sense, it narrates how the introduction of novel "discourses" has created tension between old and new, and thereby dramatically transformed both Shi'ism and Iranism. In short, the book aspires to Eric Hobsbawm's goal of presenting not just political history or social history, but a history of the whole society.[8]

CHAPTER I

"Royal despots": state and society under the Qajars

Kingdoms known to man have been governed in two ways: either by a prince and his servants, who, as ministers by his grace and permission, assist in governing the realm; or by a prince and by barons, who hold their positions not by favor of the ruler but by antiquity of blood. Such barons have states and subjects of their own, who recognize them as their lords, and are naturally attached to them. In those states which are governed by a prince and his servants, the prince possesses more authority, because there is no one in the state regarded as superior, and if others are obeyed it is merely as ministers and officials of the prince, and no one regards them with any special affection. Examples of the two kinds of government in our time are those of the Turk and the King of France.

Nicolò dei Machiavelli, *The Prince*

THE QAJAR STATE

Nineteenth-century Europeans tended to depict the Qajars as typical "oriental despots." Their despotism, however, existed mainly in the realm of virtual reality. In theory, the shah may have claimed monopoly over the means of violence, administration, taxation, and adjudication. His word was law. He appointed and dismissed all officials – from court ministers, governor-generals, and tribal chiefs, all the way down to village and ward headmen. He made and unmade all dignitaries, bestowing and withdrawing honors and titles. He even claimed to own all property, treating the country as his own private estate. Lord Curzon, after exploring the country in person and making liberal use of the India Office archives, concluded his monumental *Persia and the Persian Question* with the grand claim that the shah was the "pivot of the entire machinery of public life" and that he fused the "legislative, executive, and judicial functions of government."[1] In reality, however, the power of the shah was sharply limited – limited by the lack of both a state bureaucracy and a standing army. His real power ran no further than his capital. What is more, his authority carried little weight at the local level unless backed by regional notables. "The Qajars," in the words of a recent study, "had few government institutions worthy of the name" and had no choice but to "depend on local notables in dealing with their subjects."[2] In Machiavelli's schema, the shah resembled more the French king than the Ottoman sultan.

The Qajars, a Turkic-speaking tribal confederation, conquered the country piece by piece in the 1780–90s, established their capital in Tehran in 1786, founded their dynasty in 1796, and proceeded to reign for more than a century. They presided over the center through ministers (*vezirs*), courtiers (*darbaris*), princes (*mirzas*), hereditary *mostowfis* (accountants), and nobles (*ashrafs*) with such titles as *al-saltaneh* (of the realm), *al-dowleh* (of the government), and *al-mamaleks* (of the kingdom). But they reigned over the rest of the country through local *a'yans* (notables) – *khans* (tribal chiefs), *arbabs* (landlords), *tojjars* (wealthy merchants), and *mojtaheds* (religious leaders). These notables retained their own sources of local power. Even after a half-century of half-hearted attempts to build state institutions, Nasser al-Din Shah ended his long reign in 1896 leaving behind merely the skeleton of a central government. It amounted to no more than nine small entities – bureaus without bureaucracies. Five ministries (interior, commerce, education and endowments, public works and fine arts, and post and telegraph) were new and existed only on paper. The other four (war, finance, justice, and foreign affairs) were of older vintage but still lacked salaried staffs, regional departments, and even permanent files. They were ministries in name only.

The ministries were sparsely manned by families of scribes who had held similar positions since the early days of the Qajars – some ever since Safavid times in the seventeenth century.[3] They treated government documents as private papers; and, since the monarch did not pay them regular salaries, they considered their positions as assets to be bought and sold to other members of the scribe families. To recognize their sense of corporate identity, Nasser al-Din Shah had decreed that "men of the pen" should wear the *kolah* – a round grey-shaded bonnet hat. By the end of the century, they were easily distinguishable from the *ulama* (clerics), *sayyeds* (descendants of the Prophet), *tojjars* (merchants), and *hajjis* (those who had been on the pilgrimage to Mecca) who wore black, white, or green turbans. The kolah was also distinguishable from the red fez worn by officials in the rival Ottoman Empire. This term "men of the pen" carried much significance. It came from ancient Zoroastrian and Greek thought via the Persian genre of "mirror for princes" literature. This literature divided the population into four classes, each representing the four basic elements in nature as well as the four "humors" in the human body. "Men of the pen" represented air; "men of the sword," warriors, represented fire; "men of trade," merchants and tradesmen, represented water; and "men of husbandry," the peasantry, represented earth. The prince was depicted as a doctor whose main duty was to preserve a healthy balance between the four humors in the human body. In fact, "justice" meant the preservation of a healthy balance.[4]

The finance ministry, the oldest and most substantial of the four institutions, was staffed both at the center and in the provincial capitals by hereditary *mostowfis* (accountants) and *moshirs* (scribes). The Mostowfi al-Mamalek family – whose origins reach back to the Safavids – passed on the central office from father to son throughout the nineteenth century and until the 1920s. Other mandarin families – many of whom came from either the region of Ashtiyan in central Iran or Nur in Mazanderan – assisted the main governors in collecting taxes. The term *mostowfi* came from *ifa* and *estefa* meaning "collector of government payments." For tax purposes, the country was divided into thirty-eight regions – by the 1910s they had been reduced to eighteen. Each region was "auctioned" every *Nowruz* (New Year's Day); and the successful bidder – usually a notable offering the highest *pishkesh* (gift) – received the royal *farman* (decree) along with a royal robe making him local governor for the duration of the coming year. As such, he held the fief (*tuyul*) to collect the *maliyat* (land tax) – the main source of revenue for the central government. The tuyul was a hybrid fief linked sometimes to the land tax, sometimes to the actual land itself. These tuyul-holding governors had to work closely both with mostowfis, who had to verify the receipts and who possessed tax assessments from previous generations, and with local notables who could hinder the actual collection of taxes. The mostowfis also continued to administer the ever-diminishing state and crown lands. In the words of one historian, "even in 1923 the government continued to farm out taxes simply because it lacked the administrative machinery to collect them."[5] Morgan Shuster, an American brought in to reorganize the finance ministry in 1910, tried in somewhat condescending but useful terms to make sense of the complex mostowfi system:[6]

There has never been in Persia a tax-register or "Domesday Book" which would give a complete, even if somewhat inaccurate, survey of the sources of internal revenue upon which the Government could count for its support. Persia is divided for taxation purposes into seventeen or eighteen taxation regions each containing a large city or town as its administrative center . . . Beyond a very indefinite idea in the heads of some of the chief mostowfis, or "government accountant," at Tehran as to what proportion of these amounts should come from the first class of districts within the province, the Central Government knows nothing of the sources of the revenue which it is supposed to receive . . . The chief collector has in his possession what is termed the *kitabcha* (little book) of the province, and each of the sub-collectors has the kitabcha of his particular district. These little books are written in a peculiar Persian style, on very small pieces of paper, unbound, and are usually carried in the pocket, or at least kept in the personal possession, of the tax-collector. They are purposely so written as to make it most difficult, if not impossible, for any ordinary Persian to understand them. There is in Persia, and has been for many generations past, a particular class of men who are known as mostowfis. The profession or career of mostowfi is, in many cases, hereditary, passing from father to son. These men understand the style in which the kitabcha are written, and the complicated and intricate system by which the local taxes are computed and collected. Whether one of them is a chief collector of a province, or the collector of a taxation district, he considers the corresponding kitabcha to be his personal property, and not as belonging to the Government. He resents most bitterly an attempt on the part of any one to go into details or to seek to find out whence the taxes are derived or what proportion of them he himself retains . . . It is clear, therefore, that in Persia the Central Government has but a most meager knowledge either of the revenues which it could expect to receive, or of the justice or injustice of the apportionment of the taxes among the people of Persia.

Curzon estimated annual government revenues to have been no more than 52.4 million qrans ($8.2 million) in the late 1890s – 80 percent came from the land tax. The other 20 percent came from the mint and the telegraph system.[7] Expenditures went mostly to the court – its stables, workshops, guards, cavalry, and pensions. They also went to state granaries and subsidies for clerical and tribal leaders. Of the 43 million qran expenditures, 18 million went to the army, 8 million to government pensions, 3 million to the "royal house," another 5 million to the royal guards, 2 million to pensions for the nobility, 1.5 million to the clergy and the accountants, 600,000 to the Qajar khans, and 1 million to the foreign ministry. The latter, according to Curzon, was the only ministry with a regular full-time staff. It had permanent representatives in Istanbul, London, Paris, Berlin, Vienna, St. Petersburg, Washington, Antwerp, and Brussels. It also had representatives in the provincial capitals within Iran – mainly to keep an eye on local governors.

The war ministry claimed a mighty force of more than 200,000. In reality, the regular army, the only force with any semblance of discipline and full-time pay, numbered fewer than 8,000. It consisted of a 5,000-man artillery contingent with four outdated guns on display in Cannon Square, Tehran's main parade ground; and a 2,000-man Cossack Brigade created in 1879 to replace the traditional palace guard of some 4,000

Georgian slaves. These Cossacks were officered by Russians; but their rank
and file came partly from the Shahsaven tribe and partly from Turkic-
speaking *mohajers* (immigrants) who in the 1820s had fled the Russian
advance into Erivan. Many had received tuyuls in the fertile region of
Sefid Rud in Mazanderan in return for serving in the military.[8] The palace
guard was supplemented with some 100 Bakhtiyaris officered by their own
khan who had married into the Qajar family and received tuyuls in the
Chahar Mahal region outside Isfahan. The main governors, such as Prince
Zill al-Sultan of Isfahan, retained their own praetorian guards.

The paper army of 200,000 consisted mostly of tribal contingents
officered by the own clan leaders.[9] They were equipped with obsolete
muzzle-loading guns bought at bargain prices in the 1870s when European
armies had converted to the new breech-loading rifles. As one British
traveler noted, "the tribes compose the whole military force of the kingdom
except for the standing army which is not much more than a body guard for
the Shah and his princely governors."[10] What is more, by the end of the
century, the main tribes had increased their relative power vis-à-vis the
central government by gaining access to breech-loading rifles. According to
British travelers, gun runners did a brisk business in the Gulf smuggling
modern rifles to the Bakhtiyaris, Qashqa'is, Boir Ahmadis, Turkmans,
Shahsavens, Arabs, and Baluchis.[11] These tribes, it was generally agreed,
could now easily "out-gun" the regular army.[12] As Nasser al-Din Shah
bemoaned, "I have neither a proper army nor the ammunition to supply a
regular army."[13] Similarly, one of his ministers, Amin al-Dowleh, remarked
that "heirs to the ancient Iranian throne would not be able to hold their
heads high until they created a proper army."[14]

The justice ministry, although in existence since 1834, had little presence
outside Tehran. Abdallah Mostowfi, a leading accountant, reminisced in
his memoirs in somewhat nostalgic terms that society itself managed to take
care of legal matters without interference from the central government.[15]
Among the tribes, justice was administered by clan khans; among peasants,
by *kadkhudas* (headmen), village elders, and landlords; and among craftsmen and tradesmen, by their own guild elders. In the main cities, the formal
judicial system was divided in a somewhat ambiguous fashion into *shari'a*
(religious) and *'urf* (state) courts. The former were headed by clerical *qazis*
(judges) and hereditary *sheikh al-islams* (heads of Islam); the latter by
government-appointed *hakims*. Shari'a courts dealt with civil and personal
matters; 'urf courts with offenses against the state – these could include theft
and drunkenness as well as banditry, sedition, and heresy. The latter could
base their verdicts on the shari'a, precedent, reason, circumstantial

evidence, state expediency, and even local custom. In fact, 'urf could mean customary as well as state law. Curzon even equated it with English "common law." In theory, only the shah and his immediate representatives – the princely governors possessing the royal dagger – had the authority to take life. In practice, most judicial decisions, even those of life and death, were left to local authorities. What is more, the budget of the justice ministry remained so meager that even at the end of the century provincial departments survived by selling notary stamps.[16]

A British diplomat observed that the Qajars were willing to leave most legal matters to religious judges, tribal chiefs, village headmen, and guild elders so long as they retained in theory the ultimate authority over life and death.[17] This was no small matter in a country where the government had few instruments of control but could use the public gallows to put on gruesome displays. According to one diary covering the period 1873–1904, the provincial capital of Shiraz had 82 public executions – 48 decapitations, 17 hangings, 11 drawing-and-quarterings, 4 live burials, and 2 disembowelings. It also had 118 amputations: 41 of fingers, 39 of feet, and 38 of ears; and 110 public floggings, 11 of which proved fatal. The diary noted that these spectacles were designed to deter criminals as well as to display royal power to the wider public – "especially to nomadic tribesmen prone to rural banditry."[18]

The newer ministries were equally modest. The interior ministry had recruited an Austrian and an Italian officer in 1873 to establish a police force in Tehran. By 1900, this force, known as the *Nazmieh*, had no more than 460 policemen. The Education Ministry spent most of its limited resources on the *Dar al-Fanon* (Abode of Learning), a high school established in 1852 to train personnel for the army and the civil service. It had explicit instructions to recruit from the "sons of a'yans, ashrafs, khans, and rich families." By 1900, it had 300 students. One instructor complained that teaching these "pampered children was like bringing order to a bunch of wild desert animals."[19] Instructors were recruited mostly from France to counter British and Russian influence. The commerce ministry was confined to the few ports on the Caspian and the Persian Gulf. The ministry of posts and telegraph – "owned" until the 1910s by the Mukhber al-Dowleh family – was nominally in charge of both the postal system established in 1876 and the telegraph lines introduced by the British in 1856 to link London with Bombay. By 1900 the telegraph had been expanded to link Tehran to all the provincial capitals. Some of these lines, however, were administered by a British firm employing Armenians. According to the Italian police officer: "Only the Ministries of Army, Interior, and Foreign Affairs have any resemblance of formal organizations. The others have no regular place, no regular employees, and no regular budget. Their ministers move around with servants carrying their papers."[20]

Curzon identified six men as having most influence in the last years of Nasser al-Din Shah: Muzaffar al-Din, the heir apparent, who in line with tradition governed the strategically vital province of Azerbaijan; Zill al-Sultan, the shah's forceful son, who governed Isfahan and at one time had also governed Fars, Kurdestan, Arabestan, and Lurestan; Kamran Mirza (Naib al-Sultaneh), the shah's third son, the governor of Tehran who nominally headed the military both as army minister and as commander-in-chief (Amir Kaber) – he was also married to the daughter of the future Muhammad Ali Shah; Amin al-Sultan, the grandson of a Georgian slave who had risen to become the *Sadar A'zam* (Chief Minister) as well as minister of finance and interior and governor of the Persian Gulf ports; Amin al-Dowleh, another Georgian deemed to be Amin al-Sultan's chief rival; and finally, Musher al-Dowleh, the shah's brother-in-law and justice minister, who, being a liberal-inclined mostowfi, had educated his sons in Europe and helped set up the School of Political Science in Tehran.[21] His eldest son, who inherited his title, was to play a major role in the Constitutional Revolution.

The other cabinet posts were held by: Mukhber al-Dowleh, the minister of posts and telegraph, who also held the portfolio for the ministry of education and endowments – he was related to the shah through marriage; and Abbas Mirza, the shah's eldest brother, who was minister of commerce as well as governor of Qazvin. The other major province, Khurasan, was governed by Rukn al-Dowleh – another royal brother. These governors were entrusted not only with the royal dagger as a symbol of ultimate authority but also with the task of ensuring that the state granaries were well stocked in case of emergencies. In appointing his son governor of Tehran, Nasser al-Din Shah warned him that if food shortages ever afflicted the capital he personally would be held responsible and would be bastinadoed for the whole world to see that "on such a vital issue even the shah's son could be held accountable."[22]

Lacking a central bureaucracy, the Qajars relied on local notables – tribal chiefs, clerical leaders, big merchants, and large landlords. In most localities, whether town, village, or tribal areas, local elites enjoyed their own sources of power as well as links to the central court. Some were related to the royal family through marriage or blood. Fath Ali Shah, the second Qajar ruler, had systematically created bonds between himself and the provincial families by marrying more than one thousand wives and leaving behind some hundred children.[23] Nasser al-Din Shah was more modest; he married only seventy times. "Every region," people quipped, "is infested with camels, fleas, and royal princes (*shahzadehs*)."[24] Local notables also bought titles, offices, and tuyuls. Mostowfi complained that the creation of some two hundred honorific names flooded the market and by the end of the century "anyone who was anyone claimed to have a title."[25]

These notables can be described as a landed aristocracy. They derived much of their income from agriculture and were known colloquially as *arbabs* (land proprietors) and *omdeh-e maleks* (large landowners). Mehdi Bambad, in his multi-volume biographies of the Qajar era, identifies 1,283 personages. Of these, 771 (60 percent) were state functionaries – courtiers, mostowfis, and *monshis* (scribes); 286 (23 percent) were literary and scholarly figures – almost all linked to the court; 98 (8 percent) were princes; another 98 were ulama; and 19 (1 percent) were merchants.[26] Although Bamdad is not specific about their finances, almost all, including the ulama, had investments in agriculture – either as owners of large estates or part-owners of villages.[27]

local notable

In addition to owning land, the senior ulama enjoyed extensive authority. As *maraj-e taqlids* (sources of emulation), they were respected as spiritual and legal guides. The devout consulted them on personal and ethical as well as legal and religious matters. As *nayeb-e imams* (imam's representatives), they received two types of tithes – the Shi'i *khoms* known as the "Imam's share" and the regular Muslim *zakat* earmarked for the poor. Contributions came mostly from landlords, merchants, and guild elders. As heads of religious endowments (*awqafs*), they supervised mosques, shrines, seminaries, and Koranic schools. Endowments came mostly in the form of agricultural and urban land. And as *mojtaheds*, they taught at the seminaries, distributed scholarships, and helped appoint shari'a judges, mosque preachers, prayer leaders, and school teachers. In short, the Shi'i ulama, in contrast to their counterpart in the Sunni world, enjoyed their own sources of income. Thus they were more independent of the central government.

senior ulama

To counter this, the Qajars shrouded themselves in a religious aura. They declared themselves Protectors of Shi'ism, Keepers of the Koran, Commanders of the Faithful, and Girders of Imam Ali's Sword. They made well-publicized pilgrimages to Shi'i shrines – to the Imam Reza Mosque in Mashed where the Eighth Imam was supposedly buried; to the Fatemeh Mosque in Qom where Imam Reza's sister was interred; and even to the Ottoman Empire to visit Karbala where Imam Hussein had been martyred, Najaf where Imam Ali was buried, and Samarra where the Twelfth Imam had lived. They gold-plated the large dome at the Samarra Mosque. They also built up Mashed, which literally means the "place of

Qajars' religious facade

martyrs," to rival Mecca and Medina. They patronized theological centers in Najaf, Mashed, and Isfahan, and in Qom they founded the Fayzieh Seminary. They buried their own relatives at the Shah Abdul 'Azim Mosque on the outskirts of Tehran which was reputed to contain not only their own ancestor but also the Seventh Imam's son. They built the country's very first rail line connecting Tehran to this Abdul 'Azim Mosque. Of course, they continued to appoint members of the ulama to be *qazis*, *sheikh al-islams*, and *imam jum'ehs* (heads of the main Friday mosques). The *imam jum'eh* of Tehran married into the royal family. Samuel Benjamin, the first official American representative in Iran, claimed in somewhat exaggerated terms that the most senior mojtahed in Tehran was so powerful – even though he rode a mule and had only one attendant – that "with one word he could hurl down the Shah."[28] The Qajars also perpetuated the Safavid practice of inventing genealogies linking themselves both to ancient Iranian dynasties and to the Shi'i Imams. Equally important, they continued to popularize the myth that Imam Hussein had married Shahbanou, the daughter of the last Sassanid shah. Thus the Fourth Imam and his heirs were all supposedly direct descendants not only of the holy Prophet but also of the Sassanid shahs.

What is more, the Qajars patronized the annual Muharram ceremonies commemorating the martyrdom of Imam Hussein. They financed *dastehs* (flagellations), *rowzehkhanis* (recitations), *taziyehs* (passion plays), *husseiniehs* (religious centers), and *takiyehs* (theaters). After his 1873 tour of Europe, Nasser al-Din Shah built the vast Takiyeh Dowlat (Government Theater) in Tehran to house the annual passion plays. This canvas-covered rotunda was so grand it could house 20,000 spectators – some thought it was inspired by London's Albert Hall.[29] The American representative claimed that it featured a life-sized portrait of Prophet Muhammad.[30] It was probably the portrait of Imam Ali or Imam Hussein. The passion plays, whose origins go back to the Safavid era, dramatized in blow-by-blow accounts the final days of Imam Hussein and his seventy-two companions.[31] They began on 1st Muharram with Imam Hussein arriving on the plains of Karbala near the town of Kufa, and raising the black banner of revolt against Yezid, the Ummayid Caliph. They end on Ashura, 10th Muharram, with Imam Hussein willingly accepting his martyrdom – a fate which according to tradition he had predetermined even before his arrival at Karbala.

Nasser al-Din Shah built other takiyehs. Tehran alone had more than forty of them throughout the various wards – many were financed by local notables. Rowzehkhanis also reenacted powerful scenes from the life of Imam Hussein and his companions. By the end of the century, taziyehs incorporated happier scenes to celebrate such joyous occasions as safe returns from travel or recoveries from serious illness. Although Muharram was a solemn occasion, street actors were not averse to entertaining the public with parodies.[32] What is more, Ashura was immediately followed with the Feast of Zahra, also known as the Feast of Laughter, celebrating Caliph Omar's assassination at the hands of a Persian Muslim. Colorful clothes replaced dark ones, women painted their nails, men dyed their hair, the rich put on firework displays, and neighborhood children burnt effigies of Caliph Omar on large bonfires. English visitors found the scene familiar.

Muharram commemorations also bore striking similarities to medieval Christian passion plays. Both were seen as the fulfillment of divine predestination. Both depicted holy martyrs dying for human sins. Both exemplified human frailty as neither the people of Kufa nor those of Jerusalem rose to the occasion. Both deaths were seen as redemptive acts through which penitent believers could gain salvation in the next world. Both also fostered a sense of community against the outside world and thereby draw the masses closer to the elite. Nasser al-Din Shah dutifully attended the annual play in the Government Theater, and from the royal box watched with binoculars not only the actors but also the audience – all sitting according to rank and class. Some joked that he took a special interest in the women. Actors often improvised. They clothed the enemy in Ottoman dress, referred to Imam Hussein's infants as *shahzadehs* (royal princes), and introduced Europeans who were so moved by Imam Hussein's tribulations that they promptly converted to Shi'ism.[33] Street flagellators, meanwhile, cursed and stomped on the names of the Sunni Caliphs – Abu Bakr, Omar, and 'Uthman. Senior clerics shied away, deeming such displays unseemly, inflammatory, and, perhaps most important of all, encroachments on to their own turf. The American representative reported that it was mostly the "ignorant classes who joined in these processions."[34]

The pitch to popular religion resonated well since more than 85 percent of the country was Shi'i. Sunnis, who constituted less than 10 percent, were confined to the periphery: Baluchis in the southeast; Turkmans in the northeast; some Kurds in the northwest; and some Arabs in the southwest. Non-Muslims, meanwhile, constituted less than 5 percent of the country (see Table 2). They included some 80,000 Assyrian Christians around Lake Urmiah; 90,000 Armenians in and near Isfahan, as well as in Rasht, Tehran, and western Azerbaijan; 50,000 Jews in Yazd, Shiraz, Tehran, Isfahan, and Hamadan; and 15,000 Zoroastrians in Yazd, Kerman, Tehran, and Isfahan. The Qajars continued the Safavid tradition of treating their Christian, Jewish, and Zoroastrian minorities as legitimate "People of the Book" – legitimate

Table 2 *Communal composition of Iran, 1900*

Main language groups	
Persians	6,000,000 (50%)
Azeris	2,500,000
Mazanderanis	200,000
Gilakis	200,000
Taleshis	20,000
Tatis	20,000
Major tribes	(30%)
Kurds	850,000
Arabs	450,000
Bakhtiyaris	300,000
Qashqa'is	300,000
Baluchis	300,000
Lurs	150,000
Boir Ahmadis	150,000
Mamasanis	150,000
Afshars	150,000
Shahsavens	100,000
Hazaras (Berberis)	80,000
Timouris	60,000
Turkmans	50,000
Qareh Daghis	50,000
Afghans	30,000
Basseris	25,000
Jamshidis	20,000
Tajiks	20,000
Qarehpakhs	20,000
Smaller tribes	
Qajars, Bayats, Qarahgozlus, Baharlus, Imanlus, Nafars, Kamatchis, Maqadamdamis, Javanshiris, Shakkaks	
Non-Muslims	
Bahais	100,000
Assyrians	90,000
Armenians	80,000
Jews	50,000
Zoroastrians	15,000

Note: Since no national censuses were taken in the nineteenth century and traveler accounts are highly impressionistic, these estimates are educated guesses using scattered reports in the British Foreign Office, taking into account migration, and projecting back the first state census of 1956. For attempts to estimate the size of the tribes, see H. Field, *Contribution to the Anthropology of Iran* (Chicago: Field Museum of Natural History, 1939); and S. I. Bruk, "The Ethnic Composition of the Countries of Western Asia," *Central Asian Review*, Vol. 7, No. 4 (1960), pp. 417–20.

both because they had their own holy books and because they were recognized as such in the Koran and the shari'a. They were permitted to have their own leaders and organizations, their own schools and tax levies, and their own laws and places of worship. The shahs transacted with them through their own religious leaders. The Armenians were represented by their Archbishop in Isfahan, the Assyrians by their Patriarch in Urmiah, the Jews by their Grand Rabbi in Yazd, and the Zoroastrians by their High Priest also in Yazd.

The largest minority, the Bahais, however, lacked legal status. Initially known as Babis, they originated in the 1840s when a merchant from Shiraz had declared himself to be the Bab (Gate) to Imam Mahdi, the Twelfth Imam who had gone into Occultation. He claimed to have come to herald Judgment Day and the reappearance of the Mahdi. Although he was executed and his followers were mercilessly persecuted as heretics, especially after they tried to assassinate Nasser al-Din Shah in 1852, the movement managed to survive under the Bab's heir who took the name Baha'allah (Glory of God) and preached strict abstinence from all active politics. He declared himself to be the Hidden Imam as well as Christ, with an entirely new message propagating social reform as well as respect for established authority. He published his own holy book, replacing the Koran and the Bible. His brother, however, named himself Sub-e Azal (Morn of Eternity), declared himself to be the Bab's true heir, and continued to denounce the whole establishment. Thus the Babi movement split into the activist Azali and the quietist Bahai sects. The former survived mostly in Tehran; the latter in Yazd, Shiraz, Isfahan, and Najafabad. Estimates for their total numbers in the late nineteenth century vary from 100,000 to 1 million.[35] Both sects were clandestine. Both were headed by leaders who took refuge in the Ottoman Empire. And both were demonized by the authorities, especially the clergy, not only as foreign-connected conspiracies but also as mortal threats to Shi'i Islam.

The Qajars also tapped into pre-Islamic Iranian sentiments. They patronized public readings of the *Shahnameh* and even renamed the crown after the mythical Kayan dynasty described in that epic. They named sons after Ferdowsi heroes – names such as Kamran, Bahman, Ardashir, and Jahanger. They discovered genealogical links between themselves and the ancient Parthians. They celebrated the ancient *Nowruz* (New Year) with fireworks. They decorated their palaces with Achaemenid and Sassanid motifs. They designed a new coat of arms bearing the Lion and Sun, and, in bestowing knighthoods, declared this insignia to have been the mark of "distinction between good and evil since the days of Zoroaster."[36] They improvised on the ancient insignia, placing Imam Ali's famed two-fanged sword in the palm of the Lion.[37] Even though some clerics objected that this Lion and Sun originated in Armenia, the insignia soon became the national symbol, clearly distinguishable from the Ottoman Crescent Moon.[38]

The Qajars also emulated the Achaeminids and Sassanids by commissioning huge carvings of themselves on mountain cliffs – some right next to the ancient rock reliefs. Fath Ali Shah placed one on the well-trodden road to Abdul ʿAzim Mosque. One court chronicler argued that the "pious" shah commissioned this because "rulers from ancient times had left pictures of themselves cut in stone."[39] What is more, the Qajars recruited Persian mostowfis into their court administration, describing them as "men of the pen" to distinguish them from their "men of the sword" – the Turkic tribal chiefs. This literati was well versed not only in Ferdowsi but also in such famed Persian poets as Hafez, Mowlavi, Rumi, and Saʾadi. The appeal to Persian literature resonated well among not only mostowfi families but also the Persian-speaking population in the central heartlands – in Isfahan, Shiraz, Kerman, Qom, Yazd, and Ashtiyan. Europeans were surprised to find that even off the beaten track the rural population could cite – however incorrectly – long passages from the *Shahnameh*.[40] Edward Browne, the famed English historian of Persian literature and no fan of Ferdowsi, conceded that the *Shahnameh*, "enjoyed from the first until the present day an unchanging and unrivalled popularity" throughout Iran.[41] Of course, such blatant exploitation of Persian and Shiʾi sentiments did not always work. For example, in one of his periodic pilgrimages to Shah Abdul ʿAzim Mosque, Nasser al-Din Shah found himself pelted with stones thrown by soldiers angry for being left in arrears. Even the Shadow of God was not exempt from earthly wrath.

QAJAR SOCIETY

The Qajars governed not so much through religion and bureaucracy as through local notables. Sir John Malcolm, a British diplomat, in a perceptive aside noted that the shahs in theory appointed all tribal chiefs, governors, magistrates, and town ward headmen, but in practice had to choose those already "respected" in their own community – "just as members of corporation are in any English town."[42]

Although these officers are not formally elected, the voice of the people always points them out: and if the king should appoint a magistrate disagreeable to the citizens, he could not perform his duties, which require all the weight he derives from personal consideration to aid the authority of office. In some towns or villages the voice of the people in nominating their kadkhuda, or head, is still more decided;

if one is named of whom they do not approve, their clamour produces either his resignation or removal. These facts are important; for no privilege is more essential to the welfare of the people, than that of choosing or influencing the choice of their magistrates. It is true, these magistrates cannot always screen them from the hand of power, and are often compelled to become the instruments of oppression; still their popularity with their fellow-citizens, which caused their elevation, continues to be their strength; and in the common exercise of their duties they attend to their comfort, happiness and interests. In every city or town of any consequence, the merchants, tradesmen, mechanics, and labourers have each a head, or rather a representative, who is charged with the peculiar interests of his class. He is chosen by the community he belongs to, and is appointed by the king.

The population lived in small face-to-face communities with their own structures, hierarchies, languages and dialects, and, often, until the late nineteenth century, self-sufficient economies. Physical geography lay at the root of this social mosaic. The large central desert famous as the Kaver, the four formidable mountain ranges known as the Zagros, Elborz, Mekran, and the Uplands, as well as the marked lack of navigable rivers, lakes, and rainfed agriculture, all played a part in fragmenting the population into small self-contained tribes, villages, and towns.

The tribes, totaling as much as 25–30 percent of the population, consisted of some fifteen major entities known as *ils* – Qajars, Kurds, Turkmans, Baluchis, Arabs, Qashqa'is, Bakhtiyaris, Lurs, Mamasanis, Boir Ahmadis, Hazaras, Shahsavans, Afshars, Timouris, and Khamsehs. In some sense they were "imagined communities" claiming descent from a common mytho-logical ancestor. In actual fact, they were fluid political entities, constantly losing and absorbing members. Most had their own dialects and languages, customs and traditions, histories and genealogies, local saints and pilgrim-age sights, clothes and head gear. It is hard to gauge their real size. As one Qashqa'i chief admitted, he did not know how big his tribe was, nor did he want to know since the true figure could bring on higher taxation.[43] The nomads tended to be confined to marginal regions too mountainous or too dry to sustain year-round agriculture.

Although most tribes were either nomadic or semi-nomadic, some were fully settled. For example, the Kurds were mostly settled farmers in the valleys of Kermanshah and western Azerbaijan. Similarly, the Arabs were mostly villagers living along the Persian Gulf and in the southern province of Arabestan. The Qajars themselves had experienced the typical passage into urban life outlined by the classical scholar ibn Khaldun. Having established their dynasty, they had settled in the capital and in due course merged into the urban population. Some tribes – notably the Qashqa'is, Bakhtiyaris, and Boir Ahmadis – were large confederations headed by paramount chiefs using the Turkic title of *ilkhani*. Others had multiple chiefs with the lesser title of *khan*. Arabs tended to call their chiefs *sheikhs*; Kurds theirs *begs, aghas,* or *mirs*; and Baluchis, who spoke an Iranian dialect but paradoxically traced their descent to the Prophet's heroic uncle Hamza, referred to their chiefs as *amirs*, another Arabic term.[44]

But whether led by paramount or lesser chiefs, each *il* was segmented into clans known as *tirehs* or *tayefehs* – these terms were also sometimes used to mean tribe. Each in turn was further segmented into migratory camps and villages formed of extended families. The Bakhtiyaris had seven major clans, each large enough to be described as a tireh. The Qashqa'is had twenty tirehs; the Arabs of Arabestan seventy; and the Kurds on the Ottoman border region sixty. One Qajar document enumerated twelve substantial tayefehs among the Baluchis on the Afghan border – some with as many as a hundred extended families.[45] Clans often had their own villages, grazing lands, and migratory routes; and their own hierarchy of chiefs, *kalantars* (bailiffs), *kadkhudas* (headmen), and *rish sefids* (white-beards). Many also had distinct religious identities. For example, some Kurdish clans were Sunni; some Shi'i; some Ali-Illahi – a sect that deified Imam Ali; some Qaderi – a Sufi order; and some Naqshbandi – a rival Sufi order. Here religion tended to reinforce clan identity.

For all practical purposes, the tribes were autonomous entities. In the words of one British official, the shah in theory could appoint the Qashqa'i Ilkhani, but his choice was limited to their leading families and often to the khan already favored by these families. "The Government," he explained, "either acknowledges or is unable to oppose their appointment and some-times face-savingly grants them a mandate to keep the peace in their territory, a responsibility it cannot itself undertake." He added: "Taxes are not paid to the government but tribute is rendered to the khans. Tribesmen signify their support for the Ilkhani by the offering of 'presents' which are really in the nature of a voluntary tax."[46]

The full complexity of the tribal system can be seen among the Bakhtiyaris. They inhabited a large area in the very heart of the country with Isfahan in the east, Chahar Mahal in the north, Lurestan in the east, Arabestan in the southwest, and Qashqa'i territories in the south. Most Bakhtiyari tribes spoke Persian mixed heavily with Lur and Kurdish words. Some, however, spoke Arabic or Turkic. These tribes had probably joined the confederation in more recent times. At various occasions in the seventeenth century, the Bakhtiyaris had been the main power behind the Safavid throne in Isfahan. At one point they had even raided Tehran. The confederation as a whole was divided into two branches – the Haft Lang (Seven Feet) and the Chahar

Lang (Four Feet). According to one oral tradition, the founder of the tribe, after leading his followers from Syria to its present location, left behind two rival families – one with seven sons, the other with four. According to another tradition, the numbers referred to tax payments owed to the paramount chief, with the richer branch paying one fourth and the poorer branch one seventh.

The Haft Lang was divided into four major tayefehs; the Chahar Lang into three. Each *tayefeh* had its own khan. These seven tayefehs, in turn, were divided into more than one hundred tirehs – each with a kadkhuda. Although these kadkhudas were confirmed in their offices by the Ilkhani, most were senior elders already prominent within their clan – some were even related by marriage to their khans. Some tirehs contained as many as 2,500 families; others as few as 50 families. Many were migratory, living in camps and moving each year from winter to summer grazing lands. A few lived in permanent settlements – mostly within the Bakhtiyari territories. After a period of internal strife, the Haft Lang and the Chahar Lang had agreed to share top positions. The title of ilkhani went to the Haft Lang; and that of *ilbegi*, his deputy, to the Chahar Lang. The wealthier khans owned villages outside Bakhtiyari territories – especially in neighboring Fars, Lurestan, and Arabestan. According to British reports, the shahs had little influence within the Bakhtiyari territories. They confirmed the offices of ilkhani and ilbegi for the obvious candidates; sometimes married their daughters to the leading families; appointed the khans to be regional *hakims* (governors); and, most important of all, did their utmost to keep alive the Haft Lang–Chahar Lang rivalries.[47] In short, the Bakhtiyaris, like the other tribal groups, lived in a world unto themselves.

The peasants, who constituted more than half the population, were mostly sharecroppers. In much of the country, the annual crop was normally divided into five equal portions – for labor, land, oxen, seed, and irrigated water. According to custom, village residents enjoyed the right to work on particular strips of land even though that land in theory belonged to the landlord. "Peasants," wrote one British traveler, "do not claim proprietary rights but expect to retain possession of their strips of land during their lifetime and to hand them down to their heirs. The Persian tenant enjoys security so long as he pays his share of the rent."[48] In other words, these sharecroppers – unlike their counterparts in other parts of the world – enjoyed some semblance of security. Peasants who supplied their own seed and oxen received as much as three-fifths of the harvest. In villages dependent on *qanats* (underground canals), landlords invariably took the fifth allocated for irrigated water.

The relationship between landlords and peasants was invariably influenced by the availability of labor. In the late nineteenth century, especially after the catastrophic 1870 famine, peasants could threaten to move to underpopulated regions since they, unlike medieval European serfs, were not legally bound to the land. But population growth over the course of the next century eroded their bargaining power. This helps explain the sharp contrast drawn by nineteenth- and twentieth-century European travelers. Whereas the latter invariably found rural living conditions to be abysmally poor, the former had described them as reasonably good. As peasants became more indebted, especially for seeds, they became more like bonded serfs. Lady Sheil, traveling in the 1850s with her diplomat husband, reported that peasants enjoyed a "considerable air of substantial comfort which I often envied for our countrymen."[49] Benjamin, the American diplomat, wrote that landlords could not extort too much simply because peasants had the ability to escape to other villages. "This," he explained, is why people are "not poor" and "speak up their minds . . . paupers are less numerous in Persia than in Italy or Spain."[50] Another visitor wrote that the "cultivator" was on the whole well compensated, well fed, well dressed, and well housed.[51] The same visitor wrote that landlords often had no choice but to bid against each other to keep the peasants:[52]

Where population is so thin as in Persia, and where cultivation can only be achieved at the expense of steady industry and toil – not indeed in the labour upon the land itself as in digging and maintaining qanats, and in regulating the measured supply – it is to the interest of the landowner to be on the best of terms with his tenant; and the Persian peasant, even if he can justly complain of government exaction, has not found any one to teach him the gospel of landlord tyranny. He is poor, illiterate, and solid; but in appearance robust, in strength he is like an ox, he usually has clothes to his back, and he is seldom a beggar.

The countryside was formed of some 10,000 villages owned wholly or partly by absentee landlords – by the crown, royal family, religious endowments, tribal chiefs, government accountants, rich merchants, and plain landlords known as *arbabs*, *maleks*, and *omdeh maleks*. Independent farmers were found mostly in isolated mountain valleys and rainfed villages. Not surprisingly, the landowning system became known by the early twentieth century as *fudal* (feudal). An American "military advisor" employed by a Khurasan landlord wrote in the 1920s that this was "feudalism" similar to "medieval Europe" since landlords owned numerous villages, treated peasants as "serfs," and retained their own armies. His own employer lived in a castle with a private army of 45 full-time soldiers and 800 part-timers. "These soldiers," he commented, "were the worst scoundrels in the region."[53]

Landed notables controlled many regions. Sultanabad and western Mazanderan were owned by the famous Ashtiyani families; eastern Mazanderan by Vali Khan Sepahdar; Sistan and Baluchestan by Amir Alam, famous as "the lord of the eastern marches"[54]; Arabestan by Sheikh Khaz'al of the Shi'i Ka'ab tribe; Isfahan and Fars by Prince Zill al-Sultan, the Bakhtiyari khans, Qavam al-Mulk, the Khamseh chief, and Sowlat al-Dowleh, the Qashqa'i leader; Gilan by Amin al-Dowleh; Kermanshah by the Ardalans, a Kurdish Shi'i clan; and Kerman, Fars, as well as central Azerbaijan by the Farmanfarmas – Abdul Hussein Mirza Farmanfarma, the family patriarch, was Fath Ali Shah's grandson. Meanwhile, western Azerbaijan was dominated by the Khans of Maku, who, according to Mostowfi, lived like German junkers but wore the Persian hat and prevented government officials from trespassing on their domains. He added that they had ruled the region since Safavid times and had not paid taxes since the beginning of the Qajar era.[55] Similarly, eastern Azerbaijan, especially the Maragheh region, was controlled by the Moqadams, who pre-dated the Qajars and had married into the royal family soon after the establishment of the new dynasty. According to a recent study of Maragheh:[56]

Though the Crown Prince was seated in Tabriz, only eighty kilometers or a few days' journey from Maragheh, the Moqadams continued to monopolize the roles of governor, judge, tax collector, troop commander, and landlord throughout the nineteenth century. This must be attributed in part to the fact that they never rebelled against the Qajar dynasty after their initial conquest of Maragheh. No direct controls were imposed by the central government over Moqadam rule, nor did the Qajar shahs significantly aid them in their provincial administration, or in their frequent military campaigns against the rebellious Kurds who threatened their territories. Initial attempts at rationalizing authority and administration under Nasser al-Din Shah had little impact on the style of provincial patrimonial rule of the Moqadams. Just as such reforms were unsuccessful in other parts of the empire beyond the fringes of Tehran, so too were they unsuccessful in Maragheh.

Some European historians have argued that these landlords did not constitute a true aristocracy on the grounds they lacked proper pedigrees. In fact, their pedigrees could compete with those of their European counterparts. In addition to the Ashtiyanis, who had been court accountants since the early Safavid era, many others boasted illustrious origins. The Moqadams traced themselves back to a Caucasian chief and had been prominent in Maragheh long before the emergence of the Qajars. The Alams claimed descent from an Arab chieftain sent to subdue the area in the eighth century. They continued to speak with their clients in their patois Arabic.[57] The Khaz'als of Arabestan had been signing treaties with the

British since 1761. Sepahdar, deemed the "richest landlord in the country," claimed descent from the bearer of Imam Ali's robe.[58] His family had owned land in Mazanderan since the eighteenth century. Qavam al-Mulk was the great-grandson of a wealthy eighteenth-century merchant in Shiraz. His grandfather had been a minister under the first Qajar shah. His father had been named Ilkhani of the Khamseh tribe. The Zarasvands, the paramount Bakhtiyari family, had been important since the seventeenth century. A recent study finds that almost all office-holders in Fars had been substantial landowners long before attaining any official titles.[59] By the mid-twentieth century, the landed "feudal" class became known as the *hezar famil* (one thousand families).[60] In fact, they numbered fewer than one hundred families.

The rural settlements formed close-knit communities. With the exception of those in close proximity to cities, most villages remained self-contained geographically, economically, and culturally. Even late nineteenth-century travelers were struck by their isolation. They produced their own basic foods, their own clothes, and even their own utensils. New consumer goods – notably tea, coffee, sugar, and Manchester textiles – had not yet reached them. An 1850s inventory of goods owned by prosperous peasants in the central region indicates that almost all possessions – knife, lamp, clay pipe, earthen cooking wares, spade, harness, wooden plough, skin water container, quilt, felt cap, shoes, and bracelets – had been produced locally. "The villagers," the inventory concluded, "produce their own food – wheat, barley, corn, rice, milk, butter, eggs, and chicken – and buy from the outside only salt, pepper, and tobacco."[61]

Economic isolation was reinforced by social divisions. Even in non-tribal areas, some villages were inhabited by specific clans. For example, the region of Tunkabun in Mazanderan was populated by eleven Khalatbari clans headed by the famous Sepahdar.[62] The three hundred villages constituting Fereidun and Chahar Mahal near Isfahan were inhabited exclusively by Persians, Turkic-speakers, Lurs, Kurds, Bakhtiyari Haft Lang, Bakhtiyari Chahar Lang, Armenians, and Georgians. The Georgians, like the Armenians, had been transported there in the early seventeenth century, but had converted to Islam in the course of the eighteenth century. A British survey described thirty-six of the villages as exclusively Armenian and nine as Georgian.[63] While most irrigated villages were owned by landlords, some rainfed villages were owned by the peasants themselves. Many villages dotted in and around the Kaver Desert were inhabited exclusively by Persians, Turkmans, Baluchis, Kurds, Arabs, Afghans, Hazaras, Afshars, Timouris, and even Bahais. European visitors found it was "dangerous" for Turkmans and Persians to venture into each others' territory.[64] One traveler reported in 1841 that Sunni Turkmans "consider it perfectly lawful to carry off" Persian Shi'i girls and sell them as "slaves" in Central Asia.[65] Such fears lasted well into the next century. Look-out turrets in Persian-speaking villages continued to be known as "Turkman towers."[66]

Each village was led by a *kadkhuda* (headman). Edward Burgess, an Englishman overseeing crown lands in Azerbaijan, described their appointment: [67]

> If a large majority are determined to have the kadkhuda out, not I nor even the Prince, nor the Shah himself, can prevent their doing so . . . I give the term elections to this business because I have no other word for it, but they do not meet and vote. The thing is arranged amongst themselves, they meet and talk the matter over and whenever a large majority is in favour of one man the authorities can not resist their wish, if they did the people would stand upon their rights and would not pay taxes. If, as not infrequently happens, the governor is a tyrant, he might catch and punish two or three of the ringleaders, but he could get no good by this, and all men of sense find it better to let the village have its own way.

The kadkhuda – with the help of *rish sefids* (white-beards), *paykars* (sheriffs), and *mirabs* (water regulators) – carried out an impressive array of tasks. He mediated disputes, formulated collective decisions, and enforced them. He represented the village to the outside world, especially to landlords, tribal chiefs, and city officials. He helped deliver water to the fields. He maintained common lands, woods, public baths, mosques (if there were any), and, most important of all, the village walls which most settlements had for protection. He supervised the annual rotation of strips to ensure that families had fair access to fertile lands. Peasant ethos stressed equality; in the words of an India Office report, "peasants were assigned a strip or strips so as to make the apportionment fair."[68] The kadkhuda also coordinated plough teams known as *boneh* which pooled resources not only to cultivate the land but also to pay the local blacksmith, coppersmith, carpenter, barber, and bath attendant. According to tradition, village residency entitled peasants to boneh membership; and boneh membership entitled them to land as well as to communal pastures, woods, and water. Moreover, the kadkhuda helped the village *kalantar* (bailiff) – appointed by the landlord – to collect the latter's share of the harvest, and, where custom permitted, his labor dues. The kadkhuda also assisted local authorities in collecting taxes. Although mostowfis determined how much each village was to pay in taxes, it was the local kadkhuda who decided how much each household was to contribute. In short, the kadkhuda wore many hats – that of judge, policeman, administrator, diplomat, and tax collector.

Urban dwellers, living in thirty-six towns, totaled less than 20 percent of the population. Towns varied in size from Tehran and Tabriz, with 200,000 and 110,000 respectively, to middling urban centers like Isfahan, Yazd, Mashed, Qazvin, Kerman, Qom, Shiraz, and Kermanshah, with between 20,000 and 80,000, and to smaller centers such as Semnan, Bushire, Ardabel, Amol, and Kashan, each with fewer than 20,000. Many boasted special "personality traits": their own accents and dialects; their own culinary tastes; and their own heroes and reasons for local pride. Some at one time or another had been the country's capital city.[69] By the mid-twentieth century, publishing houses did a brisk trade in regional histories stressing the theme of local resistance against outsiders – whether Arabs, Mongols, Ottomans, Russians, and even the central authorities.

The provincial capitals had governor-generals (*valis*). Other towns had ordinary governors (*hakims*). What is more, towns were divided into distinct *mahallehs* (wards), each with its own kadkhuda. The ward kadkhuda played a role analogous to that of the village and tribal headman. He represented his community in its dealings with the outside world – especially with neighboring wards and the government. He mediated internal disputes and collected taxes. He coordinated his activities not only with notables who happened to reside in his ward, but also with the town qazi, imam jum'eh, sheikh al-islam, *darugheh* (bazaar supervisor), and *muhtaseb* (weight-and-measure inspector). He supervised local tea-houses, *hamams* (baths), and guilds (*asnafs*). These guilds had their own kadkhudas, their own elders (*rish sefids*), their own arbitration courts, their own small bazaars, and sometimes even their own cemeteries. Moreover, the ward kadkhuda attended weekly gathering (*hayats*) which not only arranged prayer meetings, weddings, and receptions for returning pilgrims, but also collected money for the needy and for the repair of local mosques, schools, and takiyehs.[70]

In addition, the ward kadkhuda helped oversee local *zurkhanehs* (gymnasiums) frequented by wrestlers and body-builders known as *lutis*. Many of these lutis worked in the bazaar as petty tradesmen. They also served as night watchmen, wall guards, and Muharram procession organizers. They displayed special symbols – scarves from Kashan and notched chains from Yazd. They joined the main Sufi orders – either the Haydaris or the Nematis. In their initiation ceremonies, they vowed to live by their chivalrous code of ethics, defending the weak against the powerful, protecting the ward against the outside world, and avoiding such "dishonorable" activities as "labouring, cotton-beating, and well-digging."[71] During work-out sessions, they recited choice verses from the *Shahnameh* – even in the

Turkic-speaking city of Tabriz.[72] For some, lutis were folk-heroes; for others, they were no better than thugs. The term eventually became synonymous with petty thievery and knife-wielding (*chaqukeshi*).

Tehran contained five separate wards or *mahallehs* – Ark (Citadel), Bazaar, Ud Lajan, Chal Maydan, and Sangalaj. The 1885 census of Tehran – the first ever taken – calculated the population to be 147,206.[73] The five wards were surrounded by a polygon-shaped wall twenty feet high and eleven miles long. Each ward had its own outer gate. Ark had additional fortifications to defend the royal compound with its palace, workshops, granaries, armory, mint, imperial mosque, Cannon Square, and the Drum Tower from which, every sunset, kettle drums and blaring horns heralded the shah's royal presence. Tradition claimed that this ritual originated from Zoroastrian times. Ark also contained a recently built Haussman-like avenue connecting Cannon Square with the Dar al-Fanon, Government Theater, Cossack barracks, police headquarters, foreign office, telegraph office, and the British-owned Imperial Bank. Thus Ark became known as the "government" as well as the "royal mahalleh." In contrast, the Bazaar mahalleh was formed of narrow winding side-streets full of homes, stores, workshops, and specialty market places. Guild members tended to live and work in the same side-streets. It also contained the execution square and the main caravansary – traditional hotel for travelers. The other three mahallehs were less distinctive. They housed notables with mansions and large gardens – many streets were named after such resident notables. They also had mosques, shops, public baths, bakeries, and takiyehs – often named after the community that frequented them. These wards were crisscrossed with side-streets, winding alleys, and cul-de-sacs – often ending at the gates of aristocratic mansions.

Tehran's census counted 101,893 home-owners and 45,363 renters – in other words, 70 percent were home-owners. Households were formed of extended families with at least ten members including servants. The census listed 47 mosques, 35 madrasehs, 34 takiyehs, 170 bakeries, 190 public baths, 130 caravansaries, 20 ice-houses, 70 brick furnaces, 277 stables, and 160 Jewish homes. It described 42,638 residents as *aqayan va kasbeh* (gentlemen and tradesmen), 756 as *ghulam-e siyah* (black slaves), 10,568 as *nokar* (servants), 46,063 as *zanan-e mohtarameh* (honorable women), 2,525 as *kaniz-e siyah* (black females), and 3,802 as *kedmatkar* (wage earners). It counted 1,578 Jews, 1,006 Christians, 123 Zoroastrians, and 30 "foreigners." It estimated that new immigrants constituted as much as 27 percent of the population – 9,900 came from Isfahan, 8,201 from Azerbaijan, 2,008 from the Qajar tribe, and the others mostly from Kashan, Kurdestan, and

Arabestan. A contemporary map marked various alleyways with such labels as Turkmans, Arabs, Shirazis, Jews, Armenians, foreigners, and the "Shah's Household Slaves."

Provincial towns were equally segregated. Malcolm, the British diplomat, reported that large towns were divided into Haydari and Nemati wards, which he traced back to Sufi orders going back to Safavid times: "There is at all times a jealousy between the parties, and during the last days of Muharram they attack each other. If a mosque is decorated by one party, the other, if they can, drives them from it, and destroys their flags and ornaments."[74] A detailed tax report on Isfahan described how every year on the Day of Sacrifice ('Aid-e Qurban) thousands of the Haydaris and Nematis – led by their ward lutis – would clash in the main city square.[75] In terms of occupation, the report listed 100 clerical households – many with seminary students; 15 high-ranking officials – some with lineages going back to the Safavids; 8 princely families; 25 *hakims* (traditional doctors); 15 prayer reciters; and 197 trade and craft guilds – including those for weavers, cotton-beaters, goldsmiths, saddlers, hatters, tent-makers, silversmiths, book-binders, leather-shoe cobblers, canvas-shoe cobblers, and loose-sleeve coat makers. In terms of language, it divided the population into Persian, Turkish, Armenian, Bakhtiyari, Kayani (an ancient Persian dialect), and Ebri (patois spoken by the local Jews). It noted that some guilds kept records in their own secret terminology. And in terms of religion, it divided the population into Shi'i, Christian, Jewish, Babi, Sheikhi (another recent offshoot of Shi'ism), and seven Sufi orders – two of whom, the Haydaris and Nematis, it blamed for the annual disturbances.

Lady Sheil found the town of Sarab in Azerbaijan torn apart every Muharram with clashes between Haydaris and Nematis. Each side augmented their flagellation processions by bringing in recruits from nearby villages.[76] Ahmad Kasravi, the well-known historian, writes that many towns in the late nineteenth century were racked by these Nemati–Haydari feuds, with each striving to place their candidates in town offices, expand their wards, lower their tax assessments, and win over neighboring villages and tribes.[77] Ali Shamin, another historian, remembers how these Haydari–Nemati riots disrupted his home town of Hamadan.[78] Kasravi's own hometown, Tabriz, was divided into two rival blocs: wards controlled by the Sheikhis versus those run by the orthodox Shi'is known locally as the Mutasheris. They too clashed during Muharram; competed for city offices; married exclusively within their own community; and avoided shops, tea-houses, gymnasiums, bath-houses, takiyehs, and mosques frequented by the others.[79] Such clashes became less frequent in Tehran only because the shah

had explicitly ordered the ward kadkhudas to keep the flagellation processions strictly within their own districts.[80] In short, the urban wards of
nineteenth-century Iran constituted communities within communities.
Some Western social scientists claim that traditional Iran lacked "civil
society." But Iranian historians such as Kasravi could well retort that it
suffered from a surfeit of such society.

STATE AND SOCIETY

Since the Qajars lacked real instruments of coercion and administration,
they survived by systematically exploiting social divisions. They described
themselves as Supreme Arbitrators, and did their best to channel aristocratic
feuds into the court. In fact, notables sought to have a presence there by
either sending *vakels* (representatives) or marrying into the royal family.
Outsiders could easily fall prey to insiders. Exclusion of Turkman khans
from the court goes a long way towards explaining their persistent unrest.[81]
As one Afshar khan admitted to a British diplomat, he did not dare attack
his rivals simply because they too enjoyed court protection: "You must
know this tribe and mine have a long-standing feud . . . At present we do not
fight like brave men but like sneaking rascals, by intrigues and plots at
court."[82]

The Qajars also took advantage of communal divisions on the local level.
In some towns, such as Shiraz and Qazvin, these divisions ran along
Nemati–Haydari lines. In other towns, especially Tabriz and Kerman,
they ran along Sheikhi–Mutasheri ones. In some provinces, they reflected
town versus country interests. In other provinces, they reflected long-standing
strains between nomadic pastoralists and settled agriculturalists. In some
rural regions, the divisions demarcated ethnicity, especially when neighboring villages spoke different dialects or languages. In other regions, they
reflected tribal rivalries, both between major tribes and between clans
within the same tribe. Since the nomads were well armed and well organized, these conflicts had greater impact on the wider society than their
numbers would warrant – even though their numbers were in themselves
considerable.

Qajar manipulation of tribal rivalries can best be seen in their zigzagging
policies towards the Bakhtiyaris. The era began with Asad Khan, the Haft
Lang chief, posing a major threat to the new dynasty, and even laying siege
to Tehran. The Qajars, however, saved themselves by allowing him considerable independence – a force of 3,000 men, direct dealings with the
British, and an English officer to train his private army. At the same time,

they built up the rival Chahar Lang by giving their leader, Muhammad Taqi Khan, control over neighboring Lur and Kurdish villages. By 1851, Muhammad Taqi Khan had become so powerful that the Qajars found it expedient to assassinate him and his immediate heirs. "The Chahar Lang," said a British report, "never recovered from this blow and since that time have always remained of secondary importance to the Haft Lang."[83]

The Qajars followed up these assassinations by rehabilitating Asad Khan's son, Jafar Quli Khan. The latter promptly eliminated thirteen members of his family; crushed the rival Duraki clan; and handed down the chieftainship to his son, Hussein Quli Khan, who in 1867 obtained the ilkhani title. But in 1882 Zill al-Sultan, the governor of Isfahan, strangled him; incarcerated his heir, Esfandiar Khan, and diminished his authority by creating the post of ilbegi (lieutenant ilkhani). At first, the two posts were shared by Esfandiar Khan's rival uncles. Then in 1888 Nasser al-Din Shah released Esfandiar Khan and helped him oust his two uncles. The shah bestowed on him not only the title of ilkhani but also that of Samsam al-Saltaneh (Sword of the Kingdom). In 1890, the shah again shifted support. He transferred the ilkhanship to Imam Quli Khan, one of the deposed uncles, and appointed Reza Quli Khan, the other deposed uncle, as governor of the newly created district of Chahar Mahal. A British report tried to make sense of these complicated intrigues:[84]

Out of the killing of Hussein Quli Khan, who is still spoken of as the "late Ilkhan" by the older khans, and of the consequent jealousy between his descendants and the family of Imam Quli Khan, who succeeded him and who was known as "the Haji Ilkhani" from having made the pilgrimage to Mecca soon after his appointment as Ilkhani, has arisen the other great rift in the Bakhtiari tribe and one which, although it only concerns the Haft Lang, is of much greater importance even today than the rivalry between Chahar Lang and Haft Lang. This is the rift between what are now known as the Haji Ilkhani families and the Ilkhani families. In view of this rivalry, often, in fact, usually amounting to hatred, it became the custom after a time that the offices of Ilkhani and Ilbegi should never be held by members of the same side of the family. Thus if one of the Ilkhani khans was Ilkhani one of the Haji Ilkhani khans would be Ilbegi ... From 1890 onwards no great change has come over Bakhtiari tribal politics. The Chahar Lang gradually declined into complete though somewhat unwilling subservience to the Haft Lang, a process which was helped by inter-marriage between the khans. The Ilkhani–Haji Ilkhani feud has however continued undiminished to the present day, in spite of much inter-marriage.

The manipulative hand of the Qajars can also be seen in the creation of the Khamseh confederacy. At the beginning of the century, Qajar power in Fars was threatened by the formidable Qashqa'is. The shah lacked ready-made allies to counterbalance them. The Bakhtiyaris to the north were themselves dangerous; the Boir Ahmadis to the east were in the midst of a civil war; and the Zands, who had formerly ruled Fars, had disintegrated to the point that the body of their last leader lay buried under the palace balcony so that the shah could trample on it every day. To neutralize the Qashqa'is, the shah created the Khamseh (The Five Together) out of five separate tribes – the Persian-speaking Basseri, the Arab Il-e Arab, and the Turkic Nafar, Ainlu, and Baharlu – each of which felt threatened by the Qashqa'is. He named as their Ilkhan Qavam al-Mulk, the governor of Fars, even though the latter had no ties to them. Indeed it was rumored that he had Jewish ancestry.[85] One forefather had been a wealthy merchant in Shiraz; another had been a ward kadkhuda; and another had served the Zands as a chief minister. With the formation of the Khamseh, the Qajars were able effectively to counterbalance the Qashqa'is. In the words of one European visitor: "The Shah and his governor hope to uphold their authority by keeping alive the animosity between the two rival parties, and in this respect they only follow the policy pursued all over the empire, and that which appears time immemorial to have been the system of government in Persia."[86] Similarly, a modern anthropologist writes: "As erstwhile Governors of Fars, the Qavams came into conflict with the increasingly important and powerful Qashqa'i confederacy; and it was to counter balance the Qashqa'is, as well as to protect his caravan routes to the southern ports, that Ali Muhammad Qavam al-Mulk caused the Khamseh confederacy to be formed with himself as its chief."[87] In other words, the Qavam family, whose founder had been a merchant-turned-governor, served as the shah's main counterweight against the Qashqa'is for the rest of the century and even well into the next.

Thus the Qajars governed Iran less through bureaucratic institutions, coercion, or grand appeals to divinity and history – although they were not averse to invoking them – than through the systematic manipulation of social divisions, especially clan, tribal, ethnic, regional, and sectarian differences. Their state – if it can be called that – hovered above rather than controlled and penetrated into society. It claimed pompous, bombastic, and highly inflated powers. Its real jurisdiction, however, was sharply restricted to the vicinity of the capital. It was often depicted as a prototypical "oriental despotism." But its real authority rested heavily on local magnates, some of whom married into the royal family and most of whom had their own independent sources of power. The shah, the proud owner of sundry titles including that of Supreme Arbitrator, could well have appropriated for himself yet another one – that of Grand Manipulator. He was Shah-in-Shah, King of Kings, in more senses than one.

CHAPTER 2

Reform, revolution, and the Great War

O Iranians! O brethren of my beloved country! Until when will this treacherous intoxication keep you slumbering? Enough of this intoxication. Lift up your heads. Open your eyes. Cast a glance around you, and behold how the world has become civilized. All the savages in Africa and negroes in Zanzibar are marching towards civilization, knowledge, labor, and riches. Behold Your neighbors the Russians, who a hundred years ago were in much worse condition than we. Behold them now how they possess everything. In bygone days we had everything, and now all is gone. In the past, others looked on us as a great nation. Now we are reduced to such a condition that our neighbors of the north and south already believe us to be their property and divide our country between themselves. We have no guns, no army, no secure finances, no proper government, no commercial law. All this backwardness is due to autocracy and to injustice and to want of laws. Also your clergy are at fault, for they preach that life is short and worldly honors are only human vanities. These sermons lead you away from this world into submission, slavery, and ignorance. The monarchs, at the same time, despoil you ... And with all this come strangers who receive from you all your money, and instead furnish you with green, blue, and red cloth, gaudy glassware, and luxury furniture. These are the causes of your misery.

Tehran Sermon (1907)

ROOTS OF REVOLUTION

Iran's Constitutional Revolution – like many other revolutions – began with great expectations but foundered eventually in a deep sea of disillusionment. It promised the "dawn of a new era," the "gateway to a bright future," and the "reawakening of an ancient civilization." It produced, however, an era of strife that brought the country close to disintegration. The same reformers who had championed radical changes were withdrawing from politics by the late 1910s, distancing themselves from "youthful follies," even

34

from their own writings, and looking around for a "man on horseback" to save the nation. They did not come round to writing histories of the revolution until the mid-twentieth century. Paradoxically, the relative ease with which the revolution was both made and later unmade was linked to the same phenomenon – the lack of a viable central state. The revolution initially succeeded in large part because the regime lacked the machinery to crush opposition. Similarly, the revolution eventually failed in large part because it lacked the machinery to consolidate power – not to mention to implement reforms.

The roots of the revolution go back to the nineteenth century – especially to the gradual penetration of the country by the West. This penetration weakened the tenuous links that had connected the Qajar court to the wider society. It did so in two concurrent ways. On one hand, it introduced a mutual threat to the many dispersed urban bazaars and religious notables, bringing them together in a cross-regional middle class that became conscious for the first time of their common grievances against the government and the foreign powers. This propertied class, because of its ties to the bazaar and the clergy, later became known as the traditional middle class (*tabaqeh-e motavasateh-e sunnati*). This vital link between mosque and bazaar, which has lasted into the contemporary age, can be traced back to the late nineteenth century.[1] On the other hand, the contact with the West, especially through modern education, introduced new ideas, new occupations, and eventually a new middle class. Their members described themselves as "enlightened thinkers," adopting first the Arabic term *monvar al-fekran* and later coining the Persian equivalent *rowshanfekran* (enlightened thinkers). In many ways, they resembled eighteenth-century intellectuals in the Tsarist Empire who had coined the Russian term "intelligentsia." These new intellectuals had little in common with the traditional "men of the pen" found either in the royal court or in the theological seminaries. They perceived the world not through "Mirror for Princes" literature, but through the French Enlightenment. They venerated not royal authority but popular sovereignty; not tradition but Liberty, Equality, and Fraternity; not Shadows of God on Earth but the inalienable Rights of Man. They talked not of social equilibrium and political harmony, but of the need for radical change, fundamental transformation, and the inevitable march of human progress. They promulgated not the advantages of absolutism and conservatism, but of liberalism, nationalism, and even socialism. Their outlook was shaped not so much by the Koran, the shari'a, and the Shi'i Messiah, but by the Age of Reason and its radical notions of Natural Rights – rights citizens possess by virtue of being humans.

In the words of Ali Dehkhoda, a leading reformer who in later years compiled the first comprehensive Persian lexicon, these new concepts cried out for new terms.[2] He and his disciples popularized such words as *demokrasi, aristokrasi, oligarki, fudalism, kapitalism, sosyalism, imperialism,* and *bourzhuazi* (bourgeoisie). They introduced novel concepts such as *chap* (left) and *rast* (right), and *qorun-e vasateh* (middle ages). They gave new colorations to old words, changing the meaning of *estebdad* from "legitimate absolutism" to "illegitimate despotism"; of *dowlat* from patrimonial court to national government; of *mellat* from "religious community" to "nation"; of *vatan* from locality to fatherland/motherland; of *majles* from gathering to parliament; of *tabaqeh* from medieval estate to economic class; of *taraqi* from physical ascent to historical progress; of *mardom* from the populace to the "People"; and of *adalat* from appropriate treatment – as the shah was supposed to mete out to the various strata – to equal justice for all. The most contentious of the new terms was probably *mashruteh* (constitutional). For some, the term came from "charter" – as in Magna Carta. For others, it came from *shari'a* (holy law) and *mashru'eh* (conditional) – implying that temporal laws should be conditioned by the divine shari'a.[3] As Dehkhoda noted, the struggle over these new concepts was most visible during the revolution, but the genesis of that struggle was in the previous century.

Western penetration started early in the century. It began with military defeats, first by the Russian army, then by the British. The Russians – armed with modern artillery – swept through Central Asia and the Caucasus, defeating the Qajars in two short wars and imposing on them the humiliating treaties of Gulestan (1813) and Turkmanchai (1828). Similarly, the British, who had been in the Persian Gulf since the eighteenth century, started to expand their reach, forcing the Qajars to relinquish Herat, and imposing on them the equally humiliating Treaty of Paris (1857). Iranians began to refer to the two powers as their "northern" and "southern" neighbors. The treaties had far-reaching consequences. They established borders that have endured more or less intact into the contemporary age. They turned the country into a buffer and sometimes a contested zone in the "Great Game" played by the two powers. Their representatives became key players in Iranian politics – so much so that they had a hand not only in making and unmaking ministers but also in stabilizing the monarchy and influencing the line of succession thoughout the century. This gave birth to the notion – which became even more prevalent in the next century – that foreign hands pulled all the strings in Iran, that foreign conspiracies determined the course of events, and that behind every national crisis lay the foreign powers. The "paranoid style of politics" which many have noted shapes modern Iran had its origins in the nineteenth century.

The treaties also paved the way for other foreign powers to obtain a series of commercial and diplomatic concessions known as capitulations. They were permitted to establish provincial consulates, and their merchants were exempted from high import duties as well as from internal tariffs, travel restrictions, and the jurisdiction of local courts. The term capitulation became synonymous with imperial privileges, arrogance, and transgressions. These treaties – together with the opening of the Suez Canal and extension of the Russian railways into the Caucasus and Central Asia – initiated the commercial penetration of Iran. The process was further accelerated by the Baku "oil rush" in the 1890s. By the end of the century, some 100,000 – many undocumented, unskilled, and seasonal workers – were crossing every year into the Russian Empire. These migrants, almost all from Azerbaijan, formed the bulk of the Baku underclass.[4]

Foreign trade – dominated by merchants from the two "neighbors" – increased eightfold in the course of the century. Imports consisted mostly of guns, tools, and textiles from Western Europe; sugar and kerosene from Russia; spices, tea, and coffee from Asia. Exports consisted mainly of carpets, raw cotton, silk, tobacco, hides, rice, dried fruits, and opium. The last was transported by British merchants to the lucrative Chinese market. Zill al-Sultan, the governor of Isfahan, became so concerned about opium undercutting food production that in 1890 he decreed that for every four fields planted with poppies one had to be set aside for cereals.[5]

In 1800, Iran had been fairly isolated from the world economy. By 1900, it was well on the way to being incorporated into that economy. This was especially true for the north, which supplied agricultural goods as well as unskilled labor to the Russian market, and for the south, especially Isfahan, Fars, and Kerman, which provided carpets and shawls, as well as opium, to the British Empire. Not surprisingly, the Russian government took special interest in the port of Enzeli and its road to Tehran. The British government took equal interest in the roads connecting the Gulf to Isfahan, Shiraz, Yazd, and Kerman. In 1888, Lynch Brothers, a London firm already active on the Tigris–Euphrates, started running stream boats from Mohammarah to Ahwaz along the Karun – Iran's only navigable river. To help their merchants, the British in 1889 established the Imperial Bank of Persia. The Russians followed suit with their Banque d'Escompte de Perse. Curzon began his *Persia and the Persian Question* with the claim that the country was vital for Britain not only because of the Great Game but also because of its commercial prospects.[6] He threatened to "impeach" any "traitor" who contemplated giving Russia a foothold in the Persian Gulf: "Every claim that can be made by Russia for the exclusive control of the Caspian Sea could be urged with tenfold greater force by Great Britain for a similar monopoly of the Persian Gulf. Hundreds of British lives and millions of British money have been spent in the pacification of these troublous waters."[7] He concluded his magnum opus with this pontification:[8]

I trust that, from the information and reasoning that have been supplied in these volumes, the importance of Persia to England will have been made sufficiently manifest. The figures and calculations which I have given relating to trade, and more particularly Anglo-Persian trade, the analysis of the indigenous resources of Persia, the character and chances of the still undeveloped schemes for internal amelioration, the field thus opened for the judicious employment of capital are all of them appeals to the practical and business-like instincts of Englishmen. In the furious commercial competition that now rages like a hurricane through the world, the loss of a market is a retrograde step that cannot be recovered; the gain of a market is a positive addition to the national strength. Indifference to Persia might mean the sacrifice of a trade that already feeds hundreds of thousands of our citizens in this country and in India. A friendly attention to Persia will mean so much more employment for British ships, for British labour, and for British spindles.

The Qajars tried to limit foreign penetration by strengthening their state through measures which later became known throughout the world as "defensive modernization." These efforts, however, failed, largely because of their inability to raise tax revenues, a problem compounded over the century by a staggering sixfold rise in prices. By 1900, government deficits were running at a rate of more than $1 million a year, yet the Qajar state was too weak to raise the tax revenues it needed.[9] In an effort to break this vicious circle, the state tried selling concessions and borrowing money. Nasser al-Din Shah initiated this process in 1872 by selling the sole right to construct mines, railways, tramways, dams, roads, and industrial plants to Baron Julius de Reuter, a British citizen after whom the famous news agency was later named. The price was $200,000 and 60 percent of annual profits. Curzon described this sale as "most complete surrender of the entire resources of a kingdom into foreign hands that has ever been dreamed of, much less accomplished in history."[10] Indeed, this prospective monopoly created such a furor – especially in St. Petersburg and among pro-Russian courtiers – that it had to be cancelled. But it sowed the seeds for the oil concession that was to bring so much turbulence in the next century. In a second gambit, Nasser al-Din Shah in 1891 sold to Major Talbot, another Englishman, a monopoly for the sale and export of tobacco. This too had to be cancelled, in part because of Russian opposition and in part because of a nationwide boycott spearheaded by merchants and religious leaders. This tobacco boycott was in many ways a dress rehearsal for the Constitutional Revolution.

Although these monopolies had to be withdrawn, the Qajars were able to sell a number of more modest concessions. British firms bought the right to dredge as well as navigate the Karun; build roads and telegraph lines in the south; finance carpet factories in Isfahan, Bushire, Sultanabad, and Tabriz; establish the Imperial Bank with full control over the printing of banknotes; and, most important of all, the concession to drill for oil in the southwest. This paved the way for the D'Arcy Concession, which, in turn, paved the way for the formation of the Anglo-Persian Oil Company. Meanwhile, Russian firms bought the right to fish in the Caspian Sea; dredge Enzeli; drill for oil in the north; and build roads and telegraph lines linking their borders to Tehran, Tabriz, and Mashed. What is more, Belgians – deemed to be neutral between Britain and Russia – built in Tehran not only the railway to the Abdul 'Azim Mosque, but also a tram line, street lights, a sugar mill, and a glass factory. By the turn of the century, foreign investments in Iran totaled $60 million. This sum may not have been huge but it was enough to cause consternation among some local commercial interests.

The Qajar attempts at "defensive modernization" did not amount to much – and that little was confined to a few showpieces in the capital. The Cossack Brigade, the most visible example, could muster no more than 2,000 men. *Nazmieh*, the Tehran police force, had fewer than 4,600 men. The central mint, which replaced the many provincial ones, could now debase the coinage, and thereby provide the government with some extra cash – but, of course, at the cost of further fueling inflation. The telegraph office – centered in Cannon Square – linked Tehran to the provinces and thus provided the shah with the means of keeping closer tabs on his governors. Ironically, it also provided the opposition with the means to challenge him during the tobacco crisis and the Constitutional Revolution. The ministry of posts and telegraph, created in 1877, issued stamps and distributed mail. The Government Printing Office published two gazettes – *Ettellah* (Information), listing new appointments, and *Iran*, summarizing official views. Both tried to substitute Persian for Arabic terms.

The crown jewel of reforms, however, was the Dar al Fanon (Abode of Learning). Founded in 1852, its mission was to train "sons of the nobility" for public service. By 1900 it was a fully fledged polytechnic with more than 350 students. Top graduates received scholarships to study in Europe – mainly in France and Belgium to limit Russian and British influence. Its faculty also came mainly from France and Belgium. At the turn of the century, the government opened four other secondary schools in Tehran, Isfahan, and Tabriz; and five new colleges affiliated with the Dar al-Fanon – two military colleges and schools of agriculture, political science, and foreign languages. The last, through the Government Printing Office, published more than 160 books. These included 80 medical, military, and language textbooks; 10 travelogues – including Nasser al-Din Shah's tour of Europe; 10 abbreviated translations of Western classics such as Defoe's *Robinson Crusoe*, Dumas' *Three Musketeers*, Verne's *Around the World in Eighty Days*, Descartes' *Discourse*, Newton's *Principia*, and Darwin's *Origin of Species*; 20 biographies of world-famous figures – including those of Louis XIV, Napoleon, Peter the Great, Nicholas I, Frederick the Great, and Wilhelm I; and, most significant of all, 10 histories of Iran, including pre-Islamic Iran, written mostly by Europeans. Thus Iranians began to see their own past as well as world history mainly through Western eyes. The elder Musher al-Dowleh, the founder of the School of Political Science, was typical of the new sentiments. Returning from long service in embassies abroad, he began to write increasingly about *mellat* (nation), *melliyat* (nationality), state sovereignty, and the need for *ra'yat* (flock-subjects) to become fully fledged citizens.

Nasser al-Din Shah began his reign in 1848 encouraging contacts with Europe. But by the end of his reign he had grown so fearful of alien ideas that it was rumored that he preferred ministers who did not know whether Brussels was a city or a cabbage. Nevertheless, he continued to send diplomatic representatives abroad and a steady stream of students to France and Belgium. He also tolerated Christian missionaries so long as they limited themselves to medical-educational activities, and proselytized only among the religious minorities. French Catholics began working with Armenians and Assyrians around Lake Urmiah; they then established more than thirty facilities spread throughout the country. American Presbyterians tended to focus on the north; Anglicans on the south; and Alliance Française in Tehran, Tabriz, and Isfahan. L'Alliance Israelite, the French Jewish organization, opened schools in Hamadan, Isfahan, and Tehran. Similarly, the Zoroastrian community in India financed a school for their coreligionists in Yazd.

Meanwhile, Iranian private entrepreneurs established a number of modest enterprises: electrical plants in Tehran, Tabriz, Rasht, and Mashed – the latter illuminated the main shrine; a sugar mill in Mazanderan; a silk factory in Gilan; a cotton mill in Tehran; and printing presses as well as papermaking factories in Tehran and Isfahan. They launched stock companies with the explicit purpose of protecting home industries from foreign competition. They funded public libraries in Tehran and Tabriz as well as ten secondary schools, including one for girls. They financed reformist newspapers: *Tarbiyat* (Education) in Tehran, *Hemmat* (Endeavor) in Tabriz, *Habl al-Matin* (The Firm Cord) in Calcutta, *Akhtar* (Star) in Istanbul, *Parvaresh* (Education) in Cairo, and *Qanon* (Law) in London. They also organized semi-formal groups – the National Society, the Society for Humanity, the Revolutionary Committee, and the Secret Society modeled after the European Freemasons. By the end of the century, such groups were meeting quietly to discuss the urgent need for government reforms. In short, the country now contained a distinct intelligentsia even though its numbers totaled fewer than three thousand and most of its members came from the ranks of the old elite. Not surprisingly, when a lone dissident in 1896 assassinated Nasser al-Din Shah in the Abdul 'Azim Mosque, some felt that the age of absolutism had finally come to an end. The new monarch, Muzaffar al-Din Shah, was reputed to be far more open to the new world. The assassin's bullet ended more than Nasser al-Din Shah's life. It ended the old order.

COMING OF THE REVOLUTION

The revolution's long-term causes were rooted in the nineteenth century; its short-term ones were triggered in 1904–05 by an economic crisis brought about by government bankruptcy and spiraling inflation. Unable to meet government expenditures, Muzaffar al-Din Shah threatened to raise land taxes and default on loans from local creditors. He also turned to British and Russian banks for new loans on top of the £4 million he had already borrowed from them. They obliged on condition he handed over the entire customs system to Belgian administrators headed by a Monsieur Naus. The latter assured Britain and Russia that he would give priority to repaying their previous loans.[11] It was rumored that Naus had Jewish origins, preferred to employ Armenians over Muslims, planned to raise drastically the tariffs on local merchants, and aspired to become minister of finance even though he was completely ignorant of the traditional mostowfi system. During Muharram in 1905, his opponents distributed a photograph of him masquerading as a mullah at a fancy dress ball.[12] The British legation summed up the financial crisis:[13]

The year 1906 has been a very important epoch in Persian history, for it has brought the introduction of parliamentary institutions. The condition of Persia had been for some time growing more and more intolerable. The Shah was entirely in the hands of a corrupt ring of courtiers who were living on the spoils of the government and country. He had parted with the treasures he had inherited from his father and with most of the imperial and national domains. He had been obliged to have recourse to foreign loans, the proceeds of which he had spent in foreign travel or had lavished on his courtiers. There was a yearly deficit and the debt of the country was growing daily. There appeared to be no recourse but another foreign loan and it was generally believed that the loan would be granted under conditions which would practically extinguish the independence of the country. A certain number of young and independent men were aware of the facts, and were engaged by the government in the negotiations which were being carried on with a view to the loan.

At the same time, the whole country was suffering from acute inflation – the price of bread shot up 90 percent and that of sugar 33 percent. This inflation was caused by a combination of a bad harvest, a cholera epidemic, and a sudden disruption in the northern trade prompted by the 1905 Russo-Japanese War and the subsequent upheavals in the Tsarist Empire. By June 1905, angry women were demonstrating in Tehran, and, in the words of an eyewitness, giving the royal governor a "piece of their mind."[14] And by November 1905, the governor was trying to divert public attention by blaming the bazaar and bastinadoing three prominent sugar merchants. One was a seventy-year-old importer highly respected because of his philanthropic activities. The whole bazaar closed down and demanded the governor's dismissal. According to an eyewitness, news of the bastinadoing "flashed through the bazaars" like lightning, and prompted shopkeepers to close down their stores.[15] Meanwhile, in Mashed, bread rioters assaulted the home of a court-linked corn dealer, and the latter retaliated by having his private gunmen shoot down forty protestors who had taken sanctuary in the Imam Reza Shrine. One local senior cleric attributed the riot to the general mood of discontent.[16]

Your majesty. Your realm is deteriorating. Your subjects have been reduced to begging. They are being oppressed and exploited by governors and officials whose greed and blood thirst knows no bounds. Last year, tax payers who could not pay cash had to sell their daughters to Turkmans and Armenian merchants who then sold them into slavery in Russia. Thousands of your subjects have had to flee this oppression and go to Russia … if remedies are not found, the country will be dismantled. The British will take over Sistan and Baluchestan; the Russians other parts; and the Ottomans have their own designs … Your majesty, listen to the plight of fifteen million souls who live in fear of being imprisoned by the foreigners.

This passing mention of the slave trade in women has been used by one sociologist to claim that gender formed the "central" issue in the Constitutional Revolution.[17]

The crisis was further compounded by other conflicts. In Kerman, Sheikhi–Mutasheri riots prompted the resignation of the governor, the bastinadoing of a local mojtahed, the killing of two demonstrators, and the scapegoating of the local Jewish community, whose quarter was looted. In Tehran in the summer of 1906, the Russian Bank, needing office space, bought an adjacent abandoned cemetery. The digging up of the dead prompted widespread protests, even in Najaf, and led to physical assaults on the bank. In the ensuing week, which coincided with Muharram, the Cossacks arrested a well-known luti, deported protest organizers, and shot into the Friday Mosque, killing an elderly sayyed. The funeral for the sayyed drew large crowds with women denouncing the governor as a latter-day Yazid and men wearing white shrouds as a sign of their readiness to be martyred.

These confrontations paved the way to two major protests, which, in turn, paved the way for the drafting of a written constitution. In June 1906, Sayyed Abdallah Behbehani and Sayyed Muhammad Tabatabai – two of Tehran's three most respected mojtaheds – led a procession of some one thousand seminary students to the sanctuary of Qom. Later accounts anachronistically described these mojtaheds as ayatollahs. In fact, the clerical title of ayatollah, as well as that of hojjat al-islam, did not gain currency until well after the Constitutional Revolution. At Qom, the two were joined by Sheikh Fazlollah Nuri, the other senior mojtahed. The three threatened to move en masse to Karbala and Najaf, and thus deprive the country of religious services unless the shah dismissed both Naus and the governor, resolved the Kerman crisis, stopped the bank construction, and, most important of all, established an *Adalat Khaneh* (House of Justice). In short, the ulama were threatening to go on strike. Female demonstrators joked that if the crisis continued marriages would have to be notarized by Monsieur Naus.

In the same week, a group of Tehran merchants, some of whom had been active in the secret societies, approached the British legation in its summer retreat on the northern hills of Tehran. The Legation, in a confidential memorandum to London, explained how it got involved in the events that followed:[18]

After the shooting, it appeared as if the Government had won the day. The town was in the hands of the troops. The popular leaders had fled. The bazaars were in the occupation of the soldiers. And there appeared to be no place of refuge. Under these circumstances the popular party had recourse to an expedient sanctioned by old, and, indeed, immemorial custom – the rule of *bast* (sanctuary). It was resolved, failing all other recourses, to adopt this expediency. Two persons called at the Legation at Gulak and asked whether, in case the people took *bast* in the British legation, the Chargé d'Affairs would invoke the aid of the military to remove them.

Mr. Grant Duff expressed that he hoped they would not have recourse to such an expedient, but, he said it was not in his power, in view of the acknowledged custom in Persia, to use force if they came ... The following evening, fifty merchants and mullas appeared in the Legation and took up their quarters for the night. Their numbers gradually increased, and soon there were 14,000 persons in the Legation garden.

The protestors were drawn predominantly from the bazaar. A committee of guild elders allocated tents to the various trades and crafts. One visitor counted at least five hundred tents, "for all the guilds, even the cobblers, walnut sellers, and tinkers had their own."[19] The Legation reported that order was so well maintained that little was damaged except some "flower-beds" and "some tree barks bearing pious inscriptions." Meanwhile, the organizing committee both arranged women's demonstrations outside and strictly controlled entry of newcomers into the compound. Only faculty and students from the Dar al-Fanon were permitted in. These new arrivals transformed the compound into "one vast open-air school of political science" lecturing on the advantages of constitutional government and even of republicanism.[20] Some began to translate the Belgian constitution with its parliamentary form of government headed by a titular monarch. The organizing committee also raised money from wealthy merchants to help those who were unable to afford the prolonged strike. One participant wrote in his memoirs:[21]

I clearly remember the day when we heard that the reactionaries were busy sowing discontent among the young carpenters and sawyers. The former, angry at having been taken away from their livelihood, demanded to know what they had to gain from the whole venture. The latter, being illiterate and irrational, were reluctant to accept any logical arguments. If these two irresponsible groups had walked out, our whole movement would have suffered. Fortunately, we persuaded them to remain in *bast.*

Finally, the organizing committee, on the advice of the modern educated colleagues, demanded from the shah not just a House of Justice, but a written constitution drafted by an elected National Assembly (*Majles-e Melli).*

At first the court dismissed the protestors as "Babi heretics" and "British-hired traitors" and tried to mollify them with the promise of setting up an ambiguous-sounding Islamic Majles. But faced with an ongoing general strike, a barrage of telegrams from the provinces, threats of armed intervention by émigré communities in Baku and Tiflis, and, as the "fatal" straw, the threat of defection from the Cossacks, the court backed down.[22] As one eyewitness asked rhetorically of Edward Browne, the famous British historian, "the Shah with his unarmed, unpaid, ragged, starving soldiers, what can he do in face of the menace of a general strike and riots? The Government had to climb down and grant all that was asked of them."[23] On August 5, 1906 – three weeks after the first protestors had taken refuge in the British legation – Muzaffar al-Din Shah signed the royal proclamation to hold nationwide elections for a Constituent Assembly. August 5 continues to be celebrated as Constitutional Day.

THE CONSTITUTION

Meeting hurriedly in Tehran, the Constituent Assembly drew up an electoral law for the forthcoming National Assembly. Most of the delegates were merchants, clerics, guild elders, and liberal notables – many of whom considered themselves members of the new intelligentsia. They drafted a complex electoral law dividing the population into six classes (*tabaqats*): Qajar princes; ulama and seminary students; *a'yan* (nobles) and *ashraf* (notables); merchants with "a definite place of business": landowners with agricultural property worth at least 1,000 tomans; and "tradesmen and craftsmen" belonging to a legitimate guild and paying at least the "average rent" in the locality.[24] Low-paid occupations, such as porters, laborers, and camel drivers, were excluded. The law also divided the electorate into 156 constituencies, allocating 96 seats to Tehran. Candidates had to be able to read, write, and speak in Persian. Elections in the provinces were to be in two stages: each "class" in every district was to choose one delegate to the provincial capital where they were to elect the provincial representatives to the National Assembly. Tehran was divided into four districts each representing the four main wards outside the royal Ark. The Tehran elections were to be in one stage: four seats were allocated to Qajar princes; ten to landowners; four to clerics; and as many as thirty-two to the established guilds. The voting age was set at twenty-five. Needless to say, the issue of women's suffrage was not raised.

These dramatic events – especially the elections for the National Assembly – sparked the formation of a large array of parties, organizations, and newspapers. In the provinces, the local populations, invariably led by the bazaars, created regional assemblies (*anjumans*). In Tehran, some thirty occupational and ethnic groups formed their own specific organizations with such names as the Society of *Asnafs* (Guilds), *Mostowfiyan* (Accountants), *Daneshmandan* (Scholars), *Tolabs* (Seminarians), Zoroastrians, Armenians, Jews, Southerners, and Azerbaijanis. The last was led by merchants from Tabriz who had contacts with the Social Democratic Party in the Caucasus.

In fact, two years earlier a group of Iranian intellectuals working in Baku had formed a circle named *Hemmat* (Endeavor) and had started to work closely with the Russian Social Democratic Party.

The press was even more active. The number of newspapers jumped from six at the eve of the revolution to more than ninety at the opening of the Constituent Assembly. Intellectuals rushed to air concepts deemed too dangerous in the previous decades. These concepts, especially liberty, equality, and fraternity, inspired the names of many of the new publications – *Bidari* (Awakening), *Taraqqi* (Progress), *Tamadon* (Civilization), *Vatan* (Fatherland), *Adamiyat* (Humanity), *Omid* (Hope), *'Asr-e Now* (New Age), *Neda-ye Vatan* (Voice of the Fatherland), *Esteqlal* (Independence), *Eslah* (Reform), *Eqbal* (Progress), *Hoquq* (Rights), *Haqiqat* (Truth), *Adalat* (Justice), *Azadi* (Liberty), *Mosavat* (Equality), and *Akhavat* (Fraternity). As in other revolutions, the lifting of censorship opened up the floodgates. According to Browne, one of the most popular of the papers was *Sur-e Israfil* (Israfil's Trumpet), which, despite its religious title, was forthrightly radical and secular.[25] Written mainly by Dehkhoda, the lexicographer, it blended satire and poetry with political commentary, all in plain modern Persian. It took to task the whole upper class, including the landed ulama, for exploiting and keeping "ignorant" the "common people" (*'avam*). Its circulation of 5,000 topped that of other papers. Since Dehkhoda had studied theology and was well versed in Islam, his satires on the ulama were especially biting. Not surprisingly, it did not take long for conservatives to target *Sur-e Israfil*.

The National Assembly opened in October 1906. It contained more than sixty bazaaris – merchants and guild elders; twenty-five clerics; and some fifty landlords, local notables, and senior officials.[26] The members gradually coalesced into two fluid parties: the *Mo'tadel* (Moderates) and the *Azadikhah* (Liberals). The former were led jointly by a wholesale scarf dealer who had led the 1905 demonstrations against Naus, and by a former royal coin minter who had helped finance the venture into the British legation. They enjoyed the backing of Sayyeds Tabatabai and Behbehani, who, while not actual deputies, nevertheless participated in parliamentary debates. On most days, the Moderates could muster a majority. The Liberals were led by Hassan Taqizadeh, an eloquent speaker from Tabriz. Although he had begun his career as a cleric and still wore his turban, he had become increasingly enamored of modern ideas – in particular modern science – especially after visiting Baku. In many ways, Taqizadeh – like Dehkhoda – was typical of the first generation of the intelligentsia.

The Liberals and Moderates worked closely to draft a constitution that would be acceptable not only to Muzaffar al-Din Shah, who died soon after signing the original proclamation, but also to his successor, Muhammad Ali Shah, who tried to water down royal promises by substituting the term *mashru* (conditional) for the more modern concept *mashrutiyat* (constitutional).[27] The final two documents – known as the Fundamental and the Supplementary Fundamental Laws – were modeled after the Belgian constitution. According to eyewitnesses, the drafters of the two documents – all graduates of the Dar al-Fanon – intended to establish a constitutional monarchy with classic separation of powers between the executive, legislative, and judiciary.[28] These two documents, with minor amendments, survived as the fundamental laws of the land all the way to the 1979 revolution – at least on paper.

The fundamental laws gave the shah the nominal prerogative to head the executive, command the armed forces, declare war and peace, sign bills into laws, and appoint the highest state officials, including cabinet ministers. But the shah had to take an oath of office before the National Assembly, accept ministers elected by it, and sign into law bills passed by it. The shah retained only one real prerogative: the right to appoint thirty senators to a sixty-man upper house. But even this proved to be a hollow power since the first senate was not convened until 1949.

The Majles was designed to be the central piece of the new constitution. Described as the "representative of the whole people," it had final say over all "laws, decrees, budgets, treaties, loans, monopolies, and concessions." It even controlled the court budget. It had the power to investigate and propose any measure "deemed conducive to the well-being of the government and people." Its sessions were to last two full years during which its members were immune from arrest. It had the authority to select cabinet ministers. The constitution even spelled out that "ministers cannot divest themselves of responsibility by pleading verbal or written orders from the shah": "If the National Assembly or the Senate shall, by an absolute majority, declare itself dissatisfied with the cabinet or with one particular minister, that cabinet or minister shall resign."

The constitutional laws had many other significant provisions. They formalized the provincial assemblies and set them up as parallel institutions to the governor-generals. They gave citizens a bill of rights including protection of life, property, and honor; freedom of speech, assembly, and organization; equality before the law; habeas corpus; and safeguards from arbitrary arrest. They designated a national flag with three equal and horizontal strips of green, white, and red – colors historically associated with Shi'ism. This has remained the national flag to the present day. As a concession to the Qajars, the new tricolor incorporated the Lion and the Sun.

The most important concessions, however, went to Islam in general and to Shi'ism in particular. Shi'ism was declared to be Iran's official religion. Only Shi'i Muslims were to hold cabinet positions. The executive could ban "heretical" books, "anti-religious" associations, and "pernicious ideas." The judiciary was divided into state and religious courts with the clergy retaining the authority to implement the shari'a in the latter. The legislature was not permitted to pass laws that conflicted with the shari'a. To ensure compliance, the National Assembly was to elect senior clerics to a Guardian Council whose sole task would be to vet all legislation. This council was to function until Judgment Day and the reappearance of the Mahdi. Such a Guardian Council, however, was not convened until after the 1979 revolution.

The person instrumental in writing the constitution was a recent returnee from Europe named Mirza Hussein Khan Musher al-Mulk, who, on his father's death in 1907, inherited the title Musher al-Dowleh. In many ways, the young Musher al-Dowleh typified the new notables who were to play leading roles in national politics during the course of the next twenty years – until the emergence of Reza Shah. He had inherited large landholdings from his father who came from a long line of mostowfis from Nain and had married into a prosperous clerical family. Having studied in Moscow and Paris, Musher al-Dowleh was fluent in Russian and French. He not only drafted the first electoral system and the fundamental laws, but also designed the national flag and modeled the interior ministry after its counterpart in Russia.[29] In the next twenty years, Musher al-Dowleh headed four cabinets and served in another eighteen – eight times as minister of war and five times as minister of justice. He also served as the country's chief representative in London and St. Petersburg. In retirement, he wrote a best-seller entitled *Iran-e Bastan* (Ancient Iran) giving readers a highly patriotic account of pre-Islamic Persia. His younger brother, Mutamin al-Mulk, was active in parliament from 1909 until 1925, first as a deputy and then as Speaker of the House. With the introduction of family names in 1925, the two brothers adopted the surname Pirnia. At times the British praised them as "progressive," "honest," and "intelligent." At other times, especially when their interests did not coincide with those of London, they dismissed them as "timid," grossly "wealthy," and overly "nationalistic." This typified British attitudes towards the liberal notables.

Notables dominated the first cabinet chosen by parliament in August 1907. Musher al-Saltaneh, a relative of Musher al-Dowleh, headed the cabinet and the interior ministry. He too came from an old mostowfi family and had previously served as provincial governor and royal treasurer. The British legation described him as coming from the "old school" and having not taken part in the "reform movement."[30] Musher al-Dowleh himself inherited his father's post as justice minister. Sa'ad al-Dowleh, the foreign minister, had represented Iran in Brussels for more than ten years and had helped organize the protests against Naus. Qavam al-Dowleh, the finance minister, had studied in France and came from a wealthy landowning family. He had a flair for literature. Mostowfi al-Mamalek, the war minister, had inherited his title as well as his huge fortune from his father who had been a grand vezir under Nasser al-Din Shah. He himself had lived in Paris from 1900 until 1907. Majd al-Mulk, the commerce minister, came from a merchant family that had produced a number of vezirs and controllers of the royal mint. Nayer al-Mulk, the education minister, had been in charge of the Dar al-Fanon from 1897 until 1904. Since he was old and infirm, his son acted on his behalf as education minister. Finally, Mohandes al-Mamalek, minister of public works, was a distinguished French-educated mathematician who had accompanied Muzaffar al-Din Shah on his European trips. The British legation claimed that he used his position to extort money from British companies building roads in Iran. Not surprisingly, the new order was soon dubbed that of "al-dowlehs, al-saltanehs, and al-mamaleks."

CIVIL WAR

When Muhammad Ali Shah ascended the throne in January 1907 he had no choice but to bend to parliamentary will and sign the fundamental laws. His position, however, gradually improved in the next few months, and by June 1908 he felt strong enough to lead the Cossacks in a typical military coup against the Majles. The change of fortunes was brought about by three separate pressures.

First, the constitutionalists suffered a major setback in 1907 with the signing of the Anglo-Russian Convention. Britain, having grown fearful of the rising power of Germany, decided to resolve long-standing differences with Russia throughout Asia, including Iran. The convention divided Iran into three zones. It allocated the north, including Isfahan, to Russia; the southwest, especially Kerman, Sistan, and Baluchestan to Britain; and demarcated the rest as a "neutral zone." The two powers agreed to seek concessions only within their own zones; to retain the Belgian customs officials; and to use the customs revenues to repay the previous loans. The constitutionalists felt not only betrayed but also isolated in their dealings with the shah.[31] The convention also taught Iranians a hard lesson in realpolitik – that however predatory the two "neighbors" were, they were even more dangerous when they put aside their rivalries. The 1907 convention continued to haunt Iranians well into the mid-twentieth century.

Second, the Majles created an inevitable backlash once it tried to reform the tax system. It restricted the practice of auctioning off tax farms. It transferred state lands from the royal treasury to the finance ministry. It gave the ministry jurisdiction over provincial mostowfis. It reduced allocations to the court treasury, which, in turn, was obliged to streamline the palace stables, armories, kitchens, kilns, warehouses, harem, and workshops. It was even forced to close down the Drum Towers. Abdallah Mostowfi, in his long memoirs, reminisced that young deputies were so enamored of all things modern that they summarily dismissed such venerable institutions as medieval "relicts."[32] One Liberal suggested that the finance ministry should update the scales by which landlords paid taxes in cash rather than in kind. Another demanded the termination of all court pensions and tuyuls. Yet another suggested that the shah could pay his debts simply by selling off his family jewels.[33] He added sarcastically that he was losing sleep worrying about the financial plight of those in the royal harem. A veteran of these debates writes that a common form of abuse in those days was to call someone a "court groom" or "court doorman." "These lackeys," he explained, "had been so pampered that they had become the most fanatical advocates of absolutism in the whole population of Tehran."[34]

Third, some Liberals compounded the backlash by proposing far-reaching secular reforms. They accused the ulama of covering up slimy interests with sublime sermons. They advocated immediate improvements in the rights not only of religious minorities but also of women. They criticized the constitutional clause that gave the ulama veto power over parliamentary legislation. They even argued that the shari'a had nothing to say about state laws (*qanons*). By mid-1907, Sheikh Fazlollah Nuri, whom some considered to be the most senior of the three mojtaheds in Tehran, had broken with his two colleagues. He formed a Society of the Prophet, rebuilt bridges to the shah, and issued a major fatwa denouncing the Liberals for opening up the floodgates to "anarchism, nihilism, socialism, and naturalism."[35] This denunciation could well have been written by a counter-Enlightenment Pope. He also hammered away on the theme that Babis, Bahais, and Armenians were scheming to destroy Islam with such heretical innovations as elected parliaments, secular laws, and, worst of all, religious equality.

Sheikh Nuri showed his strength in December 1907 by holding a rally in Cannon Square. According to eyewitness accounts, the "reactionary crowd" filled up the whole expansive square.[36] It drew participants from diverse walks of life: students and former students from Nuri's seminary; lutis under his protection; pensioners; muleteers, craftsmen, doormen, and servants employed in the royal palace; peasants from the royal estates in the nearby village of Veramin; and urban poor suffering from rising food prices. One eyewitness reported that even "common folk" from the bazaar flocked to hear Sheikh Nuri speak in Cannon Square.[37] Nuri accused the Liberals of being latter-day Jacobins undermining religion and "sowing corruption on earth" – a capital offense according to the traditional interpretation of the shari'a. Aroused by such inflammatory language, vigilantes attacked pedestrians who happened to be wearing European-style hats.[38]

The shah struck in June 1908. He did so immediately after receiving £10,000 in cash from Mukhber al-Dowleh who treated the ministry of posts and telegraph as his family fiefdom.[39] The cash was promptly distributed as special bonuses among the 1,500 Cossacks who garrisoned Tehran. Declaring martial law, the shah appointed Colonel Liakhoff, the Russian Cossack commander, to be military governor of Tehran. Liakhoff banned all newspapers and public meetings, including Muharram processions; issued arrest warrants for the leading deputies; and sent his Cossacks to occupy the telegraph office and to bombard the Majles building. According to British reports, the fighting took some 250 lives.[40] Most parliamentary leaders managed to escape – into exile or took sanctuary in the Ottoman Legation. But Behbehani and Tabatabai were placed under house arrest. Six others were imprisoned in the royal gardens and accused of "sowing corruption on earth." Three of them were executed there.

The coup triggered a civil war. While Cossacks seized Tehran and royalist Shahsaven tribesmen besieged Tabriz, the parliamentary side drew support from three sources. First, some one thousand volunteers, known as *fedayis* (self-sacrificers) and *mojaheds* (holy warriors), rallied to the parliamentary cause. They came not only from Tehran, Tabriz, Mashed, and Rasht, but also from the Iranian, Armenian, and Georgian communities in the Caucasus. Some fought under the Red Flag; others under the Iranian tricolor. The volunteers from abroad were organized by the Russian Social Democrats, the Armenian nationalist Dashnaks, and the Iranian Hemmat Party in Baku – all of whom had turned their attention to Iran once the 1905 revolution had been crushed in Russia. They fought under the slogan "Love of Freedom has no Fatherland."[41] The Armenians were led by Yeprem Khan, who, because of his anti-Tsarist activities, had been exiled to Siberia before escaping to Rasht where he worked as a brick manufacturer and headed the Dashnak Party. He became known as the "Garibaldi of Persia."[42] The Tabriz volunteers were led by Sattar Khan and Baqer Khan. The former, the kadkhuda of the main Sheikhi ward, was a luti and a former horse dealer. The latter, the kadkhuda of the neighboring Sheikhi ward, was also a luti and a former bricklayer. They had first made their mark in Tabriz by forcing grain dealers to sell their goods at "just prices."[43] The volunteers from the Caucasus were particularly lethal since they brought with them hand grenades and knew how to assemble bombs. A British reporter described them as "walking arsenals."[44] These volunteers, despite their religious backgrounds, received a major boost when three of the four leading Najaf mojtaheds issued a proclamation opposing Sheikh Nuri and instead supporting Sayyeds Behbehani and Tabatabai.

Second, the parliamentary side was significantly strengthened when Muhammad Vali Sepahdar, the leading magnate in Mazanderan, threw his weight against the shah. The India Office described him as "one of the biggest feudals in the country" with estates not only in his home region of Tunkabun but also in Qazvin, Khurasan, and Gilan.[45] On various occasions he had governed Gilan, Ardabel, Talesh, and Astarabad. At the time of the coup, he was the nominal commander of the army and was sent to help the Shahsavens take Tabriz. But instead he had defected, taking with him his men – many of whom were peasants from his Mazanderan estates. He joined forces with Yeprem Khan in Rasht. This proved to be a good career move. In the following years, Sepahdar not only gained the title Sepahsalar al-A'zam (Great Army Commander), but also headed eight cabinets and ten ministries – often as minister of war. His brother also served in many of these administrations.

Third, the parliamentary side obtained the decisive support of the Bakhtiyaris. The Ilkhani patriarch, Samsam al-Saltaneh, was persuaded by his cousin Sardar As'ad, who had been moving among liberal exiles in Paris ever since his father had been murdered by Zill al-Sultan, to cast his lot with the revolutionaries. The two khans secured their flank by selling border villages at discount prices to Sheikh Khaz'al of the Arab Ka'ab tribe. They then captured Isfahan and marched on to Tehran with some 12,000 armed tribesmen – by far the largest force on the parliamentary side. They were the only tribal leaders who could afford to finance a large and prolonged expeditionary force outside their home region. This gamble paid off. In the next two decades, Samsam al-Saltaneh headed as many as six cabinets. And Sardar As'ad, even though semi-blind, worked behind the scenes to turn the finance ministry into a virtual tribal fiefdom. The two also brought into the finance ministry a number of Armenians from Chahar Mahal. These Armenians, who had originally been tutors to Bakhtiyari children, eventually became self-taught accountants.

In July 1910, Sardar As'ad, Sepahdar, and Yeprem Khan converged on Tehran. The shah fled to the Russian Legation from where he negotiated his

abdication, agreeing to go into exile in return for a generous pension. The
Majles deputies, together with representatives from the bazaar and the
victorious armies, convened a constituent assembly of some five hundred
delegates known as the Grand Majles. They replaced Muhammad Ali Shah
with his twelve-year-old son Ahmad Shah; and named as regent his aged
uncle, Azud al-Mulk, the liberal-inclined Ilkhani of the Qajar tribe.
According to tradition, the only person permitted to sit down in the
presence of the shah was the Qajar Ilkhani.[46]

The Grand Majles retained Colonel Liakhoff as commander of the
Cossacks; created a new Cossack Brigade for Tabriz; and named Yeprem
Khan to be Tehran's chief of police. Four hundred of his men were
integrated into this police force. It set up a special tribunal to punish
those responsible for the civil war. Five leading royalists, including Sheikh
Fazlollah Nuri, were executed. The Sheikh was hanged with much publicity
in Cannon Square after being found guilty of facilitating the recent executions in the royal gardens. He was charged with the capital offense of
"sowing corruption on earth" – the same charge he had levied against his
liberal opponents. It was rumored that his son, a volunteer fighter on the
parliamentary side, had celebrated these executions.

The Grand Majles, moreover, democratized the electoral system. It
abolished class and occupational representation; increased provincial representation; decreased Tehran's representation from sixty to fifteen; eradicated the ward divisions within Tehran; and created five seats for the
religious minorities – two for Armenians, one for Assyrians, one for Jews,
and one for Zoroastrians. The new electoral law also lowered the voting age
from twenty-five to twenty; and decreased the property qualification from
2,000 tomans to 250 tomans – a year later this was entirely abolished. Thus
universal male suffrage came to Iran as early as 1911. This was to have
unforeseen consequences.

The Grand Majles further elected a provisional government, leaving
vacant the post of prime minister. It elected Sardar As'ad, despite his
blindness, interior minister; Sepahdar, war minister; Mostowfi al-Mamalek,
finance minister; Abdul Hussein Mirza Farmanfarma, Fath Ali Shah's grandson, justice minister; and Abul Qassem Khan Nasser al-Mulk, the patriarch of
the Qajar Qarahgozlu clan, foreign minister. Browne, the British historian,
was convinced that Nasser al-Mulk, a class mate of Curzon from Oxford, had
survived the coup only because of British intervention. He soon succeeded
'Azud al-Mulk as regent. The British minister reported that the dominant
figures in the new government were Sardar As'ad and Sepahdar, and that the
two, especially the latter, really "belonged to the old school of politics,"

instinctively "distrusting parliamentary interference." He added that they enjoyed the "confidence of clergy and merchants" nervous about the safety of private property.[47]

Bakhtiyari influence continued to increase. By 1912, Samsam al-Saltaneh was prime minister; Sardar Muhtesham, a close relative, was war minister; one cousin headed the palace guards; another governed the newly created district of Bakhtiyar; other cousins governed Isfahan, Behbehan, Yazd, Kerman, Sultanabad, and Boroujerd. In short, the Bakhtiyaris governed much of central and southern Iran. Also they signed, without informing the government, lucrative agreements both with the British oil company to protect the latter's facilities in their territories and with Lynch Brothers to build a toll road from their winter to their summer quarters. The British minister explained that the Bakhtiyari chiefs had gained this "paramount importance" mainly because of their "energetic role" in the civil war. He even claimed that the "real power behind the throne" was Sardar As'ad "the Great."[48] The British consul in Isfahan further explained: "By obtaining fiefs from the Qajars and by dispossessing other landlords by simple robbery, the khans came to own most of the fertile district of Chahar Mahal. They added to their wealth by acquiring other lands, collecting taxes from their tribesmen, levying tolls on the Lynch road, and receiving a steady income from the Anglo-Persian Oil Company."[49]

INSTITUTIONAL DILEMMA

When the Second Majles convened in November 1910 it seemed that the constitutional struggle had finally come to a fruitful conclusion. This, however, turned out to be deceptive. The new government soon discovered that it lacked the instruments to administer, let alone to reform, the country. It faced the same dilemma as the ancient regime: it was a state without a centralized machinery. It had ministers but no real ministries. The parliamentary victory turned out to be hollow.

Financial constraints – in plain English, bankruptcy – lay at the root of the problem. Since revenues did not match expenses – even though expenses were often less than £1.5 million a year – the government had no choice but to live year-to-year by obtaining emergency loans from London and St. Petersburg. It survived a series of crises in 1911–13 by borrowing £440,000 from the British Imperial Bank.[50] Customs revenues remained in Belgian hands and all their income went to pay off existing loans, which reached £6.2 million by 1911 – shared equally by Britain and Russia.[51] Northern customs, together with income from Caspian fisheries, went to the Russians.

Southern customs, as well as income from the telegraph system, went to the British. Oil revenues did not trickle in until 1912–13. The British-owned Burma Oil Company, which took over the D'Arcy Concession in 1905, struck the first well in 1908. It soon became the Anglo-Persian Oil Company, and its first payment to Iran came in 1912–13 – totaling the paltry sum of £2,900.[52] The overall situation was so dire that in 1914 the Belgians were telling the government that it could only avoid bankruptcy by selling islands in the Gulf to Britain and parts of Azerbaijan and Gurgan to Russia.[53]

The British legation repeatedly told the government both during and after the revolution that the "only way" to solve the problem was to increase state revenues, especially the land tax; that the only way to do so was to create a new tax-collecting machinery; and that the only way to do that was to overcome entrenched "vested interests" – mostowfis eager to preserve traditional practices, landlords averse to paying taxes, and provincial governors, as well as tribal chiefs and local magnates, jealously guarding their turf.[54] It was precisely to meet this task that the Second Majles armed the finance ministry with a new police force named the gendarmerie. It hired thirty-six Swedish officers to train and lead this force. It also hired Morgan Shuster, an American financial advisor, as Iran's treasurer-general. Since Shuster was given full authority over the state budget, he was implicitly and intentionally placed on a collision course with mostowfis as well as with the Belgians, Russians, and British. His goal was a 12,000-man gendarmerie whose main function would be to collect taxes throughout the country.[55] It soon cost £150,000 a year, the largest bite from the annual budget – twice as much as the Cossacks and seven times as much as the education ministry.[56] Even so, the gendarmerie could muster no more than 1,000 men in 1911, 3,000 in 1912, and 6,000 in 1914 – most of whom guarded the roads from Tehran to Rasht, Enzeli, Qazvin, Hamadan, and Qom, and from Shiraz to Bushire. The British minister summed up the pitiful state of affairs in 1912:[57]

The Persian Government have handed to the two Legations memorandum showing that the advance of £50,000 would be no use to them in their present financial difficulties, and asking that it may be increased to £200,000. It shows that £40,000 is wanted for gendarmerie for five months; £25,000 for the police in Tehran; £15,000 for the garrison in Tehran; £35,000 for the Cossack Brigade in Tabriz for two months; £30,000 for arrears to pay due to government departments; £30,000 for purchase of arms and ammunitions; and £40,000 for reorganization of army ... The memorandum argues that Persia can not start reforms without money.

With the central government in financial straits, the provincial magnates further enhanced their power. Sowlat al-Dowleh, the Qashqa'i Ilkhani, took over trade routes passing through Fars to the Persian Gulf. The

British Political Resident in the Gulf reported that Sowlat al-Dowleh had become the "biggest magnate in Fars," levying taxes on his tribesmen, building a "large private army," and taking advantage of the "so-called constitution."[58] He added that other tribal khans along the Gulf had become virtually "independent": "The Governor of the Gulf Ports never meddles with the districts, nor sends soldiers or officials there, and it would be beyond his power at the present time to dismiss or change the khans."[59]Qavam al-Mulk, the Khamseh Ilkhani, had taken over Shiraz and mobilized his tribes against the Qashqa'is. Sheikh Khaz'al, the Ka'ab chief, by wooing the Kuhegluyeh tribes, was extending his reach out of Mohammerah into Bakhtiyari territory. For their part, the Bakhtiyaris were undermining Sheikh Khaz'al by supporting rival Arab tribes. The British consul reported that he was trying to prevent the Bakhtiyaris and the Ka'ab from fighting each other since he needed them against the Qashqa'is.[60] Meanwhile in the north, Rahim Khan of the Shahsavens continued to reap havoc in Sarab and Ardabel. Turkman chiefs rose up in support of the ousted shah. The British minister noted: "Being Sunnis, the Turkmans did not readily submit to a Parliament which, according to their views, is subservient to the dictates of a few Shiah mojtahed."[61] What is more, Salar al-Dowleh, another contender for the throne, rose up in revolt in Kermanshah. In the words of the British minister: "The situation in the provinces is far from reassuring. Robber bands appear to infest the country from one end to the other, more or less unmolested, and the central authorities are quite unable to supply the provincial governors either with men, arms, or money that they require, in order to be in a position to restore even a semblance of order."[62] Despite these upheavals, urban centers remained remarkably peaceful. Foreign travelers found it "extraordinary" that people remained "peaceful" and avoided "bloodshed" even though the "central government had almost no real power."[63]

The notables even pursued their own foreign policies. Sheikh Khaz'al sought British advice on whether to support the "nationalists" or the "royalists."[64] He was assured protection from naval attack, respect for his autonomy, and recognition for his heirs if he supported the former. The British consul commented that "Mohammerah has an Arab, not a Persian, body politic, and a constitution of its own, of which the main feature is the need for the consent of the heads of the tribes." The Consul also arranged for the oil company to build its refinery on Abadan, an island belonging to the Sheikh. The Sheikh rented it out to the company for £1,500 a year plus £16,500 in gold sovereigns. The agreement was to be "kept secret" from Tehran. He also conducted – through British mediation – his own relations with the Ottoman Empire, and accepted the sultan's sovereignty over the Shatt al-Arab estuary.[65] A British journalist remarked that the Sheikh was in actual fact an "independent" ruler since he had armed men whereas the official governor of Arabestan was more or less unarmed.[66]

Likewise, the leading Bakhtiyari khans – especially Sardar As'ad, Samsam al-Saltaneh, and Amir Mofakham – agreed to protect the oil installations on their territories in return for an annual subsidy and a 3 percent share in the Anglo-Persian Oil Company. The agreement completely bypassed the government.[67] Soon Bakhtiyari leaders were lending money to the central treasury to pay for road guards in the south.[68] Proceeds from the 3 percent were shared by the main khans. The British minister commented that the Bakhtiyari khans retained their "tribal custom" of sharing property: "This government dependence on the tribe is undesirable but unavoidable until the gendarmerie is built. The khans cannot be ignored because they are too powerful. They can, of course, always count on as many of their own men (as armed fighters) as the situation requires."[69]

The institutional dilemma was compounded by the ongoing struggles in the Second (1909–11) and Third (1914–15) Majles between the two main parties: the Moderates and Democrats. The Democrats, most of whom had been Liberals in the First Majles, were led by Taqizadeh, the well-known orator from Tabriz, and Sulayman Iskandari, a radical prince who was to be prominent in the socialist movement for the next forty years. His brother had been one of the main casualties of the 1909 coup. The Democrats could muster twenty-four to twenty-seven deputies.[70] Most came from the north. They included eight civil servants, five journalists, one doctor, and five young clerics – three from Sheikhi families and one from a former Azali household. Their party program and organ *Iran-e Now* (New Iran) called for land reform, industrialization, railway construction, improvement in women's status, equal rights for the religious minorities, abolition of the property qualification, expansion of public education, termination of capitulations, progressive taxation, national conscription, and, most immediate of all, creation of a viable central state with proper ministries and standing army.

The Moderates, led by Sepahdar, Farmanfarma, Behbehani, and Taba-tabai, could muster as many as fifty-three deputies. These included thirteen clerics, ten landlords, ten civil servants, nine merchants, and three tribal chiefs. Thus parliament became an exclusive club for the notables. In the Second Majles, 27 percent of the members were landlords, 19 percent clerics, 24 percent civil servants, and 9 percent merchants. The guild presence had drastically diminished.[71] This process was accelerated by the abolition of the property qualification. By introducing universal male suffrage, the electoral system ironically strengthened the hands of the tribal chiefs and landlords. In the Third Majles, the landed representation jumped to 48 percent. Representing the landed classes, the Moderate Party advocated support for traditional values, private property, and, most important of all, the shari'a. They also advocated religious education to instill "cooperative attitudes among the masses"; financial assistance to help the "middle class"; the convening of the senate to fulfill the laws; and a vigilant campaign against "anarchism," "atheism," and "materialism."[72]

The conflict between Moderates and Democrats began with debates over secularism, especially over minority rights, women's function in society, and the role of the shari'a in the judicial system. It intensified with the two sides jockeying to place their favorites in charge of the cabinet: the Democrats preferred to give the premiership to Mostowfi al-Mamalek or Musher al-Dowleh; the Moderates preferred Sepahdar or Farmanfarma. The conflict eventually broke into violence when fedayis linked to the Moderates assassinated a Democrat. The Democrats retaliated by assassinating Sayyed Behbahani. Clerics promptly pronounced Taqizadeh an "apostate," forcing him to flee to Europe where he launched his paper *Kaveh* named after the legendary *Shahnameh* blacksmith who had raised the banner of revolt. The crisis was contained only because of the timely intervention of Yeprem Khan. He surrounded the pro-Moderate fedayis, totaling some three hundred men led by Sattar Khan, with his own force of more than one thousand made up of policemen, gendarmes, Bakhtiyaris, and Armenian fighters. After a brief confrontation that took fifteen lives, Yeprem Khan forced the fedayis to exchange their weapons for life pensions.[73] Some claim that the wound Sattar Khan suffered in this confrontation caused his death two years later. Yeprem Khan himself was killed a few months later fighting rebels in Kermanshah.

The institutional dilemma was compounded by external pressures. In 1909, Russians occupied Azerbaijan on the pretext of establishing law and order. Their real aim was to implement the 1907 convention. In December 1911, they occupied the rest of their zone, including Tehran, after giving the government an ultimatum demanding the immediate dismissal of Shuster. They accused him of violating the 1907 convention by sending gendarmes into their zone, employing a British military advisor, and arresting wealthy tax delinquents with Russian citizenship papers. The British, who had initially welcomed Shuster's reforms, ended up supporting the ultimatum.[74] Even though the government accepted the ultimatum and dismissed Shuster, the Russians continued to tighten their hold. In Tabriz, they

hanged forty-three men in retaliation for the assassination of one of their
soldiers. Among the hanged were refugees from the Caucasus, Sattar Khan's
relatives, and, most scandalous of all, the Sheikhi mojtahed who had played
a key role in the revolution. In Mashed, they caused an even greater scandal
by bombarding the Imam Reza Shrine and thereby killing some forty
pilgrims. The British, meanwhile, dispatched troops from India to take
control of the main trade routes between Bushire, Shiraz, and Kerman.

Foreign occupation intensified during World War I. Even though Iran
declared neutrality, it soon became a battleground for the major powers. A
coalition of Democrats and Moderates, headed by Iskandari and Sadeq
Tabatabai, the son of the famous sayyed, postponed elections for the
duration of the war, and left Tehran for Kermanshah where they set up
the Government of National Resistance. The Ottomans, allied to the
Germans, in their drive to the Caucasus and Baku, first occupied Urmiah
where they armed Ismael Khan Simku, a Kurdish chief, against Iranian
authorities as well as against local Assyrians and Armenians. The Ottomans
then moved into Azerbaijan which they claimed as part of their Turkic
world. In their brief occupation of Tabriz, they deported Sheikh Khiabani,
the popular leader of the local Democrats, on the grounds that he was
helping Armenian insurgents against the Caliphate.[75] They also tried to woo
Mirza Kuchek Khan, a veteran of the civil war who had taken to the forest of
Gilan with some 300 armed men. By 1916, Kuchek Khan and his band of
guerrillas, known as *Jangalis* (Men of the Forests), controlled much of rural
Gilan and posed a major threat to the local magnates, especially Sepahdar.

To counter the Ottomans, the Russians augmented the Cossacks into full
division strength with brigades in Tabriz and Qazvin as well as Tehran.
They also strengthened their own troops in Azerbaijan, Gilan, Tehran,
northern Khurasan, and Isfahan. Zill al-Sultan, the arch enemy of the
Bakhtiyaris, found it expedient to place his properties under their protection. The British expressed understanding since they could no longer
provide him with protection against the "rapacious" Bakhtiyaris.[76] The
British, however, signed a new secret treaty with the Russians, taking over
the "neutral" zone. In return, Russia was promised the Dardanelles. The
British dispatched troops into Abadan; forged alliances with more southern
tribes; and created the South Persian Rifles. At its height, this force had
some 8,000 men and cost as much as £100,000 a week – paid mostly by the
India Office. With the Russian revolutions in 1917, the British took charge
of the Cossacks, appointing their officers, paying salaries, and providing
supplies. They also dispatched two expeditionary forces: one from India to
Mashed; the other from Mesopotamia via Kermanshah and Gilan to Baku.

The Germans were also active. Wilhelm Wassmus, their "Lawrence of Arabia," instigated uprisings among Qashqa'is, Khamsehs, Boir Ahmadis, Sanjabi Kurds, and, most serious of all, Arabs who in 1915 were able to cut the main oil pipeline. The Germans also persuaded a number of Swedish officers in the gendarmerie to desert. One historian writes: "The Swedish-officered gendarmerie, organized in 1911, had been as close as Britain could hope to come to a force in the south to maintain order; but that particular institution proved to be an unmitigated disaster during the war when most of the force defected to the Germans, refusing even to obey instructions from the Persian Government."[77] The British attributed German popularity to the "aggressive," "uncouth," and "unscrupulous" behavior of the Russians.[78]

These wartime disruptions coincided with bad harvests, cholera and typhus epidemics, and, most deadly of all, the 1919 influenza pandemic. Altogether between 1917 and 1921 as many as two million Iranians – including one quarter of the rural population – perished from war, disease, and starvation.[79] One British eyewitness wrote that by 1919 hungry tribesmen were taking to rural banditry while starving peasants were rumored to be resorting to cannibalism.[80]

Peace did not bring an end to these difficulties. Curzon, now Britain's foreign minister, saw the defeat of Germany and Russia as providing Britain with the perfect opportunity to take over the whole of Iran. As viceroy of India he had described Iran as vital for the security of the Raj, and had denounced in no uncertain terms the 1907 convention for conceding too much to Russia. He now drafted his Anglo-Persian Agreement to incorporate the whole country into the British Empire. Harold Nicolson, who served in the British legation in Tehran before turning to literature, wrote in his biography of Curzon that his protagonist aspired to create "a chain of vassal states from the Mediterranean to India."[81] "Curzon's imperialism," he added, "was founded on the belief that God had personally selected the British upper class as an instrument of the Divine Will." One London newspaper mocked that Curzon acted as if he had "discovered" the country and consequently owned it.[82] According to the Anglo-Persian Agreement, Britain obtained the sole right to provide Iran with loans, arms, advisors, military instructors, customs administrators, and even teachers. Frenchmen were to be barred from the Dar al-Fanon on the grounds that law and politics often seeped into international relations. In return, Britain was to provide Iran with a loan of £2 million. It was also to have the monopoly right to help the country build railways, combat famine, find entry into the League of Nations, and seek indemnity for damages suffered in World War I.

The 1919 Anglo-Persian Agreement was as far-reaching as the 1872 concession to Baron Reuter which Curzon had minced no words in denouncing.

The prime minister, Mirza Hassan Khan Vossuq al-Dowleh, who helped draft the agreement, received an advance of £160,000, presumably to steer it through the Majles since all foreign treaties required parliamentary ratification.[83] Vossuq al-Dowleh, a member of the famous Ashtiyani family, began his career as a liberal Democrat and served in eleven different cabinets. Ahmad Shah appointed him premier in 1919 when the Majles was not in session. He had done so for a British stipend of £6,000 per month for an indefinite time.[84] In signing the agreement, Vossuq al-Dowleh took the precaution of obtaining from Curzon the explicit promise of political asylum in case things went awry.

The agreement turned out to be an unmitigated disaster – especially when the public grasped its full implications. As Nicholson admitted, Curzon had completely "misjudged" the mood and thought that Iran remained anti-Russian and pro-British, as it had been at the time of the Constitutional Revolution. On the contrary, it was now overwhelmingly anti-British.[85] The main political figures, as well as the leading newspapers, wasted no time in denouncing the agreement. The Bolsheviks published the secret wartime treaties, including the 1915 deal, and promised to withdraw promptly from the whole of Iran if the British did so as well. The Jangalis sought Bolshevik help and set up in Gilan the Soviet Socialist Republic of Iran. Sheikh Khiabani, who had escaped from Ottoman detention, took over Azerbaijan, defied the governor, and warned that the central government was selling out the nation. Mojtaheds in Karbala issued fatwas denouncing the British and praising the Bolsheviks as "friends" of Islam.[86] Ultra-nationalists in Tehran formed a Punishment Committee and threatened to "execute" any one who supported the detested agreement. To show they were serious, they assassinated four of Vossuq al-Dowleh's close associates. This "reign of terror" prompted Vossuq al-Dowleh to resign. It also scared others away from replacing him.[87]

The British minister informed Curzon that it was impossible to find a prime minister who would be willing to submit the agreement to the Majles.[88] He added: "Persians friendly to Great Britain do not dare to publicly support the Agreement": "Our friends are unanimous in begging us to save them from a position of increasing embarrassment by giving it up. Fifty-five well disposed deputies have publicly declared themselves opposed to it in order to rebut charges freely brought against them of having been bribed by us to support it."[89] He further added: "there is widespread belief that the Agreement, and presence of British troops and advisers in Persia, has brought Bolshevik danger on the country and that the latter would disappear if these were withdrawn."[90] This sentiment was echoed by both General Dickson of the India Office and General Ironside of the British expeditionary force in Mesopotamia. They both concluded that Curzon had placed an impossible financial burden on the empire. In other words, Britain was suffering from a classic case of imperial overreach. Dickson did not mince his words:[91]

It does not appear to be realized at home how intensely unpopular agreement was in Persia and how hostile public opinion had become to Vossuq's Cabinet before it fell. It was believed that agreement really aimed at destruction of independence and that Vossuq had sold their country to Britain. Secrecy with which agreement had been concluded, fact that Majles was not summoned and attempt created to pack Majles by resorting to most dishonest methods ... all added to conviction that Great Britain was in reality no better than the hereditary foe, Russia ... The feeling grew that Britain was a bitter foe who must be rooted out of the country at any cost. Revolts in Azerbayjan and Caspian provinces were due to this feeling and to it was spread of Bolshevik propaganda, for it was thought that Bolsheviks could not be worse and might, if their profession of securing justice for the down-trodden classes were sincere, be much better.

By 1920 Iran was a classic "failed state" – to use modern terminology. The ministries had little presence outside the capital. The government was immobilized not only by rivalries between the traditional magnates and between the new political parties, but also by the Anglo-Persian Agreement. Some provinces were in the hands of "war lords," others in the hands of armed rebels. The Red Army had taken over Gilan and was threatening to move on to Tehran. The shah, in the words of the British, was "no longer accessible to reason," and was packing up his crown jewels to flee. What is more, the British, having realized they had overreached, were evacuating their families from the north, withdrawing their expeditionary forces, and preparing to streamline their South Persia Rifles. The British minister in Tehran told London that Britain had two choices: either let the "county stew in her own juices," or "concentrate in the center and south where some healthy limbs remain." He warned that the trouble with the first choice was that "British interests would inevitably form part of the stew."[92] He ended his warning with the observation that "owners of property" had grown so "desperate" that they were looking for a man on horseback with "drastic measures" to ward off "anarchy" and the "Bolshevik poison."

CHAPTER 3

The iron fist of Reza Shah

There is room in Iran for only one shah – and I will be that shah.

Reza Shah

THE COUP

In the early hours of February 21, 1921, General Reza Khan, commander of the Cossack garrison in Qazvin, took control over Tehran with three thousand men and eighteen machine guns. This coup, hailed later as the glorious 3rd Esfand (February 21) liberation, launched a new era. Reza Khan, who had risen through the ranks, was self-educated – some claim semi-illiterate. He came from a military family that fled Russian advance into the Caucasus and received a fief in the fertile village of Alasht in the Sefid Rud region of Mazanderan. His relatives, including his father and grandfather, had served in the provincial regiment – the latter had been killed in the 1848 siege of Herat. Reza Khan himself had enrolled as a teenager in the Cossack Brigade. Rumor had it that he had at one time or another served as a stable boy, either for the royal palace, the Farmanfarmas, the Dutch legation, or the American Presbyterian Mission. During the civil war and the subsequent upheavals, he made his mark as an up-and-coming officer nicknamed "Reza Khan Maxim." In later years when he built himself a palace in Mazanderan, he decorated the entryway with a large mosaic depicting a Maxim machine gun. He was multilingual: he spoke Alashti – a dialect of Mazanderani – with his neighbors; Persian with the outside world; pigeon Russian with the Tsarist Cossack officers; and variant of Turkish with his men.

In carrying out the coup, Reza Khan declared martial law, won over the local gendarmes, skirmished briefly with the city police, and assured Ahmad Shah that he had come to save him from the Bolsheviks. He also installed as premier Sayyed Ziya Tabatabai, a young journalist described by the British legation as "notorious for his Anglophilia."[1] The previous premier, Sepahdar, who for months had failed either to convene a majles or form a

63

cabinet, fled to the Turkish embassy. Before marching on Tehran, Reza Khan had given two promises to Ironside, the British general who had recently taken charge of the Cossacks and replaced Russian officers with Iranians. He had promised to facilitate the withdrawal of British troops and not to overthrow Ahmad Shah.[2] Unbeknownst to Curzon, Ironside considered the Anglo-Persian Agreement a lost cause, and was on the look-out for a suitable man on horseback to save the situation. Ironside had placed Reza Khan in charge of the Qazvin garrison and hurriedly promoted him general. Thus many 1920–21 sources still referred to Reza Khan as a colonel. Ironside also provided Reza Khan with ammunition and pay for his men – immediately after the coup the Cossacks received generous bonuses. On the eve of his march on Tehran, Reza Khan assured a joint delegation from the royal palace and the British legation that he was pro-shah and pro-British and that once the latter had withdrawn from the country he would organize a force capable of dealing with the Bolsheviks.[3] Not surprisingly, many Iranians still consider the coup a "British plot."

Reza Khan kept his promises – at least for the time being. He facilitated British withdrawal, abrogated the Anglo-Iranian Agreement, and instead signed a Soviet–Iranian Agreement. The Soviets agreed not only to withdraw promptly from Gilan, but also to cancel all Tsarist loans, claims, and concessions – everything except the Caspian fisheries. They, however, reserved the right to return in full force if a third power ever invaded the country and posed a threat to the Soviet Union. This gave Iran a protective umbrella. The British, meanwhile, with a straight face and no sense of irony, presented Tehran with a bill for weapons delivered to the Cossacks and the South Persian Rifles. The bill totaled £313,434 17s. 6d.[4] In abrogating the 1919 agreement, Reza Khan assured the British that this would "throw dust in Bolshevik eyes."[5] He also assured Theodore Rothstein, former *Manchester Guardian* editor who had just been appointed Soviet minister in Tehran, that his government was determined to eradicate British influence and pursue a policy of strict neutrality in foreign affairs. The Soviets soon elevated their legation to a full embassy. The British legation summed up the post-war situation:[6]

From an external point of view Great Britain was generally regarded as the enemy, Russia as the possible friend. Although the obvious Russian efforts to diffuse Communist ideas and propaganda caused certain uneasiness, the apparent generosity of canceling Persia's debts to Russia, of returning all Russian concessions acquired in Tsarist times, of handing over the Russian Banque d'Escompte to the Persian Government and surrendering the Capitulations had made a profound impression, and the Russian-inspired idea that Persia had everything to gain by association with a Russia purged by the fires of revolution and everything to lose by succumbing to the imperialist and colonizing ambitions of Great Britain, was sufficiently plausible to gain many Persian adherents.

Reza Khan, however, for the time being kept his promise to the Qajars even though he lost no time in making himself, in the words of the British legation, a "virtual military dictator."[7] He established himself as the real power behind the throne, first as army chief, then as war minister, and then as premier as well as commander-in-chief of the armed forces. During these years, he made and unmade ministers and premiers, including Sayyed Ziya who was packed off to exile after ninety-nine days. He did not openly venture on to the central stage until 1925–26 when he convened a Constituent Assembly, deposed Ahmad Shah, accepted the crown, named his son heir apparent, and crowned himself monarch – much in the fashion of his heroes, Napoleon and Nader Shah. It was rumored that at the coronation the Speaker of the Majles stepped forward to bestow the crown, but he took it in his own hands, declaring "This is not something someone else can place on my head."[8] The ceremony was choreographed along the lines of European as well as Safavid and Qajar coronations. It opened with a prayer by the Imam Jum'eh, and closed with a flowery oration by the prime minister with long passages from the *Shahnameh*. Reza Khan had become Reza Shah. He remained so until the Anglo-Soviet invasion of 1941. These fifteen years, together with the preceding five, can be described as the Reza Shah era.

The hallmark of the era was to be state-building. Reza Shah came to power in a country where the government had little presence outside the capital. He left the country with an extensive state structure – the first in Iran's two thousand years. It has been said of Stalin that he inherited a country with a wooden plough and left it with the atomic bomb. It can be said of Reza Shah that he took over a country with a ramshackle administration and left it with a highly centralized state. In assessing him, historians, especially Iranian ones, have invariably raised two loaded questions. Was he a true patriot or a British "agent"? Was he comparable to other contemporary strongmen, especially Ataturk and Mussolini? The first question was made obsolete by later events – especially his removal by the British. The second is anachronistic since these other rulers had inherited centralized states. A more apt comparison would be with the Tudors, early Bourbons, or sixteenth-century Habsburgs – monarchs whose goal had been to create centralized states. Reza Shah drove like a steamroller toward this goal, crushing all opposition, whether from the left or right, from the center or the provinces, from the aristocratic notables or the nascent trade

1 Coronation stamp, 1926

unions. A man of few words, he had little time for rhetoric, philosophy, or political theory. The main ideological baggage he carried stressed order, discipline, and state power. He conflated his own persona with the monarchy; the monarchy with the state; and the state with the nation. Not averse to harnessing religion, he gave the state a motto containing three words: *Khoda* (God), Shah, and *Mehan* (Nation). Some quipped that as his power increased, the middle word rose to dwarf the other two. In his eyes, however, the trinity was so interwoven that opposition to him was tantamount to opposition to the state, the nation, and even religion. In other words, political dissent was tantamount to subversion and treason.

STATE-BUILDING

Reza Shah built his new state on two main pillars: the military and the bureaucracy. During his rule, the military grew tenfold and the bureaucracy seventeenfold. In 1921, the military totaled no more than 22,000 men – some 8,000 Cossacks, 8,000 gendarmes, and 6,000 South Persian Riflemen. By 1925, it numbered 40,000 troops consolidated under one ministry of war. And by 1941, it mustered more than 127,000 men. Likewise, in 1921 the central government had been no more than a haphazard collection of semi-independent mostowfis, monshis, and titled grandees. But by 1941, it had eleven full ministries employing in excess of 90,000 salaried civil servants. The largest ministries – interior, education, and justice – had scarcely existed in 1921.

The expansion was made possible by revenues from four sources: oil royalties; extractions from tax delinquents; higher customs duties; and new taxes on consumer goods. Oil royalties, which started as a trickle in 1911 and totaled no more than £583,960 in 1921–22, grew to £1,288,000 in 1930–31, and £4,000,000 in 1940–41.[9] The other revenues began to increase once Arthur Millspaugh, another American, was named treasurer-general to restart Shuster's aborted project to create an effective tax-collecting system within the finance ministry. When Millspaugh arrived in 1922, skeptics gave him "three months to learn his job, three months to set his work in motion, and three months to collect his salary before leaving in despair."[10] But in five years, he managed to create a new department, abolish tax farms, update old rates, tighten up levies on opium sales, and, equally important, retool mostowfis as full-time civil servants. Soon he was able to present Iran's first comprehensive annual budget. In all this he was greatly helped by Reza Shah – until the latter decided that the country had room for only one shah. Millspaugh writes that he was able to collect back taxes from important magnates such as Sepahdar (Sepahsalar) simply because the new commander-in-chief threatened to seize their assets.[11] It was thought that these extractions led to Sepahdar's suicide in 1926. "Reza Khan," Millspaugh remarked, "belongs to the class of statesmen of which Henry II of England and Philip Augustus of France were the prototypes. He supplied the personal and military force necessary to establish the authority of the central government."[12] Similarly, he pressured the Bakhtiyari khans and Sheikh Khaz'al to hand over their oil shares to the central government. The British minister reported in 1923:[13]

This degree of success would not have been possible without the influential assistance of Reza Khan, which has rendered possible the collection of revenues, both arrears and current, in districts where former Governments had no power to enforce the payment of taxes. Every part of the kingdom has now been brought under the control of the Central Government, and taxes are being paid regularly into the Treasury for many districts where, in former years, not only did nothing reach the Treasury, but large sums had to be disbursed by the Government.

Government revenues also increased as trade recovered after World War I; as income tax – mainly on salaries – was introduced; and, most important, as state monopolies and taxes were imposed on a variety of consumer goods, especially sugar, tea, tobacco, cotton, hides, and opium. Customs revenue jumped from 51 million qrans in 1921 to 93 million in 1925, and further to 675 million in 1940. Revenues from consumer taxes rose from 38 million qrans (rials) in 1925 to as much as 180 million in 1940. The tax on sugar and tea – introduced in 1926 – brought in 122 million qrans in 1928, 421 million in 1938, and 691 million in 1940. In other words, the revenue from sugar and tea alone rose sixfold. Total government income rose from less than 246 million rials in 1925–26 to more than 3,610 million in 1940–41. The British estimated that by 1935 more than 34 percent of this income was being spent on the armed forces.[14]

The armed forces constituted the main pillar of the new regime. Reza Khan began work on the military immediately after the 1921 coup. He merged the Cossacks with the remnants of the gendarmerie and the South Persian Rifles to form a national army of 20,000. He replaced the Russian, Swedish, and British officers with his Cossack cronies. He took charge of road tolls and opium taxes in order to pay for this new army. Within two years, he had five divisions totaling 30,000 men – separate divisions for Tehran, Tabriz, Hamadan, Isfahan, and Mashed. According to the British, he spent "the whole of 1921–23 building up a well-disciplined force . . . the first proper such force since the days of Fath Ali Shah in 1834."[15] This new army successfully crushed a number of provincial rebels – especially Kuchek Khan and the Jangalis in Gilan, Khiabani in Tabriz, Simku in Kurdestan, and Sowlat al-Dowleh in Fars. It also crushed gendarmerie mutinies led by Major Lahuti in Tabriz and Colonel Taqi Peysan in Mashed.

The armed forces continued to grow – especially after the introduction of conscription in 1925. The conscription law can be described as the regime's central piece. With conscription came Iran's first birth certification as well as mandatory family names. The conscription law required all able-bodied males over the age of twenty-one to serve two full years in active service and another four years in the reserves. The conscripts were drawn first from the peasantry; then from the tribes; and eventually from the urban population. By 1941, the military had eighteen full divisions totaling 127,000 men – one division in each of the twelve provinces with extra ones on the northern border with Russia. The cavalry and mechanized divisions contained some 100 tanks and 28 armored vehicles. The air force had 157 planes; the navy 2 frigates and 4 gunboats.[16] The services were coordinated by a newly created joint office of the chiefs of staff. In 1939, the war minister approached the British with an ambitious proposal to buy 30 Blenheim bombers,

Table 3 *Government budgets, 1925–26 and 1940–41*
(in million qrans-rials)

	1925–26	1940–41
Revenue		
Total	245	3,613
Direct taxation	34	75
Road tax	20	85
Indirect taxes total	36	180
Customs	91	298
Expenditures	245	4,333
(Major ministries)		
War	94	565
Finance	30	265
Education	7	194
Industries	–	992
Agricultural	–	121
Roads	–	1,092
Imbalance	–	71

Note: Compiled from D. Nowruzi, "The Development of the Budget in Iran,"
Razm Nameh, Mo. 6 (November 1948), pp. 11–18; and from British minister,
"Annual Reports for Persia (1923–41)," FO 371/Persia 1924–42/34-10848 to 27180.
These reports are highly detailed and informative – so much so that in 1933 the
foreign office instructed the legation in Tehran to pare them down. It complained
that the 1932 report on Persia had been ninety-seven pages long whereas those
on the USSR, USA, France, and Italy had each been fewer than seventy-two
pages. See Foreign Office, "Note to the Legation (22 April 1933)," FO 371/Persia
l934/34-16967.

30 Wellington bombers, 35 Hurricane fighters, and 30 American Curtis
fighters. He argued that these planes could "come in useful for bombing
Baku."[17] Such proposals would not have sat well with the northern neighbor. In analyzing the military budget, the British minister commented:[18]

The main burden of the taxpayer will continue to be the army. Tanks, artillery and
other material are being acquired in increasing quantities, so much so that neighbouring States are beginning to wonder whether Iran may not be a potential
aggressor in the future. The reasons which have led the Shah to spend so much
on armaments are probably, however, quite simple: he had to have a sufficient force
to keep order and, having acquired this, his natural wish, as a soldier, was to see his
army provided with up-to-date material. Further, he has vivid recollections of the
sufferings of a weak Persia in times of war and confusion, and is determined to
avoid the recurrence of such a state of affairs.

Reza Shah also strengthened the rural gendarmerie and the urban police. He replaced Yeprem's Armenians in the Tehran police department and the Swedish advisors in the gendarmerie with his own men. He expanded the police force into provincial cities.[19] He substituted short-term detention jails with long-term prisons – institutions unknown in traditional Iran. He created two security organizations: the *sharbani* attached to the urban police; and the *Rokn-e Dovom* (Second Pillar), modeled after the French Deuxieme Bureau, attached to the army. The British minister feared that he was creating a police state: "Political suspects, however slight the ground of suspicion – an incautious remark or a visit to an unpopular friend – may find themselves in prison or banished to the provinces without any semblance of a trial."[20]

Reza Shah worked hard to harness the officer corps to his regime. He invariably appeared in public wearing military uniforms. He took personal interest in their promotions, training, and living conditions. He sold them state lands at discount prices; rewarded them with bonuses; appointed them to governorships; and turned a blind eye to their financial irregularities. He communicated with field commanders directly through the military office in the palace, bypassing the cabinet, the premier, and the war minister. He built in Tehran an impressive array of military establishments – an arsenal, a machine-gun factory, an airplane repair shop, a military hospital, an officers' club, an army bank, a staff college, and a military academy. He sent military personnel to Europe for further training – army officers, numbering as many as 300, went mostly to France; pilots and naval officers went mainly to Italy. He filled crucial military posts with such former Cossacks as Generals Muhammad Ayrom, Morteza Yazdanpanah, Ahmad Amir Ahmadi, and Fazlollah Zahedi. Ayrom, a fellow Cossack colonel in 1921, served as his chief of police until absconding to Nazi Germany with an ill-gotten fortune.

What is more, Reza Shah raised Crown Prince Muhammad Reza to be first and foremost a military officer. He was tutored in the palace with other officers' sons; spent three brief years with the same tutors and playmates in the exclusive La Rosey School in Switzerland; returned home to enter the military academy; and, upon graduation, received a commission to become special inspector in the armed forces. Reza Shah gave a similar upbringing to his six other sons. The crown prince – like his father – rarely appeared in public out of military uniform. The British legation noted that his activities outside the military were limited to the "boy scouts, athletic meetings, visiting institutions, and appearing for the Royal family at State functions."[21] This was a regime that can be truly defined as a military monarchy.

The growth in the bureaucracy was equally impressive. The four nineteenth-century ministries (foreign affairs, interior, finance, and justice), as well as the three more recent ones (public works and commerce, post and telegraph, and education and endowments), all grew to become substantial bureaucracies. What is more, three new ministries were created – industry, roads, and agriculture. Reza Shah ended his reign with eleven fully fledged ministries. The interior ministry, the central bureaucracy, was in charge of provincial administration including the urban police and rural gendarmerie. The eight old provinces were remapped into fifteen: Tehran, Azerbaijan, Fars, Gilan, Mazanderan, Hamadan, Isfahan, Kerman, Kermanshah, Khurasan, Arabestan, Kurdestan, Lurestan, Baluchestan, and the Gulf Ports. These provinces were divided into counties, municipalities, and rural districts. The shah, via the interior minister, appointed the governor-generals, who, in consultation with the minister, appointed the regional governors and town mayors. For the first time, the hand of the central government could reach the provinces. The governors were no longer semi-independent princes, as in Qajar days, but military men and civil servants totally dependent on the central government.[22] A British consul described the administrative structure in a typical province:[23]

Isfahan is the headquarters for the whole province. The province has various departments each with its own head, army (9th Division), police, municipality, finance, industry and commerce, public health, roads, registration of property and documents, census, education, agriculture, posts and telegraphs, justice, gendarmerie, conscription. In addition there are departments for the distribution of cereals, opium and tobacco. These departments have representatives in the chief towns of the district outside Isfahan. The police only operate within the municipality limits of Isfahan city and in Najafabad. Police work outside these two areas and the maintenance of general security are the tasks of the gendarmerie.

Reza Shah buttressed his two pillars with an extensive patronage network – so much so that he created the post of court minister outside the cabinet. The soldier who had risen through the ranks accumulated enough land during the course of his reign to become the wealthiest man in Iran, if not in the whole Middle East. A sympathetic biographer estimates that by the time he died he had accumulated a bank account worth £3 million and farm lands totaling 3 million acres.[24] The lands, concentrated in his ancestral Mazanderan, were mostly plantations for tea, rice, silk, cotton, and tobacco. He also had wheat farms in Hamadan, Asterabad, Gurgan, and Veramin. He accumulated these estates in part by outright confiscation, in part by dubious transfer of state properties, in part by irrigating waste lands, and in part by forcing landlords, both large and small, to sell him property at nominal prices. Sepahdar was one of his victims.

Even as early as 1932, the British legation reported that Reza Shah had developed an "unholy interest in land" and was putting whole families into prison until they agreed to sell him their properties: "His insatiable land hunger is reaching such a point that it will soon be permissible to wonder why His Imperial Majesty does not, without more ado, register the whole of Persia in his own name."[25] It added that, whereas an "increasing number of landowners are discontented," others are saying that he is merely doing what previous dynasties have done, that he is making better use of the land, and that "the whole country really belongs to him in any case."[26] The British minister was less generous: "He has continued to amass wealth by questionable means and has allowed his senior military commanders to do the same. At the same time, he loses no opportunity of discrediting them if he suspects them of becoming too powerful or of keeping too much of the wealth they amass for their own use. If they do not forget to give him a reasonable share, he condones their robbery."[27] He added: "Reza Shah is avaricious and greedy of wealth, and all means whereby he can acquire money and lands are good to him . . . A new road leading to the Chalus Valley across the Elburz (into Mazanderan) has been constructed at enormous expense, simply to gratify his private whim."[28] Many felt he drained the rest of the country to nourish his home region.

To develop Mazanderan, Reza Shah constructed not only roads but also a railway line from Tehran to the new port of Bandar Shah. He constructed luxury hotels in Babulsar and Ramsar. He placed state factories producing sugar, tobacco, and textiles in Babul, Sari, and Aliabad which he renamed Shahi. For cheap labor, he resorted to the corvee, military conscription, and even kidnapping of Isfahan textile workers. The British legation reported that his factories could not function without "slave labour."[29] In short, court patronage offered many lucrative positions, salaries, pensions, and sinecures. This placed him in good standing – at least in Mazanderan. Years later, in August 1953, when his statues were being toppled throughout the country, those in Mazanderan remained untouched.

TRANSFORMATIONS

Reza Shah is often seen as a great "reformer," "modernizer," and even "secularizer." In fact, his main aim in establishing new institutions was to expand his control by expanding his state's power into all sectors of the country – into its polity, economy, society, and ideology. The legacies he left behind were byproducts of this single-minded drive to create a strong centralized state.

He gained absolute control over the political system mainly by transforming the Majles from an aristocratic power center into a pliant rubber stamp. In the previous era, from the Second Majles in 1909 until the Fifth Majles in 1925, independent politicians and rural magnates had been able to shepherd retainers and peasants to the voting polls. In the words of Malek al-Shu'ra Bahar, the poet laureate and veteran constitutionalist:[30]

The electoral law, which continues to plague us even today (1944), is one of the most harmful and least thought-out bills ever passed by us Democrats. By introducing a democratic law from modern Europe into the paternalistic environment of traditional Iran, we weakened the liberal candidates and strengthened the conservative rural magnates who can herd their peasants, tribesmen, and other retainers into the voting polls. It is not surprising that when liberals in the Fourth Majles tried to rectify their mistake, the conservatives staunchly and successfully rallied behind the existing "democratic law."

Reza Shah retained the electoral law, but closely monitored access into parliament. He personally determined the outcome of each election and thus the composition of each Majles – from the Fifth in 1926 to the Thirteenth in 1940. The class composition may not have changed – more than 84 percent of members continued to be landowners, local notables, civil servants, and court-connected businessmen.[31] In fact, the number of deputies whose sole occupation was landowning actually increased. But the political composition did change in that only compliant candidates were permitted to enter. The control mechanism was simple. The shah – together with his chief of police – inspected the list of prospective candidates, marking them as either "suitable" or "bad," "unpatriotic," "mad," "vain," "harmful," "stupid," "dangerous," "shameless," "obstinate," or "empty headed."[32] The suitable names were passed on to the interior minister, who, in turn, passed them on to the provincial governor-generals and the local electoral boards. The sole function of these boards was to hand out voting papers and supervise the ballot boxes. Needless to say, these boards were all appointed by the central government. Unsuitable candidates who insisted on running found themselves either in jail or banished from their localities. Consequently, the successful candidates were invariably "suitable" ones who enjoyed some support in their home constituencies – often because they owned estates there. For example, in the Seventh Majles elections, the shah decided that the two largest landlords in Maragheh, Abbas Mirza Farmanfarma and Iskander Khan Moqadam, should both retain their seats on the grounds that they enjoyed considerable "local support."[33] The former had represented Maragheh in three assemblies; the latter in nine.

To ensure that deputies remained pliant, the shah took away parliamentary immunity; banned all political parties, even royalist caucuses; closed down independent newspapers; and planted what the regime itself described as "spies" and "informants." The British minister reported as early as 1926 that Reza Shah appeared to be "working towards a military autocracy" and "his sole aim seemed to be to discredit not only elder statesmen but parliamentary government itself": "He has created an atmosphere of uncertainty and fear. The Cabinet is afraid of the Majles; the Majles is afraid of the army; and all are afraid of the Shah."[34]

Deputies and other politicians who openly criticized the shah met sticky ends. For example, Samuel Haim, a Jewish deputy, was executed for "treason." Mirzazadeh Eshqi, a prominent socialist poet and editor of *Qarn-e Bestum* (The Twentieth Century), was gunned down in broad daylight. So was Kaykhosrow Shahrokh, a Zoroastrian deputy. Muhammad Farokhi-Yazdi, another deputy and former editor of the socialist paper *Tofan* (Storm), died suddenly in a prison hospital. Sayyed Hassan Modarres, who had succeeded Behbehani as leader of the Moderate Party, was exiled to an isolated village in Khurasan where he suddenly died. It was rumored that he had been strangled.[35] Unaware of these rumors, the British legation reported in 1940:[36]

Modarres leads a simple life, and is much revered by the lower classes, who used to frequent his house and ask his advice on all sorts of questions. He is quite fearless and frank and expresses his opinions freely, and nobody, not even the Shah, escaped his criticisms. An apparently organized attempt to assassinate him was made in October 1926 one morning in the street, but, although wounded in three places, he managed to escape with his life. For an old-fashioned cleric he is cute and far-sighted, but is a demagogue and obstinate.

Parliament ceased to be a meaningful institution. Instead it became a decorative garb covering up the nakedness of military rule. As one prime minister later admitted: "The Majles was retained for ceremonial purposes since the shah insisted that executive actions should get the seal of approval from the legislative branch."[37] It carried out this ceremonial task so well that the shah found it unnecessary either to convene the senate – which would have given him more power – or to make significant changes to the constitutional laws – the only change the 1925 Constituent Assembly made was to pass the crown from the Qajars to the new shah. The British minister reported as early as 1926: "The Persian Majles cannot be taken seriously. The deputies are not free agents, any more than elections to the Majles are free. When the Shah wants a measure, it is passed. When he is opposed, it is withdrawn. When he is indifferent, a great deal of aimless discussion takes place."[38]

Reza Shah also handpicked cabinet ministers to produce both docility and stability. In the previous two decades (1906–25) when parliaments had participated in the formation of governments, the country had seen as many as thirty-five changes of premier and sixty changes of cabinet. In the next fifteen years (1926–41), the country had only ten cabinets and eight changes of premier. In all, fifty men filled ninety-eight cabinet posts in these years. Thirty-five of them had started their careers in government service – mostly in the ministries of finance or foreign affairs. Another six were former Cossacks. Thirty-seven had titles or had been born into titled families. Of the others, two came from clerical families; four from landowning ones; and five from middle-level government ranks. Twenty-six had studied abroad, and fourteen had graduated from the Dar al-Fanon. Almost all were fluent in one or more European languages: thirty-four spoke French, twelve English, eleven Russian, and six German.

Although well-educated, well-trained, and well-heeled, these ministers were at the shah's beck and call. When addressing the monarchy, they aptly resorted to ancient terminology and referred to themselves as his royal highness's *chakers* (slaves). This abject subservience was encouraged by the fate that befell the "triumvirate" who had helped forge the new regime: Mirza Abdul Hussein Khan Timourtash, Ali Akbar Khan Davar, and Firuz Mirza Farmanfarma.

Timourtash (Sardar Mo'azem Khurasani), the court minister, was, in the words of the British legation, the "most powerful man in the country after the shah" until his sudden demise in 1934.[39] He came from a wealthy landed family in Khurasan, and had graduated from a military academy in Tsarist Russia. After his return in 1915, he served on financial commissions, sat in parliament as a deputy from Khurasan, and, as governor of Gilan, helped the Cossacks defeat the Jangalis. The British minister described him as "witty," "clever," "energetic," "eloquent," but a "confirmed gambler." Just before accusing him of embezzlement, the shah had bestowed on him the title *Jenab Ashraf* (Noble Highness). He died in prison from "food poisoning," thus becoming the first minister since 1848 to be put to death. For some Reza Shah was a "modernizer"; for others, he was reviving early Qajar practices.

Davar, one of the few ministers without an aristocratic title, was the son of a minor government official. He started his career in the ministry of post and telegraph and was sent to Geneva in 1910 to serve as Persian tutor to the shah's children. While there, he had obtained a Swiss law degree. After his return, he edited a newspaper that focused on the need for legal reforms; worked as an independent lawyer; represented Veramin in the Fourth and

Fifth Majles; and, in the Constituent Assembly, drafted legislation that permitted the smooth transfer of the crown. Davar was rewarded with the justice ministry. He was highly regarded as "studious," "intelligent," "well read," "hardworking," and "upcoming" – until accused of financial irregularities. He dropped dead in prison at the age of fifty, supposedly because of a "heart attack." His right-hand man, Abdul Hassan Diba, died in similar circumstances. Farah Diba, the future empress, was the latter's niece.

Firuz Farmanfarma (Nowsrat al-Dowleh) was the son of the famous Prince Farmanfarma. A graduate of the Sorbonne, he began his career in 1916 as an assistant to his father who was minister of justice. Subsequently he became foreign minister and helped Vossuq al-Dowleh negotiate the infamous 1919 Anglo-Persian Agreement. Reza Shah placed him in charge of the ministries of justice and finance before accusing him of taking bribes. After spending years in and out of prison, where he translated Oscar Wilde's *De Profundis* and wrote books on penal law and his jail experiences, he was eventually banished to his estates where he was smothered to death.[40] The British legation reported that "his ability marks him as one of the leading men in the country, whether in the Cabinet or in the Majles, and the Shah, who probably does not trust him, recognizes his usefulness." It added: "Like Timourtash, whose intimate friend he is, he is a born gambler. He owes money in every direction, including tailor's bills in London, which he declines to pay, and for which he would be liable to prosecution should he at any time return to England."[41] His probable reason for avoiding London, however, had more to do with the £160,000 "advance" he had taken for the 1919 Agreement. Like many aristocrats, high living and large retinues created cash-flow problems. And like others with similar life styles, he was seen as "corrupt" by the general public. Reza Shah could at the drop of a hat destroy such public personalities. For the elite, life was not nasty, poor, and brutish. But it could definitely be short.

Reza Shah extended state power over the economy by pursuing what was then called *étatisme*. He eased out foreign financial administrators, including Millspaugh and the Belgians. He annulled the nineteenth-century capitulations that had given foreign powers commercial and extra-territorial privileges. The British minister sounded alarm bells as early as 1927: "No one was prepared for the bombshell which fell upon the foreign community in Tehran when, following a speech by His Majesty on the occasion of the inauguration of the new law court buildings, the Persian Government addressed notes to all the foreign representatives concerned denouncing at one year's notice, the old treaties which allowed for extra-territorial jurisdiction, including the Spanish and French perpetual treaties of 1842 and

1855."[42] Similarly, the National Bank took over from the British Imperial Bank the right to print money. This came in handy when paper money helped finance industrialization in the late 1930s. This fueled a 54 percent rise in basic prices.

The other ministries also expanded their reach. The ministry of post and telegraph nationalized the Indo-European Telegraphy Company, started a telephone network, and in 1939 launched Radio Iran to compete with the BBC and Radio Moscow. The commerce ministry controlled foreign trade by setting up tariff walls and issuing import-export licenses. The industries ministry built some 300 plants producing sugar, tea, cigarettes, rice, canned food, soap, cotton oil seed, glycerin, jute, sulfuric acid, cement, lumber, copper, batteries, and, most important of all, electricity – by 1938 most towns had some electrical lighting. It also gave low-interest loans to businessmen to start manufacturing companies – especially for cotton textiles, carpets, matches, beer, hides, and glass wares. The roads ministry constructed 1,000 kilometers of paved roads linking Tehran to Mashed, Tabriz, Julfa, Mahabad, Isfahan, Shiraz, and Bushire. It also constructed 5,000 kilometers of gravel roads linking Tehran to most provincial capitals. By the late 1930s, these roads carried as many as 27,000 vehicles, including some 5,000 cars, 8,000 trucks, and 7,000 buses.[43] The regime's main showpiece, however, was the Trans-Iranian Railway. Cutting through some of the most difficult terrain in the world, it was contracted out in small parcels to numerous foreign companies – German, French, Scandinavian, Swiss, Czech, Italian, American, British, and Belgian. By 1941, the Trans-Iranian Railway connected Tehran to Shahi and Bandar Shah in the north; Semnan on the way to Mashed in the east; Zanjan on the way to Tabriz in the west; and all the way to Ahwaz and Abadan in the south. It was financed mostly by taxes on sugar and tea. When a cabinet minister was overheard complaining that the money could be better spent on roads, he found himself in prison accused of being part of the British "conspiracy" to keep the country backward.

The state also extended tentacles deep into society. Military conscription did more than expand the armed forces. It extracted males from traditional environments and immersed them for the very first time in a nationwide organization where they had to speak Persian, interact with other ethnic groups, and pay daily allegiance to the shah, the flag, and the state. Two-thirds of the conscripts spent their first six months learning Persian. In fact, the draft was designed in part to turn peasants and tribesmen into citizens. The draft, of course, created the need for identity cards and thus family names. Reza Shah himself adopted the name Pahlavi – after the ancient

2 Road construction stamp, 1934

3 Stamps set depicting Pahlavi ideology, 1935

3.1 Persepolis

3.2 Tehran airport

3.3 Sanatorium near Tehran

3.4 Cement factory in Abdul 'Azim

3.5 Gunboat

3.6 Railway bridge over Karun

3.7 Tehran post office

3.8 Justice: woman with scales and sword

3.9 Education: angel teaching youth

4 Stamp set celebrating ancient Iran

4.1 Persepolis: ruins of Main Palace

4.2 Persepolis: lion carving

4.3 Persepolis: Darius

4.4 Persepolis: warrior

4.5 Pasaraga: Cyrus' tomb

4.6 Carving at Naqsh-e Rostam: God Mazda's investiture of Ardashir

4.7 Carving at Naqsh-e Rostam: Shahpour
accepting Emperor Valerian's submission

language that had evolved into modern Persian. He forced a family that was already using that name to relinquish it. He also forced his own children from previous marriages – one to a Qajar – to find themselves other surnames. In mandating names, he abolished aristocratic titles. Many notables shortened their names. For example, Vossuq al-Dowleh became simply Hassan Vossuq; his brother, Ahmad Qavam al-Saltaneh, became Ahmad Qavam; and Firuz Mirza Farmanfarma (Nowsrat al-Dowleh) became Firuz Farmanfarma. Ordinary citizens often adopted names that reflected their occupational, regional, or tribal backgrounds. Reza Shah also abolished the royal tradition of using bombastic designations and announced that he would in future be addressed simply as His Imperial Majesty.

In the same vein, Reza Shah implemented a series of measures to instill in the citizenry a feeling of uniformity and common allegiance to himself and his state. He introduced the metric system; a uniform system of weights and measures; and a standard time for the whole country. He replaced the Muslim lunar calendar with a solar one which started the year with the March 21 equinox, the ancient Persian New Year. Thus 1343 (AD 1925) in the Muslim lunar calendar became 1304 in the new Iranian solar calendar. Muslim months were replaced with such Zoroastrian terms as Khordad, Tir, Shahrivar, Mehr, and Azar. The standard time chosen was intentionally half an hour different from neighboring time zones.

Reza Shah also implemented a new dress code. He outlawed tribal and traditional clothes as well as the fez-like headgear that had been introduced by the Qajars. All adult males, with the exception of state "registered" clergymen, had to wear Western-style trousers and coat, as well as a front-rimmed hat known as the "Pahlavi cap." In the past, bare heads had been

Table 4 *Expansion of public education, 1923–24 and 1940–41*

	1923–24	1940–41
Pupils in kindergartens	0	1,500
Primary schools	83	2,336
Pupils in primary schools	7,000	210,000
Secondary schools	85	241
Pupils in secondary schools	5,000	21,000

considered signs of madness or rudeness, and headgear identified the person's traditional or occupational ties. The Pahlavi cap was now seen as a sign of national unity. It was soon replaced by the felt-rimmed fedora known in Iran as the "international hat." Men were also encouraged to be clean shaven, or, if they insisted on moustaches, to keep them modest – unlike large ones sported by Nasser al-Din Shah and the famous or infamous lutis. In the past, beardless men had been associated with eunuchs. In the words of one government official, the intention of the dress code was to "foster national unity" in lieu of local sentiments.[44] In decreeing the early dress code for men, Reza Shah instructed the police not to harass women – to permit unveiled women to enter cinemas, eat in restaurants, speak in the streets to unrelated members of the opposite sex, and even ride in carriages with them so long as they pulled down the carriage hoods. By the mid-1930s, there were at least four thousand women, almost all in Tehran, who ventured into public places without veils – at least, without the full-length covering known as the *chadour* (tent).[45] These four thousand were mostly Western-educated daughters of the upper class, foreign wives of recent returnees from Europe, and middle-class women from the religious minorities.

A uniform educational system was another target of reform. In 1923, students at Iran's institutions of learning, including those administered by the state, private individuals, clerical foundations, missionaries, and religious minorities, totaled no more than 91,000. State schools had fewer than 12,000 students.[46] According to Millspaugh, the total number of schools did not exceed 650. They included 250 state schools, 47 missionary schools, and more than 200 clerically administered *maktabs* (religious primary schools) and madrasehs.[47] Female pupils – almost all in missionary schools – numbered fewer than 18,000. By 1941, the state administered 2,336 primary schools with 210,000 pupils, and 241 secondary schools with 21,000 pupils including 4,000 girls.[48] The missionary schools, as well as those started by religious minorities, had been "nationalized." Similarly, the maktabs had been absorbed into the state secondary system. The state system was modeled on the French lycees with primary and secondary levels each formed of six one-year classes. It emphasized uniformity, using throughout the country the same curriculum, the same textbooks, and, of course, the same language – Persian. Other languages, even those previously permitted in community schools, were now banned. The policy was to Persianize the linguistic minorities.

language – Persian

Higher education experienced similar growth. In 1925, fewer than 600 students were enrolled in the country's six colleges – law, literature, political science, medicine, agriculture, and teacher training. In 1934, these six merged to form the University of Tehran. And in the late 1930s, the university opened six new colleges – for dentistry, pharmacology, veterinary medicine, fine arts, theology, and science-technology. By 1941, Tehran University had more than 3,330 students. Enrollment in universities abroad also grew. Although wealthy families had been sending sons abroad ever since the mid-nineteenth century, the numbers remained modest until 1929 when the state began to finance every year some 100 scholarships to Europe. *euro edu.* By 1940, more than 500 Iranians had returned and another 450 were completing their studies. Tehran University – like the school system – was designed on the Napoleonic model, stressing not only uniformity but also the production of public servants.

The state also exerted influence over organized religion. Although the seminaries in Qom, Mashed, Isfahan, and, needless to say, Najaf, remained autonomous, the theology college in Tehran University and the nearby Sepahsalar Mosque – the latter supervised by a government-appointed imam jum'eh – examined candidates to determine who could teach religion and thus have the authority to wear clerical clothes. In other words, the state for the first time determined who was a member of the ulama. Of course, clerics who chose to enter government service had to discard turbans and gowns in favor of the new hat and Western clothes. Ironically, these reforms gave the clergy a distinct identity. The education ministry, meanwhile, not only mandated scripture classes in state schools but also controlled the content of these classes, banning ideas that smacked of religious skepticism. Reza Shah aimed not so much to undermine religion with secular thought as to bring the propagation of Islam under state supervision. He had begun his political career by leading Cossacks in Muharram processions. He had given many of his eleven children typical Shi'i names: Muhammad Reza, Ali Reza, Ghulam Reza, Ahmad Reza, Abdul Reza, and Hamid Reza. He invited popular preachers to broadcast sermons on the national radio station. What is more, he encouraged Shariat Sangalaji, the popular preacher in the Sepahsalar Mosque, to declare openly that Shi'ism was in dire need of a "reformation." Sangalaji often took to the pulpit to argue that Islam had nothing against modernity – especially against science, medicine, cinema, radios, and, the increasingly popular new pastime, soccer.

Reza Shah perpetuated the royal tradition of funding seminaries, paying homage to senior mojtaheds, and undertaking pilgrimages – even to Najaf and Karbala. He granted refuge to eighty clerics who fled Iraq in 1921. He encouraged Abdul Karim Haeri Yazdi, a highly respected mojtahed, to settle in Qom and to make it as important as Najaf. Haeri, who shunned politics, did more than any other cleric to institutionalize the religious establishment. It was in these years that the public began to use such clerical titles as ayatollah and hojjat al-islam. Sheikh Muhammad Hussein Naini, another mojtahed, supported the regime to such an extent that he destroyed his own early book praising constitutional government. Reza Shah also exempted theology students from conscription. He even banned the advocacy of any ideas smacking of "atheism" and "materialism." Some ministers waxed ecstatic over *'erfan* (mysticism) in general, and Sufi poets such as Rumi and Hafez in particular. They equated skepticism with materialism; materialism with communism. In the words of a minister and textbook writer, "the aim of elementary education is to make God known to the child."[49] Reza Shah would have subscribed to Napoleon's adage: "One can't govern people who don't believe in God. One shoots them." Not surprisingly, few senior clerics raised their voices against the shah.

Reza Shah created cultural organizations to instill greater national awareness in the general public. A new organization named Farhangestan (Cultural Academy) – modeled on the French Academy – together with the Department of Public Guidance, the National Heritage Society, the Geography Commission, the journal *Iran-e Bastan* (Ancient Iran), as well as the two main government-subsidized papers, *Ettela'at* (Information) and *Journal de Teheran*, all waged a concerted campaign both to glorify ancient Iran and to purify the language of foreign words. Such words, especially Arab ones, were replaced with either brand new or old Persian vocabulary.

The most visible name change came in 1934 when Reza Shah – prompted by his legation in Berlin – decreed that henceforth Persia was to be known to the outside world as Iran. A government circular explained that whereas "Persia" was associated with Fars and Qajar decadence, "Iran" invoked the glories and birthplace of the ancient Aryans.[50] Hitler, in one of his speeches, had proclaimed that the Aryan race had links to Iran. Moreover, a number of prominent Iranians who had studied in Europe had been influenced by racial theorists such as Count Gobineau who claimed that Iran, because of its "racial" composition, had greater cultural-psychological affinity with Nordic peoples of northern Europe than with the rest of the Middle East. Thus Western racism played some role in shaping modern Iranian nationalism. Soon after Hitler came to power, the British minister in Tehran wrote that the journal *Iran-e Bastan* was "echoing" the anti-Semitic notions of the Third Reich.[51]

The Geography Commission renamed 107 places before concluding that it would be impractical to eliminate all Arabic, Turkish, and Armenian names.[52] Arabestan was changed to Khuzestan; Sultanabad to Arak; and Bampour to Iranshahr. It also gave many places royalist connotations – Enzeli was changed to Pahlavi, Urmiah to Rezaieh, Aliabad to Shahi, and Salmas to Shahpour. It decreed that only Persian could be used on public signs, store fronts, business letterheads, and even visiting cards. The Cultural Academy, meanwhile, Persianized administrative terms. For example, the word for province was changed from *velayat* to *ostan*; governor from *vali* to *ostandar*; police from *nazmieh* to *shahrbani*; military officer from *saheb-e mansab* to *afsar*; and army from *qoshun* to *artesh* – an entirely invented term. All military ranks obtained new designations. The qran currency was renamed the rial. Some purists hoped to replace the Arabic script; but this was deemed impractical.

Meanwhile, the Society for National Heritage built a state museum, a state library, and a number of major mausoleums. The shah himself led a delegation of dignitaries to inaugurate a mausoleum for Ferdowsi at Tus, his birthplace, which was renamed Ferdows. Some suspected that the regime was trying to create a rival pilgrimage site to the nearby Imam Reza Shrine. In digging up bodies to inter in these mausoleums, the society meticulously measured skulls to "prove" to the whole world that these national figures had been "true Aryans." These mausoleums incorporated motifs from ancient Iranian architecture. The society's founders included such prominent figures as Taqizadeh, Timourtash, Musher-al-Dowleh, Mostowfi al-Mamalek, and Firuz Farmanfarma.[53] Politics had become interwoven not only with history and literature, but also with architecture, archeology, and even dead bodies.

Reza Shah placed equal importance on expanding the state judicial system. Davar and Firuz Farmanfarma, both European-educated lawyers, were assigned the task of setting up a new justice ministry – a task that had seen many false starts. They replaced the traditional courts, including the shari'a ones as well as the more informal tribal and guild courts, with a new state judicial structure. This new structure had a clear hierarchy of local, county, municipal, and provincial courts, and, at the very apex, a supreme court. They

Table 5 *Changes in place names*

Old name	New name
Barfurush	Babul
Astarabad	Gurgan
Mashedsar	Babulsar
Dazdab	Zahedan
Nasratabad	Zabol
Harunabad	Shahabad
Bandar Jaz	Bandar Shah
Shahra-e Turkman	Dasht-e Gurgan
Khaza'alabad	Khosrowabad
Mohammerah	Khorramshahr

Table 6 *Changes in state terminology*

Old term	New term	English equivalent
Vezarat-e Dakheleh	Vezarat-e Keshvar	Ministry of interior
Vezarat-e Adliyeh	Vezarat-e Dadgostari	Ministry of justice
Vezarat-e Maliyeh	Vezarat-e Darayi	Ministry of finance
Vezarat-e Mo'aref	Vezarat-e Farhang	Ministry of education
Madraseh-ye Ebteda'i	Dabestan	Primary school
Madraseh-ye Motavasateh	Daberestan	Secondary school

transferred the authority to register all legal documents – including property transactions as well as marriage and divorce licenses – from the clergy to state-appointed notary publics. They required jurists either to obtain degrees from the Law College or to retool themselves in the new legal system. They promulgated laws modeled on the Napoleonic, Swiss, and Italian codes. The new codes, however, gave some important concessions to the shari'a. For example, men retained the right to divorce at will, keep custody of children, practice polygamy, and take temporary wives. The new codes, however, did weaken the shari'a in three important areas: the legal distinction between Muslims and non-Muslims was abolished; the death penalty was restricted exclusively to murder, treason, and armed rebellion; and the modern form of punishment, long-term incarceration, was favored over corporal punishments – especially public ones. By accepting modern codes, the law implicitly discarded the traditional notion of retribution – the notion of a tooth for a tooth, an eye for an eye, a life for a life.

To meet the inevitable need, Davar and Firuz Farmanfarma drew up plans to build five large prisons and eighty smaller ones.[54] Many were not completed until the 1960s. Qasr, the largest, was completed in the 1930s and came to symbolize the new regime. Located on the ruins of a royal retreat on the northern hills of Tehran, its full name was Qasr-e Qajar (Qajar Palace). Its thick, high walls not only absorbed the inmates but also concealed the wardens and the occasional executions from public view. One former inmate writes that passersby were easily intimidated – as they were supposed to be – by its formidable walls, barbed wire, armed guards, searchlights, and gun turrets.[55] Some dubbed it the Iranian Bastille. Others called it the *faramush-khaneh* (house of forgetfulness) since the outside world was supposed to forget its inmates and the inmates were supposed to forget the outside world. Ironically, Firuz Farmanfarma became one of its first inmates. He did not tire of boasting to fellow prisoners about the modernity and cleanliness of the place. But Ali Dashti, a Majles deputy who spent a few months there, complained that being confined there was like being "buried alive in a cemetery." He chastised the West for inventing such "horrors" and complained that incarceration was "torture far worse than death."[56] The reforms also restricted the traditional custom of taking and giving *bast* (sanctuary). Protestors and criminals could no longer seek shelter in telegraph offices, royal stables, and holy shrines. A British visitor noted in 1932: "The general opinion is that at last *bast* has shot its bolt."[57] It reappeared intermittently in the 1941–53 period, but only inside the parliament building and the royal gardens.

Reza Shah built more than prisons in the cities. A great advocate of urban renewal, he pulled down old buildings and constructed government offices, expansive squares, and Haussman-like boulevards. He named avenues after himself and placed his statue in the main squares – the clergy had prevented his predecessors from doing so. The government buildings often incorporated motifs from ancient Iran, especially Persepolis. To erase the Qajar past, he destroyed some two thousand urban landscape photographs on the grounds that they demeaned Iran.[58] He built not only state offices and schools, but also playgrounds for soccer, boy scouts, and girl guides. By the end of the 1930s, electrical plants – both state and private – had come to the main towns, providing energy to government buildings, street lights, and factories, as well as to middle- and upper-class homes. Telephones linked some 10,000 subscribers throughout the country. And more than forty cinemas had opened up in the main cities. In short, the overall urban appearance had drastically changed. The old mahallehs based on sect – especially Haydari–Nemati and Sheikhi–Motasheri identities – had withered away. The new districts were based more on class, income, and occupation.

The regime failed in one major area: public health. With the exception of Abadan, an oil company town, other cities saw little of modern medicine and sanitation in terms of sewage, piped water, or medical facilities. Infant mortality remained high: the main killers continued to be diarrhea, measles, typhoid, malaria, and TB. Even the capital had fewer than forty registered doctors.[59] Other towns gained little more than health departments whose main function was to certify modern *dokturs* and *farmasis* (pharmacists), and, in the process, disqualify traditional *hakims* practicing folk medicine based on the Galenic notions of the four "humors." For the modern-educated, these notions reeked of medieval superstitions. Some hakims, however, retooled themselves as modern doctors. The son of one such hakim recounted his father's experience:[60]

Until 1309 (1930) he practiced mostly old medicine. When it was time to take the exam he went to Tabriz. There he studied with Dr. Tofiq who had studied medicine in Switzerland. Because there were no medical books at that time in Persian, he used Istanbul-Turkish translations of European medical texts. He studied both theory and practice. He learned from him how to use a stethoscope, to take blood pressure, and do examination of women. He then took the licensing exam and passed it. This was the most important thing in changing the way he practiced medicine.

Of course, it was Tehran that saw the most visible changes. Its population grew from 210,000 to 540,000. Reza Shah destroyed much of the old city, including its twelve gates, five wards, takiyehs, and winding alleyways, with the explicit goal of making Tehran an "up-to-date capital." He gave the new avenues such names as Shah, Shah Reza, Pahlavi, Cyrus, Ferdowsi, Hafez, Naderi, Sepah (Army), and Varzesh (Athletics). He began building a grand Opera House in lieu of the old Government Theater. He eliminated gardens named after such aristocrats as Sepahsalar and Farmanfarma. He renamed Cannon Square as Army Square, and placed around it a new telegraph office as well as the National Bank and the National Museum. He licensed five cinemas in northern Tehran. They had such names as Iran, Darius, Sepah, and *Khorshed* (Sun). Their first films included *Tarzan*, *The Thief of Baghdad*, *Ali Baba and the Forty Thieves*, and Chaplin's *Gold Rush*.[61] Around these cinemas developed a new middle-class life style with modern cafés, boutiques, theaters, restaurants, and bookstores.

Reza Shah also built in the capital a train terminal; modern factories nearby in the southern suburbs; and the country's two state hospitals. One hospital was featured on a postage stamp – probably the only one to do so anywhere in the world. The city's face changed so much that the new generation could no longer locate places that had been familiar to their parents and grandparents – places such as Sangdalaj, Sepahsalar Park, the Arab Quarter, and *Paqapaq* – the old execution square.[62] Early in the reign, the British minister had noted that municipal authorities were "ruthlessly pulling down homes," paying little in compensation, and exploiting the opportunity to line their own pockets. "Their destructive propensities," he emphasized, "pass all rational bounds."[63] He sounded the same note at the end of the reign: "The capital continues to grow: new avenues, paved with asphalt, replace the old lanes; factories and residential quarters increase; and the city already attracts immigrants from all parts of the country. As in so many cases, it must be open to doubt whether the large sums devoted to reconstruction have always been judiciously spent. There is still, for instance, no clean water supply in the town."[64]

STATE AND SOCIETY

The new state attracted a mixed reception. For some Iranians and outside observers, it brought law and order, discipline, central authority, and modern amenities – schools, trains, buses, radios, cinemas, and telephones – in other words, "development," "national integration," and "moderniza- tion" which some termed "Westernization." For others, it brought oppres- sion, corruption, taxation, lack of authenticity, and the form of security typical of police states. Millspaugh, who was invited back to Iran in 1942, found that Reza Shah had left behind "a government of the corrupt, by the corrupt, and for the corrupt." He elaborated: "The Shah's taxation policy was highly regressive, raising the cost of living and bearing heavily on the poor ... Altogether he thoroughly milked the country, grinding down the peasantry, tribesmen, and laborers and taking a heavy toll from the land- lords. While his activities enriched a new class of 'capitalists' – merchants, monopolists, contractors, and politician-favorites – inflation, taxation, and other measures lowered the standard of living for the masses."[65] Similarly, Ann Lambton, the well-known British Iranologist who served as her coun- try's press attaché in wartime Tehran, reported that "the vast majority of the people hate the Shah."[66] This sentiment was echoed by the American ambassador who reported: "A brutal, avaricious, and inscrutable despot, his fall from power and death in exile ... were regretted by no one."[67]

In actual fact, public attitudes were more ambivalent – even among the notables. On one hand, the notables lost their titles, tax exemptions, authority on the local level, and power at the center – especially in the cabinet and the Majles. Some lost even their lands and lives. On the other hand, they benefited in countless ways. They no longer lived in fear of land reform, Bolshevism, and revolution from below. They could continue to use family connections – a practice that became known as *partybazi* (literally, playing party games) – to get their sons university places, European scholarships, and ministerial positions. They prospered selling their agricultural products, especially grain, to the expanding urban centers. They took advantage of a new land registration law to transfer tribal properties to their own names. They shifted the weight of the land tax on to their peasants. Even more significant, they obtained for the first time ever the legal power to appoint the village headman (*kadkhuda*). Thus, in one stroke the state came down in solid support of the landlords against the peasants. "Modernization" was not without its victims.

What is more, the notables who were willing to swallow aristocratic pride were accepted into the corridors of privilege – even into the court. Reza Shah took as his third wife a member of the Dowlatshahi family – a Qajar clan related by marriage to such old households as the Ashtiyanis, Mostowfis, and Zanganehs. He married off one daughter, Princess Ashraf, to the Qavam al-Mulk family that had governed Shiraz and the Khamseh for generations. He married off another daughter, Princess Shams, to the son of Mahmud Jam (Muder al-Mulk), a patrician collaborating fully with the new order. He kept on as his special confidant – both as chief of staff and as special military inspector – General Amanollah Jahanbani, a fellow officer from the Cossacks and a direct descendant of Fath Ali Shah. He also enhanced his family status by marrying the crown prince to Princess Fawzieh, the daughter of Egypt's King Farouk. In more ways than one, Reza Shah, who some claimed had started life as a stable boy, had found his way into the top ranks of the old elite.

The new regime aroused opposition not so much among the landed upper class as among the tribes, the clergy, and the young generation of the new intelligentsia. The tribes bore the brunt of the new order. Equipped with troops, tanks, planes, strategic roads, and, of course, the Maxim gun, Reza Shah waged a systematic campaign to crush the tribes. For the very first time in Iranian history, the balance of military technology shifted drastically away from the tribes to the central government. Reza Shah proceeded not only to strip the tribes of their traditional chiefs, clothing, and sometimes lands, but also to disarm, pacify, conscript, and, in some cases, "civilize" them in "model villages." Forced sedentarization produced much hardship since many "model villages" were not suitable for year-round agriculture. In the course of the reign, the troublesome tribal chiefs were all brought to heel. Simku, the Kurdish leader, was murdered after being enticed to return to the country. Sowlat al-Dowleh, the Qashqa'i Ilkhani, and Sheikh Khaz'al, the Arab leader, were both carted off to house detention in Tehran where years later they died under suspicious circumstances. Imam Quli Khan Mamassani, a Lur chief, Dost Muhammad, a Baluch leader, Sartip Khan, a Boir Ahmadi, and Hussein Khan, another Qashqa'i chief, were all executed. Others, such as the Vali of Pasht-e Kuh, who, in the words of the British minister, had "enjoyed a semi-autonomous position (in Lurestan)," decided that "discretion was the better part of valour."[68] By 1927, the British minister could write that the army had finally "broken the power of the great tribal families" that had ruled for more than one hundred and fifty years.[69]

Reza Shah delayed the fall of the Bakhtiyaris mainly because he needed them to counter the Qashqa'is, Arabs, Baluchis, and Boir Ahmadis. In 1925–27, he gave the ministry of war and the governorship of Arabestan to Ja'far Quli Khan Sardar As'ad, the son of the famous constitutional leader. But in 1927–29, when he no longer needed their contingents, he moved to break their power. He enflamed feuds between the Ilkhanis and the Hajji Ilkhanis, and between the Haft Lang and the Chahar Lang. He shifted the tax burden on to the Haft Lang, and took away their 1909 privilege of retaining armed men. Consequently, when the Haft Lang rebelled in 1929, the Chahar Lang sided with the central government. Reza Shah seized the opportunity to disarm the Haft Lang and force them to sell land, transfer oil shares to the central government, and hand over to the army the strategic task of protecting the petroleum installations. He also imprisoned seventeen khans including Sardar As'ad. Having dealt with the Haft Lang, he turned against the Chahar Lang. He disarmed them and placed them under military administration; and carved up their region among the neighboring provinces of Isfahan and Khuzestan. Finally, in 1934, in the midst of wild rumors that Lawrence of Arabia had entered Iran to instigate tribal revolts, he eliminated seven leading Bakhtiyari khans: two, including Sardar As'ad, died suddenly in prison; and five others, serving prison sentences, were summarily executed. Other khans found it expedient to "sell" their oil shares to the government and their prized villages in Chahar Mahal to landlords and merchants in Isfahan.

Conflict with the clerical opposition, which had simmered ever since Reza Shah violated the sanctuary of Qom in 1928, did not come to a head until 1935 – and even then it was confined to Mashed. Reza Shah provoked the crisis with a series of controversial acts which some suspected were designed to show the world who was boss. He decreed a new dress code, replacing the Pahlavi cap with the "international" fedora which, because of its brim, prevented the devout from touching their foreheads on the ground – as strict rules stipulated. The same decree encouraged – but did not initially obligate – women to discard the veil. Reza Shah obliged senior officials to bring their wives to public functions without veils, and expressed the hope that all women would eventually discard them. He also announced that female teachers could no longer come to school with head coverings. One of his daughters reviewed a girls' athletic event with an uncovered head. He himself opened the new Majles without either an officiating cleric or any hat whatsoever – an affront to both religion and convention. He allowed women to study in the colleges of law and medicine. He permitted the latter to dissect human bodies, a practice frowned upon in religious circles. He moved his official birthday to Nowruz. He extended the ban on titles to include sayyed, hajji, Mashedi, and Karbalai, titles used by those who had made the pilgrimage to Mecca, Mashed, or Karbala. He restricted public mourning observances to one day, and obliged mosques to use chairs for such occasions – this, of course, ran counter to the tradition of sitting on mosque floors. He banned street commemorations for Muharram, the Day of Sacrifice, and the Feast of Zahra – the famous festive bonfire day. He opened up the Mashed shrine as well as the main Isfahan mosque to foreign tourists. He even toyed with the idea of raising the marriage age – eighteen for men and fifteen for women.

The predictable backlash came in 1935. On July 10 – the anniversary of the Russian bombardment of the Mashed shrine in 1911 – a local preacher took the occasion to denounce not only these "heretical innovations" but also rampant government corruption and the heavy consumer taxes. This inspired many from the bazaar and the nearby villages to take sanctuary inside the shrine. They chanted: "The Shah is a new Yezid"; and "Imam Hussein protect us from the evil Shah." Local authorities watched helplessly for four full days since the city police and the provincial army battalion refused to violate the shrine. The British consul reported that frightened officials ran back and forth with their new hats hidden under their coats, ready to produce them only if they encountered other officials.[70] The standoff ended only when reinforcements from Azerbaijan arrived on the scene and broke into the shrine. Two hundred civilians suffered serious injuries; and more than one hundred, including many women and children, lost their lives. In the following months, the shrine custodian and three soldiers who had refused to shoot were executed. A British diplomat warned: "The Shah, in destroying the powers of the Mullahs, has forgotten Napoleon's adage that the chief purpose of religion is to prevent the poor from murdering the rich. There is nothing to take the place of religious influence, save an artificial nationalism which might well die with the shah, leaving anarchy behind."[71]

The Mashed outburst, however, did not have much impact on the rest of the country. The mojtaheds, especially the leading ones in Qom and Isfahan, kept their silence. The shah, for his part, stepped up his controversial measures. He ended the tradition both of announcing the arrival of Ramadan with a volley of guns, and of shorter work hours during the fast. He transferred the administration of clerical foundations from the office of religious endowments to the ministry of education. What is more, he now banned outright the full-length chadour from all public places: from streets, government offices, cinemas, public baths, city buses, and even street carriages.[72] He also ordered ordinary citizens to bring their wives to public functions without head coverings. Even road-sweepers, shopkeepers, and carriage drivers were compelled to do so. British consuls reported that those who failed to do so were summoned to police stations. The wife of one governor committed suicide. Many women took to wearing long scarves and high collars.[73] In describing this crisis, the British consul tried to place it within the larger picture.[74]

Next to their daily bread, what affects the people most widely is what touches the code of social habit that, in Islam, is endorsed by religion. Among Moslems the Iranians are not a fanatical people. The unveiling of women inaugurated in the preceding year attacks the people's social conservatism as much as their religious prejudice. Above all, like conscription, it symbolizes the steady penetration into their daily lives of an influence that brings with it more outside interference, more taxation. But one can easily exaggerate the popular effect of unveiling; it is a revolution for the well-to-do of the towns, but lower down the scale, where women perform outdoor manual labour, its effects both on habit and on the family budget diminish until among the tribal folk of all degrees they are comparatively slight. Hence resistance among the greater part of the people has been passive, and, where existing, has manifested itself in reluctance of the older generation to go abroad in the streets. It is one thing to forbid women to veil; it is another thing to make them mingle freely with men.

The opposition of the intelligentsia to the new regime was confined mostly to the young generation that had not lived through the age of troubles. The older generation tended to be much more ambivalent. Kasravi, the well-known historian, is a good case in point. As a teenager in Tabriz during the civil war, he had sympathized with the reformers, and had written his major work to praise the whole constitutional movement. As a young man, he had watched in trepidation as the country was torn asunder by foreign invasions and internal conflicts. The main underlying theme of his magnum opus was the danger of national fragmentation. As a madraseh-trained scholar interested in the modern sciences, he had joined the judiciary, discarded his turban, attained a judgeship, and approved of legal reforms, but then quietly resigned when he realized that the shah was misusing the courts to line his own pockets. After Reza Shah's fall, however, he argued: "Our younger intellectuals cannot possibly understand, and thus cannot possibly judge Reza Shah. They cannot because they were too young to remember the chaotic and desperate conditions out of which he arose."[75] In a series of articles in his paper *Parcham* (Flag), he assessed the pros and cons of Reza Shah.[76] He gave him high marks for creating a centralized state; pacifying the "unruly tribes"; disciplining the "superstitious" clergy; spreading the Persian language and replacing Arabic words with Persian ones; opening new schools; improving the status of women; eliminating titles and undermining "feudal" structures; introducing military conscription; building modern towns and factories; and, most important of all, striving to unify the country with one language, one culture, and one national identity. But at the same time, he gave him low marks for trampling the constitution; making a mockery of the fundamental laws; favoring the military over the civilian administration; murdering progressive leaders; and, most serious of all, accumulating money and thereby creating a culture of corruption.

Much of the opposition to the regime came from the new intelligentsia – especially from young professionals who had been influenced by the left while studying in France and Germany during the turbulent early 1930s. They found little to admire in the shah. They deemed him to be not a state-builder but an "oriental despot"; not a selfless patriot but a selfish founder of his own dynasty; not a reformer but a plutocrat strengthening the landed upper class; not a real "nationalist" but a jack-booted Cossack trained by the Tsarists and brought to power by British imperialists. Some found his use – or rather, misuse – of history to be racist, chauvinistic, and designed to "keep them quiet."[77] This distrust intensified in 1933–34 when the shah signed a new agreement with the Anglo-Iranian Oil Company. In return for a measly 4 percent increase in royalties, the shah extended the concession all the way to 1993. This confirmed the suspicion that the shah, despite all his patriotic talk, was in fact beholden to London. The British minister himself warned that "all his sins are attributed to us."[78] "Few," he added, "expect the present system of government to outlive its author."[79] Such opposition poured out into the open as soon as Reza Shah was forced to abdicate in 1941.

CHAPTER 4

The nationalist interregnum

The Majles is a den of thieves.

Mossadeq

NOTABLES REEMERGE

The 1941 Anglo-Soviet invasion destroyed Reza Shah – but not the Pahlavi state. The two Allies – joined by the United States in December 1941 – realized that the Iranian state could be useful in achieving the two goals for which they had invaded the country: physical control over oil – the British nightmare in World War II, even more so than in World War I, was loss of these vital supplies; and a land "corridor" to the Soviet Union since the alternate route through Archangel was frozen much of the year. Ironically, the Trans-Iranian Railway as well as the new roads made Iran a more tempting "corridor." To facilitate the flow of both oil to Britain and supplies to the Soviet Union, the Allies found it expedient to remove Reza Shah but to preserve his state. As Sir Reader Bullard – the British minister who was soon elevated to the rank of ambassador – made clear in his typically blunt and frank reports, the Allies kept his state but engineered his removal in part to curry much-needed favor among Iranians. "The Persians," he wrote, "expect that we should at least save them from the Shah's tyranny as compensation for invading their country."[1]

On September 15, three weeks after the initial onslaught, Reza Shah abdicated in favor of his twenty-one-year-old son, Crown Prince Muhammad Reza, and went into exile, first to British Mauritius and then to South Africa, where he died in 1944. His army, which had been equipped to deal with internal opposition and not with foreign invasion, had been able to resist for only three brief days. The Allies raised few other demands besides the abdication. They insisted that he should take with him into exile headstrong members of his family. They arrested as a Nazi "Fifth Column" some two hundred Iranian officers and technicians as well as Germans

97

working on the railways. They took direct control over the main transport routes from the Gulf to the Soviet Union, and split Iran into two zones – much like in World War I – with the Russians taking the north and the British the south – including the oil regions. Otherwise, they left the actual administration of the country to the central government. They guaranteed Iran's territorial integrity; promised to withdraw within six months of the war's end; supplied the government with grain to ward off famine; discouraged tribes from causing trouble; and, most crucial of all for the new shah, agreed to retain his armed forces at the minimum strength of 80,000 soldiers and 24,000 gendarmes.

In preserving the armed forces, the Allies tacitly agreed to leave the regular army under the young shah's direct control. He continued to communicate directly with his chiefs of staff and field commanders, bypassing the war minister. He also continued to cultivate the officer corps – much as his father had done. He managed throughout the 1940s to get as much as 24–26 percent of the annual budget allocated to the war ministry.[2] He took personal interest in all matters military, including inspection, uniforms, barracks, maneuvers, and arms purchases. He often appeared in public wearing military uniforms. He – like much European royalty – enjoyed flying modern planes. He jealously guarded all senior appointments to the war ministry and general staff. He personally vetted all promotions above the rank of major in the army – especially in the tank brigades. He was soon arguing that as commander-in-chief he had the prerogative to control the armed forces and that the main function of the war ministry was to provide the military with necessary supplies. He treated the ministry as a mere office of military supplies and the minister as a regimental quartermaster.

In return for keeping control of the armed forces, Muhammad Reza Shah agreed to cooperate fully with the Allies. He offered to contribute troops for their war effort and talked of expanding the army to half a million men.[3] It is often said that the 1970s oil bonanza fueled the shah's megalomania. In fact, he harbored such aspirations long before the oil boom. Bullard, the British representative, politely declined the offer of troops and talked instead of more realistic goals. He wrote that the Allies had agreed to give the young shah a "trial (period) subject to good behavior, which would include the granting of extensive reforms, the restoration to the nation of the property illegally acquired by his father, and the exclusion of all his brothers from Persia."[4] The new shah handed over to the government with much fanfare some 600 million rials.[5] He also quietly transferred to his bank account in New York a $1 million "nest egg in case of an emergency."[6] Immediately after the invasion, Britain came to the crucial decision that it was in its best interests to preserve not only the Iranian state, but also the Pahlavi dynasty and the latter's special relations with its armed forces.[7] It concurred with the royalist motto: "No Monarchy, No Military." The British even tried to get the shah to improve his family image by persuading his Egyptian-born wife, Queen Fawzieh, to spend less time buying clothes and more time learning Persian. Fawzieh, however, did not last long, preferring to return in 1943 to more cosmopolitan Cairo. The shah remarried seven years later, taking as his new wife Soraya Esfandiyari, a Swiss-educated daughter of a Bakhtiyari khan. The new royal couple communicated in French.

On his accession, the shah took a number of other well-publicized measures to improve his public standing. He took his oath of office before the Majles wearing civilian clothes; vowed to reign – not rule – as a constitutional monarch respecting the fundamental laws; sought out civilian advisors; and highlighted his democratic credentials, notably his Swiss education. He earmarked the sum he had transferred to the government to be spent on hospitals, medical laboratories, and public libraries; on a water system and shelter for the poor in Tehran; on new medical colleges in Tabriz, Mashed, and Shiraz; and on a nationwide campaign against malaria and eye diseases.[8] He handed over his father's estates to the government so that the latter could return them to the original owners – these estates, however, became a major bone of contention.[9] He also relinquished the religious endowments which his father had transferred to the ministry of education. He took a number of well-publicized pilgrimages – including to Mashed and Qom. What is more, he assured Grand Ayatollah Aqa Hussein Qomi, the senior mojtahed in Najaf, that the state would no longer wage its campaign against the veil. Women – or rather, their immediate communities – could decide whether or not to wear the veil – and what form the veil should take. The British legation reported that the propertied classes, as well as the shah and the government, were eager to forge an alliance with the clergy so as to "turn men's minds away from communism to religion."[10]

The 1941 invasion thus inaugurated an interregnum that lasted a full thirteen years. It put an end to the era when the monarch had ruled supreme through his undisputed control of the army, bureaucracy, and court patronage. It began a period when the new monarch continued to hang on to much of the armed forces, but lost control over the bureaucracy and the patronage system. This interregnum lasted until August 1953 when the shah, through a coup engineered by the Americans and the British, reestablished royal authority, and, thereby, recreated his father's regime. In these thirteen years power was not concentrated in one place. On the contrary, it was hotly contested between the royal palace, the cabinet, the Majles, and the urban masses, organized first by a socialist movement and then by a nationalist one. In this contest, the center of political gravity shifted away from the shah, back to the notables who had ruled the country from 1906 to 1921, but who had been relegated to the background in the period from 1921 to 1941. They now reemerged on the national scene in full force. One British diplomat drew striking parallels with his own country's experience: "The situation resembles England before 1832, with the landowning class in charge of Parliament and of the Cabinet, and with two classes in the country – one bloated with wealth, and the other abjectly poverty-stricken and power-less."[11] Bullard, who harbored few illusions about long-term prospects for democracy, cautioned: "It seems extremely likely that once foreign troops have gone, some form of dictatorship, however disguised, will be set up, doubtlessly with the army as a base. But at present it is best (for us) to support the Majles."[12]

The notables dominated on multiple levels – in the cabinet, in the Majles, and, equally significant, at the local level. The latter level determined who went into the Majles, which elected the prime minister as well as the cabinet ministers. The cabinet ministers, in turn, controlled the state bureaucracies. The country had returned to the rule of the notables with the landed elites again herding their clients, especially peasants and tribesmen, to the polls, and, thereby, dominating both the cabinet and the Majles.

The notables were most visible in the cabinet. In these thirteen years, 148 politicians filled 400 cabinet posts, and 12 headed 31 different cabinets. Of the 148 ministers, 81 were sons of titled notables; 13 were Western-educated technocrats linked to the prominent families; 11 were senior army officers; and 8 were wealthy businessmen. Of the 12 prime ministers, 9 came from titled families and themselves had used titles before their 1925 abolition (the old titles crept back into common usage after 1941). The 3 non-aristocratic premiers, nevertheless, were well connected to the landed upper class. General Ali Razmara, the only non-civilian among them, was the son of a cavalry officer and had studied at St. Cyr before experiencing a meteoric rise through the military by leading successful campaigns against the Kurds, Lurs, and the Khamseh. He was related by marriage to both the Farmanfarmas and the Qavam al-Mulks. Ali Soheily, the second non-aristocrat, was the son of an Azerbaijani merchant and had entered government service in the 1910s through the patronage of Taqizadeh, the famous Tabriz deputy. In later years, Soheily attached himself to Reza Shah, becoming his minister of roads, interior, and foreign affairs, as well as governor of Kerman, director of the Caspian fisheries, and ambassador to London. Similarly, Abdul-Hussein Hezhir, the third non-aristocratic premier, was the son of an armed volunteer from Tabriz who had fought in the civil war and had been brought into government service by Taqizadeh. He had enjoyed the patronage of Davar and Timourtash.

The other nine premiers were household names. Ali Foroughi (Zaka al-Mulk) was a seminary-trained jurist who had been tutor to the young Ahmad Shah and minister of justice on numerous occasions in the 1910s. He had represented Iran at the 1919 Versailles Conference, thrice served as war minister in the early 1920s, and headed the cabinet during both the 1925 coronation and the 1934 Mashed crisis. The latter had led to his resignation. Some thought he had resigned because he had opposed the anti-veil campaign. Others thought he had resigned because the executed custodian of the Mashed shrine had been his son-in-law. In 1941, Foroughi oversaw Reza Shah's smooth abdication, privately telling the British that if the latter remained in Iran he would inevitably scheme to return to his "old arbitrary ways."[13] Even though Foroughi was instrumental in preserving the monarchy, he placed little trust in the new shah. Bullard commented: "Foroughi hardly expects any son of Reza Shah to be a civilized man."[14] Bullard, in his constant frustration to get Iranian politicians to do his bidding, added caustically: "He is one of the three honest men in Persia."[15]

Ibrahim Hakimi (Hakim al-Mamalek), another patrician, was the son of the court doctor and himself had served as a doctor at the Qajar court. He inherited his title from his father. Despite his family position, Hakimi participated in the 1906 protest in the British legation and sat in the First Majles as a Democrat. He studied medicine in Paris; served as minister of education and finance before being forced into retirement by Reza Shah; but was brought back in 1933 to be minister of agriculture. It was thought that he had regained the shah's confidence by turning his large estate outside Tehran into a highly successful cotton plantation. Ali Mansur (Mansur al-Mamalek) typified part of the old elite that had swallowed its pride and submitted to Reza Shah. He served as his prime minister and interior minister before being arrested for financial irregularities. A few years later, he was forgiven and reappointed minister of industry. Muhammad Sa'ed (Sa'ed al-Vezareh), also known as Maraghehi, came from a landed family that had moved to Azerbaijan from Herat more than a hundred years before. In addition to representing his constituency in the Majles, Sa'ed had a long career in the foreign office, mostly in the Caucasus.

Mohsen Sadr (Sadr al-Ashraf) typified part of the old elite with links to the religious establishment. A seminary-trained jurist, he was a son of a religious tutor in Nasser al-Din Shah's court and himself had served both as a tutor at court and as a custodian of the Mashed shrine. He was also a major

Table 7 *Prime ministers (August 1941–August 1953)*

	Original name	Cabinet	Approximate birth date	Career	Education	Foreign languages
Foroughi Ali	Zaka al-Mulk	August 1941–March 1942	1873	Judge	Dar al-Fanon	French, English
Soheily Ali		March–August 1942; January 1943–March 1944	1890	Foreign ministry	Dar al-Fanon	French, Russian Turkish
Qavam Ahmad	Qavam al-Saltaneh	August 1942–February 1943; February 1946–December 1947; July 1952	1875	Ministries	France	French
Sa'ed Muhammad	Sa'ed al-Vezareh	March–December 1944; November 1948–March 1950	1885	Foreign ministry	Caucasus, France	Russian, Turkish, French
Bayat Morteza	Saham al-Saltaneh	December 1944–May 1945	1882	Landowner, deputy	Switzerland	French
Hakimi Ibrahim	Hakim al-Mulk	May–June 1945; December 1945–February 1946; December 1947–June 1948	1870	Court doctor	France	French
Sadr Mohsen	Sadr al-Ashraf	June–December 1945	1873	Landowner, judge	Traditional	Arabic
Hezhir Abdul-Hussein		June–November 1948	1895	Ministries	Dar al-Fanon	French, Russian, English
Mansur Ali	Mansur al-Mamalek	March–June 1950	1888	Ministries	Dar al-Fanon	French
Razmara Ali		June 1950–March 1951	1900	Military	St. Cyr	French, Russian
Ala Hussein	Mu'en al-Vezareh	March–May 1951	1884	Landowner, Foreign Ministry, landowner	England	English
Mossadeq Muhammad	Mossadeq al-Saltaneh	May 1951–August 1953	1885		Switzerland	French

landlord in Qom and Mashed who increased his own properties while serving as a judge and administering the royal estates. Morteza Bayat (Saham al-Saltaneh) came from the wealthiest family in Arak. Although one of the few politicians with no experience in public administration, he briefly headed the finance ministry in 1926–27. He had spent much of his life as a gentleman farmer and as a venture capitalist with a coal mine in northern Iran.

Hussein Ala (Mu'in al-Vezareh), another major landlord, was the son of Ala al-Mulk, also titled al-Saltaneh. In 1922, the India Office described the family as one of the most influential in the whole southeast of Iran.[16] Educated at Westminster School, Hussein Ala deputized for his father as foreign minister on and off from 1906 until 1915. He also served as Reza Shah's English translator, and as the country's representative in London and Washington. He was married to the daughter of Nasser al-Mulk who had been Ahmad Shah's regent. A Qajar himself, Nasser al-Mulk's side of the clan adopted the family name Qarahgozlu.

The other two premiers were also prominent patricians. Muhammad Mossadeq (Mossadeq al-Saltaneh), the future national hero for many Iranians, came from a prominent mostowfi and landed family. Ahmad Qavam (Qavam al-Saltaneh), Mossadeq's cousin, best represented the notables eager to reassert aristocratic power at the expense of the Pahlavis. Qavam had been prominent in national politics ever since 1906, when he, with his masterful calligraphy, had written the royal proclamation granting the country a written constitution. He came from a long line of mostowfi families going back five generations to the famous Mohsen Ashtiani. The Ashtiani family had married into the Qajars, Farmanfarmas, Alas, and Qarahgozlus. Vossuq al-Dowleh, the foreign minister who had signed the 1919 Anglo-Persian Agreement, was Qavam's elder brother. In the era before Reza Shah consolidated power, Qavam himself headed four different cabinets and an impressive array of ministries – of war, justice, finance, and interior. After a brief exile in France, he had been permitted to retire to his tea plantation in Gilan. One observer wrote that he reentered politics in 1941 "openly baring his teeth at the royal family."[17] Another suspected that he planned to set up a republic with himself as president.[18] The shah complained to Bullard that Qavam was a "dangerous schemer" who was "eager to implement some desperate design" and had surrounded himself with "a gang of cut-throats."[19] Bullard himself described Qavam as the most shrewd, energetic, skillful, courageous, ambitious, and authoritative of the old time politicians.[20] In some ways, Qavam in the 1940s was what Sepahdar had been in the 1910s and Mushir al-Dowleh in the 1900s.

Qavam reentered politics with Muzaffar Firuz Farmanfarma, the son of the famous Farmanfarma murdered by Reza Shah, as his right-hand man. Educated at Harrow and Cambridge, Muzaffar Firuz rushed home determined, in Bullard's words, to "avenge the murder of his father": "he would sacrifice anything to bring about the downfall of the Shah."[21]

Notables also dominated the four parliaments that sat in these thirteen years: the Thirteenth (1941–43), Fourteenth (1944–46), Fifteenth (1947–49), and Sixteenth Majles (1950–52). For example, of the 134 deputies in the Fourteenth Majles – the first elected after the abdication – 27 percent were large landlords, 16 percent were civil servants with substantial land, 11 percent were wealthy businessmen, and 6 percent were clerics with land.[22] More than 62 percent had been born into landowning families. Professionals and civil servants without land numbered fewer than a handful.

What is more, notables dominated Majles through parliamentary parties known as *fraksiuns* – the term was borrowed from the German Reichstag. For example, the Fourteenth Majles was divided into four major fraksiuns. The *Azadi* (Freedom or Liberal) Fraksiun was led by: Muhammad Vali Mirza Farmanfarma, the family's patriarch; by Abul-Qassem Amini, the grandson of the Amin al-Dowleh who had served as chief minister to both Nasser al-Din Shah and Muzaffar al-Din Shah – the Aminis were descendants of the famous Ashtiyani family; and by Sardar Fakher Hekmat of the Mushar al-Dowleh family that had struggled for generations with the Qavam al-Mulks and the Qashqayis for mastery of Fars. The *Demokrat* Fraksiun – also known as the *Fraksiun-e 'Eshayer* (Tribal) – was led by: Samsam and As'ad Bakhtiyari; Sowlat Qashqayi, son of the late Sowlat al-Dowleh; and Abbas Qobadian (Amir Makhsus), chief of the Kalhur tribe in Kurdestan. Qobadian, like many Bakhtiyari and Qashqayi khans, had been incarcerated by Reza Shah. The *Ettehad-e Melli* (National Union) Fraksiun was led by: Sayyed Muhammad Tabatabai and Sayyed Ahmad Behbehani – sons of the two mojtaheds who had led the early constitutional movement; and by Ezatollah Bayat, brother of the premier with the same name, both of whom were major landlords in Arak. The *Mehan* (Fatherland) Fraksiun was led by Hadi Taheri, Muhammad Namazi, and Hashem Malek-Madani – three wealthy businessmen who had represented Yazd, Shiraz, and Mallayer respectively during the previous twenty years. The Majles also contained a number of prominent independent (*mostaqel*) deputies: Mossadeq; Sayyed Ziya, the short lived premier of the 1921 coup; Timourtash, son of the murdered minister; and Rahman Khalatbari, heir to the famous Sepahdar.

The deputies, especially the fraksiun leaders, played crucial roles. They dominated the committees that steered legislation into and through parliament – all bills had to be passed by the Majles. They chose premiers and cabinet ministers, and could, at any time, terminate them through a vote of no-confidence. Not surprisingly, cabinets on average lasted less than five months and premiers less than eight months. Exasperated by this revolving door, a British diplomat complained: "It is clear that Persia is not ready for parliamentary democracy. These deputies are an intolerable nuisance unless sat upon."[23] Despite the turnover, the ministries continued to function reasonably well under permanent under-secretaries. The government even gained an additional ministry – that of health. The shift of gravity towards the notables can best be seen in the process of electing ministers. In the previous twenty years, the shah had been accustomed to issue a royal *farman* (decree) to his handpicked premier to head a cabinet, choose for him his ministers, and then dispatch them to the Majles to obtain the needed seal of approval. But in these thirteen years, the normal process was for the Majles, or rather the fraksiun leaders, first to choose their candidate for premier; their candidate then automatically received the royal farman to form a cabinet. The new premier then selected his ministers, drew up a government program, and went to the Majles to receive the needed vote of approval both for his program and ministers. This vote of confidence could be withdrawn at any time. The deputies regained other constitutional powers: immunity from arrest; the right to investigate any subject; and the authority to administer to the shah his oath of office stressing allegiance to the constitutional laws.

The main source of power for the notables lay at the local level. They controlled not only the peasant tenants whom they could herd to the polls but also the electoral boards that supervised the ballot boxes and handed out the ballot papers. As one British consul correctly predicted in 1943: "landlords are justifiably confident that, in spite of radicalism in the towns, the majority of the peasants will continue to follow their lead on election day."[24] They were influential even in the industrial towns. For example, in Isfahan the main power behind the scenes was Akbar Mas'oud (Sarem al-Dowleh), the eldest son of the famous Zill al-Sultan who had governed the province for nearly half a century. Even though Mas'oud had lost much credibility both because he had signed the 1919 Anglo-Persian Agreement and because he had been involved in an "honor killing," he remained a significant force on the local level because of his wealth and family contacts. Many officials as well as police and gendarme officers were reputed to be in his pay. After serving Reza Shah as governor of Hamadan, Fars, and Kermanshah, he had retired to his estates to hunt and develop a "model village." The British embassy reported that after the fall of Reza Shah he had shunned public office but "had become the unofficial controller of almost everything in Isfahan."[25] He had so much influence on the electoral board that he was able to "arrange" behind the scenes a suitable outcome for the Fourteenth Majles elections.

The campaign for this election began with five strong candidates competing for the city's three parliamentary seats: Taqi Fedakar, a young lawyer representing the trade unions organized recently by the Tudeh Party in the city's large textile mills; Haydar Ali Emami, a merchant turned industrialist with strong links to local landlords; Sayyed Hashem al-Din Dowlatabadi, the son of a prominent cleric and the main spokesman for the local guilds and merchants – especially merchants who had acquired expropriated Bakhtiyari lands; Sheifpour Fatemi (Mosbeh al-Sultan), a close ally of the Bakhtiyaris and himself a major landlord in the region; and Ahmad Quli Khan Bakhtiyari, the eldest son of Morteza Quli (Samsam) Khan, the patriarch of the Ilkhani family. After 1941, Morteza Quli Khan had returned to reclaim his lands, reassert his authority over the Hajji Ilkhani branch, and free his tribesmen from military control. By 1944, he had accomplished much of his goal. He had obtained the governorship of the recreated district of Bakhtiyar stretching from Dezful to Chahar Mahal. He had reasserted authority over the Hajji Ilkhani and regained some of his family lands – although not those acquired by the Isfahani merchants. What is more, he had armed some 4,500 tribesmen and forced the military and the gendarmerie to withdraw from the Bakhtiyari region. The British consul reported that the military withdrew when it discovered that the soldiers were more eager to "shoot their officers than the tribesmen."[26] The same consul reported:[27]

Under Reza Shah, the land and mill owners – who are mostly ignorant, believing that money can do everything, reactionary to a degree, and solely interested in making as much money as possible – reigned supreme in Isfahan with the help of the central government. But with the change of regime in 1941 and removal of the ban on communist propaganda, the Russian-backed Tudeh, led locally by Fedakar, began to develop by taking advantage of this struggle between labour and capital. At present Isfahan is the center of the struggle because of the existence of an easily organized body of uneducated opinion among the millhands.

Despite these tensions, Akbar Mas'oud brokered an amicable deal. Ahmad Quli Khan Bakhtiyar and Sheifpour Fatemi took the less prestigious seats of nearby Shahr-e Kurd and Najafabad respectively. Meanwhile, Fedakar, Dowlatabadi, and Emami took the three Isfahan seats. In fact, these three urged supporters to cast their three votes for each other. In the final count, Fedakar received 30,499 votes; Dowlatabadi 29,470; and

Emami 27,870. This gave Isfahan a voter turn-out of nearly 50 percent. The turn-out in Tehran was less than 15 percent.[28] Of course, it was even lower in rural constituencies. This provided the landed magnates with the perfect opportunity to determine the outcome. They packed the electoral boards which distributed the ballots; the kadkhudas herded the peasants to the polls; and the electoral boards counted the votes. The rule of the notables can be labeled "feudal democracy."

THE SOCIALIST MOVEMENT (1941–49)

The first real challenge to the notables came from the socialist movement. Within a month of Reza Shah's abdication, a group of recent graduates from European universities and former political prisoners led by Iraj Iskandari met in the home of his uncle Sulayman Iskandari, the veteran constitutional revolutionary, and announced the formation of the Tudeh Party. Iraj Iskandari, who remained at the party's helm until 1979, was the son of Yahya Iskandari, the radical prince who had been prominent in the 1906 revolution, had been arrested in the 1909 coup, and had died soon after – some suspect that this imprisonment hastened his early death. Despite aristocratic lineage, the family was not wealthy. Iraj Iskandari had won a government scholarship to Europe where he was influenced by the socialist and communist movements. Soon after his return in the mid-1930s, he, together with a group of like-minded intellectuals, was arrested and accused of propagating *eshteraki* (socialism-communism). They became famous as the "Fifty-three." Upon their release from prison in August 1941, Iraj Iskandari together with his closest colleagues decided to form a party with a broad appeal that would attract not only their own generation of young radicals but also communists and progressive patriots from the older generation. Thus they named their organization Hezb-e Tudeh (Party of the Masses).

In his memoirs, Iraj Iskandari recalls that they intended to overcome past sectarianism by creating a broad movement of "democratic, patriotic, and progressive forces."[29] They succeeded in persuading the aged and highly respected Sulayman Iskandari to accept the party's chairmanship. The latter had been prominent in national politics ever since 1906. He had been among the deputies arrested in the 1909 coup. He had headed the Liberal Party in the first Majles, the Democratic Party in the 1910s, and the Government of National Resistance in World War I; he had been interned in India by the British and had been later exchanged for a prisoner released by the Jangalis. He had also founded and led the Socialist Party in the 1920s. His relatives had been instrumental in founding women's organizations. He had originally supported Reza Khan's reforms – he had even served as his minister of education – but had broken with him over the change of dynasty. He favored the replacement of the Qajar monarchy with a republic. During Reza Shah's reign, he had lived quietly in a two-room flat. Probably because of his modest living, the British legation described him as "an obscure Qajar Prince."[30] He remained chairman of the Tudeh until his death in 1944. Thus his life spanned forty years of radicalism. In accepting the Tudeh chairmanship, he probably laid down the condition that the party, despite its social radicalism, should not antagonize the devout with anti-religious propaganda. He was convinced that in the past the socialist movement had undermined itself by unnecessarily antagonizing the devout. He credited his own survival in the 1909 coup to the fact that when guards came to take him to his trial and probable execution they found him in the midst of his morning prayer. He, like other founding members of the Tudeh, wanted to create a broad-based organization that would appeal to socialistic, patriotic, democratic, and even constitutionalist sentiments. The party's very first program declared:[31]

Our primary aim is to mobilize the workers, peasants, progressive intellectuals, traders, and craftsmen of Iran. Our society has two major classes: those who own the main means of production; and those who have no significant amounts of property. The latter include workers, peasants, progressive intellectuals, craftsmen and traders. They work but do not receive the fruit of their labor. They are also oppressed by the oligarchy. They have little to lose but much to gain if the whole social structure were radically transformed and the main means of production were owned by the people ... When we say that our aim is to fight despotism and dictatorship we are not referring to specific personalities but to class structures that produce despots and dictators. In August 1941 many thought that Reza Shah's abdication had ended overnight the dictatorial system. We now know better; for we can see with our own eyes that the class structure that produced Reza Shah remains. What is worse, this class structure continues to create petty Reza Shahs – oligarchs in the form of feudal landlords and exploiting capitalists, who, through their ownership of the means of production, continue to control the state.

This appeal was highly successful. By 1945–46, Tudeh had become the party of the masses in more than name. It had six parliamentary seats in addition to that of Isfahan. It had three cabinet ministries: education, health, and trade. Its main newspaper, *Rahbar* (Leader), boasted a record-breaking circulation of more than 100,000 – triple that of the semi-official *Ettela'at*. The party also claimed 50,000 core members and 100,000 affiliated members. It opened branches in seventy-eight towns – in other words, almost every town with a population of more than 10,000. Its May Day and Constitution Day celebrations attracted huge crowds in all the major cities – in Tehran they drew as many as 40–60,000. It also forged alliances with other progressive groups, such as the Iran Party, Socialist Party, and Jangali Party.

Impressed by these showings, the *New York Times* wrote that Tudeh and its allies could win as much as 40 percent of the vote in fair elections.[32] It added that Tudeh was "stimulating the masses to think and act politically for the first time." Bullard stressed that "Tudeh is the only coherent political force in the country and is strong enough to nip in the bud any serious opposition since it has almost complete control of the press and of labour throughout the country."[33] His American counterpart reported that "Tudeh is the only large, well organized, and functioning political machine in Iran."[34] A member of the British cabinet commented: "I cannot get it out of my mind that the Tudeh Party, though admittedly a revolutionary party, may be the party of the future which is going to look after the interests of the working man in Persia."[35] British consuls in the provinces were equally impressed. The Abadan consul reported that "the security of the refinery and the fields, and the safety of the British personnel depend on the good will and pleasure of the Tudeh Party."[36] British officials touring the Caspian reported: "Tudeh had gained so much influence in Gilan and Mazanderan that the control of affairs had virtually passed into their hands."[37] "Persian politics," said one British report, "has become a struggle between the have and the have-nots with the Left championing the latter."[38] The British consul in Mashed was more explicit:[39]

The state of the middle and lower classes is little better than in the dark latter days of Reza Shah. Public Bandit No 1 has gone, only to make way for a coterie of officials who, taken as a whole exploit the masses nearly as thoroughly as he did. Not only is the man in the street and at the plough looted directly by local officials, police, and gendarmerie in the good old ways, but a new technique has been evolved by which he is squeezed daily by big business in the shape of monopoly departments and officially protected private racketeers ... Their only fear is the Tudeh engineering a popular uprising.

The Tudeh Party drew most of its support from urban wage earners and from the salaried middle class – especially the intelligentsia. By 1945, the British reported that the Tudeh-led Central Council of Federated Trade Unions had thirty-three affiliates with more than 275,000 members.[40] This constituted 75 percent of the industrial labor force with a presence in most of the country's 346 modern industrial plants. Its membership included 45,000 oil workers, 45,000 construction laborers, 40,000 textile workers, 20,000 railwaymen, 20,000 carpet weavers, 11,000 dockers, 8,000 miners, and 6,000 truck drivers. The Central Council showed its full strength in May

1946 by organizing a general strike throughout the oil industry. The British embassy reported that the Anglo-Iranian Oil Company had no choice but to concede the eight-hour day, Friday pay, overtime scales, higher wages, and better housing since the unions had de facto control over Khuzestan as well as over the refinery, the oil wells, and the pipelines.[41] The Tudeh Party followed up this success by pressuring the government to decree the first comprehensive labor law in the Middle East. This promised the eight-hour day; Friday pay; six day's annual holidays, including May Day; worker's insurance and unemployment pay; minimum wages based on local food prices; outlawing of child labor; and the right of workers to organize independent unions. British consuls privately admitted that employers – including the oil company – had through "greed," "arrogance," "exploitation," and "disdain" for their employees brought the country to the brink: "We are seeing the rise of a new social movement. The advantages which workers have won are considerable and they will certainly continue to make the employers feel their newly discovered power."[42] This success prompted the British Conservative government to appoint a Labour Attaché in Tehran with the explicit mission of detaching "individual members from the Tudeh Party."[43]

Tudeh strength among the salaried middle class was equally impressive. It attracted not only an impressive array of professional and white-collar associations, but also much of the intelligentsia. Among its members and sympathizers – some would say "fellow-travelers" – were many of the country's intellectual luminaries.[44] Their list reads like a Who's Who of modern Iran: Sadeq Hedayat, Bozorg Alavi, and Sadeq Chubak, the three leading lights of modern prose writing; Ahmad Shamlu and Nima Yushej, the two path-blazers of modern poetry; Bahar, the poet laureate of traditional literature; Said Nafisi, Mehdi Bamdad, Muhammad Tamaddon, Morteza Ravandi, Yahyi Arinpour – five leading historians; Noshin, Loreta, and Hussein Khair-Khaw, the founders of modern theater; Ghulam-Hussein Saedi, the playwright; Jalal al-e Ahmad and Behazin, two well-known essayists; Golestan, one of Iran's first film directors; and such literary figures as Parviz Khanlari, Nader Naderpour, Muhammad Tafazolli, Muhammad Mo'in, Fereidun Tavalolli, Fereidun Tankubani, and Siavesh Kasrai. Their ranks also included prominent lawyers, doctors, surgeons, engineers, architects, musicians, artists, sculptors, and university professors. These intellectuals socialized in Tudeh clubs as well as in private cafés near the cinemas and theatres of northern Tehran. Their main gathering places were the Noshin's Sa'adi Theater and Ferdowsi Café favored by Sadeq Hedayat and Bozorg Alavi. In the words of the London

Times, Tudeh at its height attracted the "most talented and the best educated of the young generation."[45]

The Tudeh Party, however, suffered major setbacks in 1945–46. These were caused by the Soviet demand for an oil concession in northern Iran and their sponsoring of autonomy movements in Kurdestan and Azerbaijan. The oil demand took Tudeh by surprise – especially since their Majles deputies had just denounced the government for offering concessions in Baluchestan to American companies, and their labor organizers in Khuzestan had been calling for the nationalization of the Anglo-Iranian Oil Company. Tudeh tried "damage limitation," arguing that the Soviet willingness to share future profits equally was far more generous than the 20 percent received from the British. The demand, however, became an embarrassing litmus test dividing leftists from nationalists. Bullard reported that many Tudeh leaders had privately informed the prime minister that they opposed the Soviet demand and instead supported the official policy of postponing all oil negotiations until after the war.[46]

The Kurdish and Azerbaijan movements were even more damaging. In September 1945, the Soviets, for reasons best known to themselves, suddenly sponsored Kurdish and Azerbaijan groups demanding provincial autonomy. Jafar Pishevari, a veteran communist who edited his own paper and disdained the young Marxists leading the Tudeh Party, suddenly rediscovered his Azeri "roots" and realized that his native Azerbaijan had long been deprived of its "national rights." Supported by the Soviets, he established his own Democratic Party of Azerbaijan, and, together with armed volunteers, took over the province. A parallel "uprising" took place in neighboring Kurdestan. The Soviets continued to provide them with protection until they withdrew from Iran in May 1946. These crises further divided staunch leftists from mainstream nationalists. Iraj Iskandari later revealed that the Tudeh leaders had publicly supported the Azerbaijan and Kurdish Democratic Parties for the sake of socialist solidarity with the Soviet Union, but privately they had remained "bewildered," "surprised," and "shocked."[47] They had even sent a protest letter to the Soviet Communist Party. One leader wrote to Moscow insinuating that the whole disastrous scheme had been cooked up by local leaders in Baku to further their own "personal interests and dictates" against both Iran and the Soviet Union.[48] Tudeh again tried damage limitation. It argued that these provincial movements wanted regional autonomy and cultural rights, not separation and political independence. It also focused on their reforms, especially in Azerbaijan, where the provincial government introduced women's suffrage; laid the foundations for Tabriz University; renamed streets after local heroes in the

Constitutional Revolution; and carried out the country's first land reform, distributing state lands, confiscating large estates, and increasing sharecroppers' portion of the harvest. These reforms, however, did little to save the provincial governments once the central army returned with full force in 1946. The two provincial governments lasted only twelve months.

The government struck additional blows at Tudeh. Accusing the party of having aided and abetted the "secessionists," it issued arrest warrants for its leaders including Iraj Iskandari who was forced to go into exile. The government, together with the British, orchestrated a revolt of southern tribes – Qashqa'is, Bakhtiyaris, Boir Ahmadis, Kalhur Kurds, and Arab Ka'abs – targeting Tudeh organizations in Bushire, Yazd, Shiraz, Kerman, and Kermanshah. It declared martial law in Tehran, clamped down on the trade unions, and closed down many Tudeh clubs and party offices throughout northern cities. Even more drastic, the shah in February 1949 took advantage of a failed attempt on his life by a lone assassin to declare nationwide martial law, outlaw Tudeh, close down its newspapers, round up as many leaders as possible, and sentence to death in absentia those who managed to escape. He also arrested opposition figures such as Qavam who in no way were related to Tudeh; banned newspapers critical of the royal family; and convened a Constituent Assembly to enhance his royal prerogatives. This assembly gave him the authority both to dissolve parliament on condition he convened a new one within six months, and to assemble an upper house of sixty senators – half of whom he could nominate as stipulated under the 1906 constitution. He packed this Senate with elderly notables, such as Taqizadeh and Hakimi, who were now willing to concede to him total control over the armed forces. The Senate promptly bestowed the title *Kaber* (The Great) on the deceased Reza Shah; and gave him a state funeral even though clerical leaders refused to have him buried on hallowed ground in Mashed, Qom, or Shah Abdul 'Azim Mosque. Instead, he was buried in a Napoleonesque mausoleum in southern Tehran. The Senate also quietly transferred Reza Shah's vast estates from the state back to the royal family. The shah had reasserted control over court patronage. Not surprisingly, many, including the British and American ambassadors, concluded that the shah had transformed the assassination attempt into a royalist *coup d'état*.

Although Tudeh's political clout was short lived, its intellectual and cultural influence endured. The party introduced into Iran the notion of mass politics, mass participation, and mass organizations with party cells and branches, party conferences and congresses, and party newspapers, politburos, and central committees. Others readily borrowed such terms as "democratic centralism" and "mass democracy." Tudeh published the first Persian-language political dictionary popularizing such words as colonialism, imperialism, fascism, united front, bourgeoisie, aristocracy, oligarchy, reactionary, progress, masses, and toilers. It popularized the notion of class identity, class conflict, and class dynamics – so much so that even conservatives began to use such language, claiming that "benevolent" and "paternalistic" landlords were best qualified to protect peasants and workers. Moreover, Tudeh reinforced the general conviction that the state had the moral responsibility to provide citizens with basic necessities. Its popular slogan was: "Work for All, Education for All, Health for All." Rights became associated more with social democracy than with laissez-faire liberal democracy. Furthermore, it introduced into politics the demand for land reform and for root-and-branch transformation of landlord–peasant relationships. It championed the cause of "Land to the Tiller." Finally, it introduced into politics the idea that women should have the same political rights as men – especially the right to vote.

Tudeh also reinforced the national identity of Iran as an ancient civilization with cultural features distinct from its neighbors. While it mocked the racial theories of the former regime and previous generation, it stressed the importance of pre-Islamic Iran. It celebrated the equinoxes, praised ancient Iran, and waxed eloquent about Persian literature – especially the *Shahnameh*. Noshin, the famous dramatist and founding member of Tudeh, was one of the very first to reinterpret the epic as a radical text, denouncing monarchs and instead praising folk rebels such as Kaveh the Blacksmith. Similarly, Tudeh glorified the Constitutional Revolution as a democratic and patriotic movement led by the progressive intelligentsia. It located itself in the long narrative of the constitutional movement. What is more, Tudeh raised for the first time the demand for nationalization of the British-owned oil industry. On May Day in 1946, the British consul in Khorramshahr noted in alarm that a female speaker had not only demanded a comprehensive labor law with equal pay for equal work, but had also called for the total nationalization of the oil industry, accusing the British company of exploiting the "jewel of Iran" and of spending more on dog food than on wages for its Iranian workers.[49] This was probably the very first time that the call for oil nationalization had been heard in Iran. It would not be the last.

THE NATIONALIST MOVEMENT (1949–53)

Tudeh's decline in the late 1940s provided an opportunity for the nationalist movement to emerge in the early 1950s. The movement was led by the charismatic Muhammad Mossadeq who had been prominent in national politics ever since the Constitutional Revolution of 1906, having served as parliamentary deputy, provincial governor, and cabinet minister before being forced into retirement by Reza Shah. He was best known for championing two major causes: strict constitutionalism at home and an equally strict policy of "negative equilibrium" abroad to assure independence from foreign domination. Mossadeq argued that traditional politicians had jeopardized Iran's very existence with their misguided policy of "positive equilibrium" and "capitulating" to the great powers. Such a policy, he warned, prompted other powers to demand equivalent concessions, endangering national sovereignty. For these reasons, he denounced both the 1919 Anglo-Iranian Agreement and the 1945–46 oil negotiations with both the Americans and Soviets. For the same reasons, he took up the cause of oil nationalization, demanding that the government should take over the Anglo-Iranian Oil Company. He insisted that Iran had the inalienable right to have full control over the production, sale, and export of its own oil resources.

In internal affairs, Mossadeq was known as a strict constitutionalist. As a young man, he represented the "aristocratic" stratum in the First Majles. Educated in Switzerland, he had written a law thesis advocating the full-scale introduction of Western jurisprudence into Iran. He opposed the 1921 coup and the establishment of the Pahlavi, which led to his brief imprisonment, followed by banishment to his village of Ahmadabad some one hundred miles away from Tehran. After 1941, he returned to politics and again became prominent in parliament where he argued that the shah – like his counterparts in Belgium and Britain – should reign not rule. He took the young shah to task for retaining power over the armed forces and thus violating the spirit as well as the tenets of the constitutional laws; for using the military to interfere in parliamentary elections; and for regaining control over the royal estates which had been promised to be returned to their original owners. He questioned the legitimacy of the 1949 Constituent Assembly on the grounds that its election was rigged. He also advocated drastic changes in the electoral law, such as banning the military from the vicinity of ballot boxes, guaranteeing the independence of electoral boards, and creating more urban seats – especially for Tehran.[50] He even advocated taking away the vote from illiterates on the grounds that "this would be the best way to weaken the entrenched power of the landed oligarchy."[51] Although often depicted as an "Anglophobe," he was in fact an unabashed admirer of nineteenth-century British liberal parliamentary government.

Despite his aristocratic origins, Mossadeq obtained much of his support among the middle classes. From a long line of prominent mostowfis and a direct descendant of the famous Mohsen Ashtiani, Fath Ali Shah's chief minister, Mossadeq was related by blood and marriage to many other notables – including Farmanfarma, Qavam, Vossuq, Bayat, and the Imam Jum'eh of Tehran. Nonetheless, Mossadeq enjoyed the reputation of being "incorruptible" both because he denounced the extravagancies of fellow aristocrats and because he himself lived a middle-class style of life. He shunned his title of al-Saltaneh, and preferred to be addressed as Dr. in recognition of his higher degree from Europe. His contemporaries tended to refer to anyone with a higher degree either as *doctor* or *mohandes* (engineer). Once elected prime minister, Mossadeq refused to be addressed as His Excellency – the British embassy saw this as proof of his demagogy, irrationality, and unpredictability. Iranians took it as yet more evidence that he was not like other notables.

Campaigning both against the British and against the shah, Mossadeq created the National Front (*Jebe'eh-e Melli*) and mobilized within it a broad spectrum of middle-class parties and associations. The most important groups were the Iran Party, the Toilers Party, the National Party, and the Tehran Association of Bazaar Trade and Craft Guilds. The Iran Party started as an engineers' association but had developed into a nationwide organization with a program that was both socialistic and nationalistic. Originally allied with the Tudeh, it gravitated towards Mossadeq after 1946. It was to become Mossadeq's mainstay, providing him with his most reliable ministers, technocrats, and even military supporters. The Toilers Party contained a number of prominent intellectuals who had broken with Tudeh because of the Soviet oil demands and the crises over Azerbaijan and Kurdestan. Chief among them were Al-e Ahmad, the well-known writer, and Khalel Maleki, an older member of the "Fifty-three" who had been prominent in Tudeh and in later years became the main Iranian theorist of the "Third Way" – a non-communist and non-capitalist road to development. The National Party was a chauvinistic organization confined to Tehran University. It harped on the glories of pre-Islamic Aryan Iran and the return of "lost territories" – especially Bahrain and parts of Afghanistan and the Caucasus. Influenced by fascism, its propaganda targeted the minorities – especially Jews, Armenians, and Bahais – and accused them of being unpatriotic "fifth columns." The educated middle class in Iran – like its counterparts the world over – was not always liberal, tolerant, and progressive.

Mossadeq also had the support of a number of prominent figures – especially Ayatollah Sayyed Abul-Qassem Kashani, the most politically active cleric of his day. As a theology student in Najaf, Kashani had taken part in the Shi'i revolt against the British in Iraq during the early 1920s. It was rumored that his father, also a cleric, had been killed fighting the British. Kashani himself had been imprisoned a number of times – by the British in 1943 because of his links to the German "fifth column," by Qavam in 1945 for opposing the Soviet oil negotiations, and by the shah in 1949 for presumed links to the would-be assassin. The British embassy reported that Kashani "nurses a bitter enmity towards us" and provided Mossadeq with much "politico-religious support" but could be bought off since he and his sons were "venal" and willing to accept a "deal" – if the offer was "lucrative enough."[52]

In addition to many connections to the bazaar, Kashani had informal ties to the secretive *Fedayan-e Islam* (Self-Sacrificers of Islam) – one of the first real fundamentalist organizations in the Muslim world. Formed of a small circle of minor clerics and bazaar apprentices, the Fedayan-e Islam not only demanded the strict application of the shari'a but was also willing to use violence against those it deemed to be "apostates." In 1946, it hacked to death the historian Kasravi for writing books critical of Shi'ism. In 1949, it assassinated Hezhir, the former premier, after Kashani had pronounced him a "secret Bahai." In March 1951, it murdered Razmara, the premier, after Kashani had denounced him for negotiating an unfavorable oil deal with the British. In later years, Fedayan-e Islam shot and wounded Mossadeq's right-hand man and foreign minister on the suspicion he was a secret Bahai. They also plotted to kill Mossadeq himself because of his refusal to implement the shari'a and appoint true believers to high positions. Not surprisingly, some suspected that the Fedayan-e Islam and Kashani, despite appearances, had in later years developed secret links with foreign powers.

With middle-class support and using such strategies as petitions and street demonstrations, Mossadeq was able to mobilize a mass movement calling for the nationalization of the oil industry. With a Tudeh-led general strike in the oil industry in April 1951, he was able to pressure the Majles in May 1951 to accept his nationalization bill and give him the vote necessary to form a government to implement the nationalization law. Not surprisingly, Mossadeq was deemed to be a double-edged sword which threatened not only the oil company and the British Empire but also the shah and his continued control over the armed forces. The royalist speaker of the Majles exclaimed in exasperation: [53]

Statecraft has degenerated into street politics. It appears that this country has nothing better to do than hold street meetings. We now have meetings here, there, and everywhere – meetings for this, that, and every occasion; meetings for university students, high school students, seven-year-olds, and even six-year olds. I am sick and tired of these street meetings . . .

Is our prime minister a statesman or a mob leader? What type of prime minister says "I will speak to the people" every time he is faced with a political problem? I always considered this man to be unsuitable for high office. But I never imagined, even in my worst nightmares, that an old man of seventy would turn into a rabble rouser. A man who surrounds the Majles with mobs is nothing less than a public menace.

As prime minister, Mossadeq acted to implement his programs. He placed colleagues from the National Front in key ministries and parliamentary committees. He created the National Iranian Oil Company (NIOC) and began negotiations with the Anglo-Iranian Oil Company (AIOC) for a smooth transfer of control. When the latter resisted, he ordered NIOC to take over AIOC – its oil wells and pipelines as well as its refinery and offices throughout the country. When the British government – in support of AIOC – evacuated all company personnel, blocked the export of oil from Iran, and lodged a complaint with the United Nations, he personally appeared before the National Security Council, and, accusing Britain of subversion, broke diplomatic relations and closed down the latter's consulates as well as embassy. Britain retaliated by freezing Iranian assets and reinforcing its naval presence in the Persian Gulf. By the end of 1951 Mossadeq was embroiled in a full-blown crisis with Britain. In a postmortem on the whole crisis, the foreign office admitted that Mossadeq had been able to mobilize the "discontented against the upper class closely identified with the British."[54]

The crisis with the shah came to a head in mid-1952, precipitated by Mossadeq's attempt to reform the electoral law to weaken the monarch and the landed magnates. Failing to reform the law, he stopped the elections for the Sixteenth Majles just after urban centers had completed voting and enough deputies had been chosen to produce a parliamentary quorum. He then instigated a confrontation with the shah by asserting that he, as premier, had the constitutional authority to appoint the war minister as well as other members of the cabinet. This was the first time that royal control of the military had been seriously threatened. When the shah resisted, Mossadeq took his cause directly to the public. In a radio broadcast, he argued that he needed supervision over the armed forces to prevent nefarious forces from plotting to undo oil nationalization. The public promptly poured into the streets, and after three days of general strikes and bloodshed, forced the shah to back down. The crisis became known as 30th Tir (July 21).

Mossadeq followed up with a series of hammer blows. He designated 30th Tir a "national uprising" with "national martyrs." He took over the portfolio of the war minister, changed the name of the ministry to that of defense, vowed to buy only defensive weapons, appointed the chief of staff, purged 136 officers, transferred 15,000 men from the army to the gendarmerie, cut the military budget by 15 percent, and appointed a parliamentary committee to investigate past arms procurements. He also transferred the royal estates back to the state; cut the palace budget; appointed a fellow anti-royalist notable to be court minister; placed royal charities under government supervision; forbade the shah to communicate with foreign ambassadors; forced Princess Ashraf, the shah's politically active twin sister, into exile; and refused to close down newspapers that were denouncing the palace as "a den of corruption, treason, and espionage." When faced with resistance in the two houses of parliament, Mossadeq dissolved the Senate and asked his supporters to resign from the Majles, thereby ending the required quorum. By July 1953, some of his colleagues were openly talking of a constitutional committee – with Dehkhoda, the famous lexicographer and veteran of the 1906 revolution, as its chairman – to explore the feasibility of replacing the monarchy with a democratic republic. Mossadeq himself called for a referendum to ratify parliament's dissolution:[55]

The people of Iran – and no one else – have the right to judge this issue. For it is the people who brought into existence our fundamental laws, our constitution, our parliament, and our cabinet system. We must remember that the laws were created for the people, not the people for the laws. The nation has the right to express its views, and, if it wished, to change the laws. In a democratic and constitutional country, the nation reigns supreme.

THE COUP (1953)

The 1953 coup has often been depicted as a CIA venture to save Iran from international communism. In fact, it was a joint British–American venture to preserve the international oil cartel. Throughout the crisis, the central issue was who would control the production, distribution, and sale of oil. Although the word "control" was scrupulously avoided in public pronouncements, it was very much the operative term in confidential reports issued in both London and Washington. For London, the AIOC had in Iran the world's largest refinery, the second largest exporter of crude petroleum, and the third largest oil reserves. It also provided the British Treasury with £24 million in taxes and £92 million in foreign exchange; supplied the British navy with 85 percent of fuel needs; and the AIOC with 75 percent of its annual profits – much of which went to its shareholders in England as well as to oil ventures in Kuwait, Iraq, and Indonesia.

For Washington – as well as for London – Iranian control would have far-reaching disastrous consequences. It would not only strike a direct blow at the British. It would give control to Iran. It could inspire others – especially Indonesia, Venezuela, and Iraq – to follow suit, and thus drastically shift control over the international petroleum market away from Western oil companies towards the oil-producing countries. This would threaten American as well as other Western companies – not to mention the US as much as the British government. British confidential memos were quite explicit in spelling out these long-term dangers:

Iran would be content to see the industry running at a low level without foreign management. This raises a problem: the security of the free world is dependent on large quantities of oil from Middle Eastern sources. If the attitude in Iran spreads to Saudi Arabia or Iraq, the whole structure may break down along with our ability to defend ourselves. The danger of buying oil produced on reduced scale has, therefore, potentialities with dangerous repercussions.[56]

The first effect of nationalization would be to put control into Persian hands. Seen from the United Kingdom point of view the present problem was not solely one of the fate of a major asset. It concerns *the* major asset which we hold in the field of raw materials. Control of that asset is of supreme importance. The point has already been made of the importance of the asset to our balance of payments and to our rearmament programme, but in the sphere of bilateral negotiations the loss of this, our only major raw material, would have cumulative and well-nigh incalculable repercussions. Moreover, it is false to assume an identity of interests between the Western world and Persia over how much oil should be produced and to whom it would be sold and on what terms. The Persians could get all the oil and foreign exchange they need from much reduced operations. For all these reasons, the United Kingdom has to keep control of the real resources involved.[57]

The British were willing to increase royalties, share management with other Western companies, and even accept the principle of nationalization so long as it was not put into effect and actual control remained out of Iranian hands. The British ambassador admitted that London was willing to go beyond the normal 50/50 deal and give Iran as much as 60 percent of the profits so long as real "control" remained in Western hands: "It seems very unlikely we can do anything at all to meet Iran (on the question of control) . . . We must keep effective control. We have explored a number of devices by which we could disguise this hard fact but found nothing that was not either too dangerous or too transparent for even the Persians to accept."[58]

In public, the British hammered away on the theme that it was impossible to reach a settlement because Mossadeq was "fanatical," "crazy," "erratic," "eccentric," "slippery," "unbalanced," "demagogic," "absurd,"

(margin note: Iran's nationalization at odds w/ GB+USA interests)

"childish," "tiresome and single-minded," "inflammatory," "volatile and unstable," "sentimentally mystical," "wild," "wily Oriental," "unwilling to face fact," "dictatorial," "xenophobic," "Robespierre-like," "Frankenstein-like," "unprepared to listen to reason and common sense," and "swayed by martyrdom complex." The British ambassador told his American counterpart that Iran – like Haiti – was "immature" and therefore needed to remain under a firm foreign hand for at least another two decades.[59] Drew Pearson – the venerable dean of American journalism – warned that it would be far too dangerous for America to have gas prices and the future of the "Free World" in the hands of such men as Mossadeq and his foreign minister whom he accused falsely of having been convicted of corruption and jury tampering. "Such men," he exclaimed, "will decide whether we have oil rationing – or possibly, whether we go into World War III."[60] The British press attaché in Washington spread the rumor that Mossadeq "indulged freely in opium."[61] A handwritten note in the foreign office mentioned in passing that the Tehran embassy was sending to the press attaché in Washington "a steady supply of suitable poison too venomous for the BBC." It added that Washington was "making full use of this poison."[62] The British and American governments also falsely claimed that Mossadeq was giving too many concessions to the Tudeh Party, bringing fellow-travelers into his administration, and secretly negotiating with the Soviet Union. In private memos, however, the foreign office admitted that the Tudeh Party was not a real threat.[63] Similarly, Dean Acheson, Truman's secretary of state, later admitted that the supposed Tudeh danger had never been considered to be serious.[64]

The British and the Americans differed less over interests and strategy than over timing and tactics. Whereas the British argued consistently and insistently from the very beginning that Mossadeq would never give way on the issue of control, the Americans spent fourteen months – from April 1951 until July 1952 – searching for ways to persuade or hoodwink him into settling for a "compromise" in which Iran in theory would retain the nationalized industry, but in practice would hand over the actual running of that industry to a consortium of AIOC and other major Western companies. It was not until the July 1952 crisis that Washington came around to the British view that the only way to deal with Mossadeq was to overthrow him. The day after the crisis, the American ambassador reported that "only a *coup d'état* could save the situation": "He has so flattered the mob as the sources of his powers that he had, I fear, made it impossible for a successor to oust him by normal constitutional methods."[65]

The CIA and its British counterpart, MI6 (SIS), began in late 1952 to make plans for an eventual military coup. Both brought to the plan major assets. The British had a long-standing and extensive network inside Iran. They had a number of Persian-speaking experts – some of whom had worked in and on Iran for more than thirty years. They also had contacts with numerous old-time politicians, religious figures, tribal chiefs, business leaders, and senior military officers. Over the years, MI6 had compiled a comprehensive military "Who's Who," keeping tabs on their political leanings, family relations, career patterns, and personal foibles. This proved invaluable – especially since the CIA had not bothered to collect such information. One lesson the CIA drew from the whole venture was the need to compile similar dossiers for other countries: "we need personal information however trivial": "who the officer is, what makes him tick, who his friends are, etc."[66] The Americans, meanwhile, brought to the table their large embassy compound; some one hundred advisors embedded in the Iranian army and gendarmerie; young officers, many of them tank commanders, recently trained in the USA; and a clandestine network in the Tehran bazaars, especially in gymnasiums, known as *zurkhanehs*. The CIA also sent to Tehran Kermit Roosevelt who, as a member of the illustrious family, could reassure the shah that Washington would follow up the coup with generous financial support, with a face-saving oil agreement, and with guarantees to protect the monarchy. In fact, the shah did not commit himself to the plan until the nominal head of the coup, General Fazlollah Zahedi, had signed his own pre-dated letter of resignation as future prime minister. The shah had no desire to replace Mossadeq with some potentially dangerous general.

The planned coup came on 28th Mordad (August 19). While gangs from the bazaar zurkhanehs – encouraged by preachers linked to the royalist Ayatollah Behbehani and probably Ayatollah Kashani – provided mostly sound effects, thirty-two Sherman tanks rolled into central Tehran, surrounded key positions, and, after a three-hour battle with three tanks protecting Mossadeq's home and the main radio station, proclaimed Zahedi to be the shah's designated and lawful prime minister. According to eyewitnesses, the "motley crowd" of five hundred was augmented with some two thousand military personnel wearing civilian clothes.[67] The *New York Times* estimated that the battle had left more than three hundred dead.[68] The shah, however, praised 28th Mordad as a bloodless but heroic people's revolution to protect their beloved monarch. President Eisenhower – without any trace of irony – informed the American public that the Iranian "people" had "saved the day" because of their "revulsion against communism" and "their profound love for their monarchy."[69]

The 1953 coup left a profound and long-lasting legacy. By destroying Mossadeq, the shah would be haunted by his mystique – which, in many ways, was comparable to that of other great contemporary national heroes such as Gandhi, Nasser, and Sukarno. The coup seriously undermined the legitimacy of the monarchy – especially in an age already rampant with republicanism. It identified the shah with the British, the Anglo-Iranian Oil Company, and the imperial powers. It also identified the military with the same imperial powers – especially the CIA and MI6. It tarnished the Americans with the British brush – Iranians began to see the main imperial enemy as no longer just Britain but Britain in cahoots with America. It destroyed the National Front and the Tudeh Party – both suffered mass arrests, destruction of their organizations, and even executions of their leaders. This destruction paved the way for the eventual emergence of a religious movement. In other words, the coup helped replace nationalism, socialism, and liberalism with Islamic "fundamentalism." In an age of republicanism, nationalism, neutralism, and socialism, the Pahlavi monarchy had become inseparably and fatally identified with imperialism, corporate capitalism, and close alignment with the West. One can argue that the real roots of the 1979 revolution go back to 1953.

CHAPTER 5

Muhammad Reza Shah's
White Revolution

The monarchy has a special meaning for Iranian families. It is in our way of life. It has been an integral part of our history for 2,500 years.

Empress Farah

The shah's only fault is that he is really too great for his people – his ideas are too great for us.

Assadollah Alam, court minister

Interviewer: "Your Majesty, where have your supporters gone?" The shah: "Search me."

Press interview in 1978

STATE EXPANSION (1953–75)

Muhammad Reza Shah continued after 1953 where his father had been forced to leave off in 1941. He restarted at full speed the drive to expand the three pillars that held up his state: the military, the bureaucracy, and the court patronage system. In many ways, his reign was a continuation of his father's – with some minor variations. Whereas the father had ruled in the age of fascism and talked bluntly of making trains run on time, the son lived at the height of the Cold War and thus shied away from the language of autocracy and racism. But even he, at the peak of his power, could not resist adding to his exalted list of royal titles the brand new one of Arya Mehr (Aryan Sun). Muhammad Reza Shah fulfilled Reza Shah's dream of building a massive state structure.

This dream was achieved thanks to rising oil revenues. These rose in part because of increased production – Iran became the world's fourth largest oil producer and the world's second largest oil exporter; in part because the 1954 consortium agreement gave Iran a 50 percent share of profits; but for the most part because the Organization of Petroleum Exporting Countries (OPEC) took advantage of the 1973 Arab–Israeli War to quadruple international oil prices. Iran's oil revenues rose from $34 million in 1954–55 to

Table 8 *Oil revenues, 1954–76*

Year	Oil revenues ($ million)	Oil revenues as % of foreign exchange receipts
1954–55	34.4	15
1956–57	181	43
1958–59	344	60
1960–61	359	60
1962–63	437.2	70
1964–65	555.4	76
1966–67	968.5	65
1968–69	958.5	53
1970–71	1,200	54
1972–73	2,500	58
1973–74	5,000	66
1974–75	18,000	72
1975–76	20,000	72

Source: Data derived from F. Fesharaki, *Development of the Iranian Oil Industry* (New York: Praeger, 1976), p. 132.

$5 billion in 1973–74, and further to $20 billion in 1975–76. In the course of these twenty-three years, oil provided Iran with more than $55 billion. In any average year, it gave the government more than 60 percent of its revenues and 70 percent of its foreign exchange. Iran became a petroleum state – or, as some would say, a rentier state – in the full sense of the term.[1]

Of the three pillars holding up the Pahlavi state, the military continued to receive preferential treatment. The shah launched the new era by changing the name of the defense ministry back to ministry of war to make it clear that civilians had no business meddling in military matters. Iran became one of the few countries in the world with a ministry of war rather than of defense. In the period between 1954 and 1977, the military budget grew twelvefold and its share of the annual budget went from 24 to 35 percent – from $60 million in 1954 to $5.5 billion in 1973, and further to $7.3 billion in 1977. Its manpower expanded from 127,000 to 410,000. By 1977, the regular army had in excess of 220,000 men, the air force 100,000, the gendarmerie 60,000, and the navy 25,000. Much of the military budget went into ultra-sophisticated weaponry. Arms dealers joked that the shah devoured their manuals in much the same way as other men read *Playboy*. By 1975, the shah had the largest navy in the Persian Gulf, the largest air force in Western Asia, and the fifth largest army in the whole world. His arsenal included more than 1,000 modern tanks, 400 helicopters,

28 hovercraft, 100 long-range artillery pieces, 2,500 Maverick missiles, 173 F4 fighter planes, 141 F5s, 10 F14s, and 10 Boeing 707 transport planes. A US Congressional report estimated that Iran's military purchases were "the largest in the world."[2] As if this were not enough, the shah placed orders in 1978 for another $12 billion worth of arms. These included 160 F16s, 80 F14s, 160 F16s, 209 F4s, 3 naval destroyers, and 10 nuclear submarines – making Iran a power in the Indian Ocean as well as in the Persian Gulf. He also signed contracts with West Europeans for nuclear plants – with obvious military implications. A Congressional report stated:[3]

Iran's military expenditures surpassed those of the most powerful Indian Ocean states, including Australia, Indonesia, Pakistan, South Africa and India. The Shah also planned to spend an estimated $33 billion (some experts say probably three times as much) for the construction of some 20 nuclear reactors by 1994. If constructed with German, French, and American aid, they would have made Iran the largest producer of nuclear energy in the entire Indian Ocean area.

The shah did not confine his military interest to arms purchases. He continued to take a keen interest in all things military – in training, maneuvers, barracks, and the general well-being of the officers. He showered them with generous salaries, pensions, and fringe benefits, including comfortable housing, frequent travel abroad, periodic bonuses, modern medical facilities, discount department stores, and real estate gifts. He performed state functions in military uniform; placed officers in high administrative positions; vetted all promotions above the rank of major; and praised the officer corps for having saved the country in 1953 on that "blessed day" of August 19 (28th Mordad). The day was celebrated every year as a national holiday. The military and the monarchy became so interwoven that the shah, in an interview with a foreign academic, inadvertently identified himself not as the state, *à la* Louis XIV, but as the army – much as his father had done.[4]

The shah also took measures to forestall the possibility of a military coup. From personal experience, he had a healthy fear of colonels hovering in the background. He forbade the chiefs of the services as well as the heads of the security agencies from communicating with each other directly.[5] All communication was channeled through the royal palace. He named family members and officers with "underwhelming" personalities to head the key military positions.[6] This was to have disastrous consequences in 1978–79. He expanded the Imperial Guards to more than 8,000 well-trained men; created an Imperial Inspectorate under his childhood friend General Fardoust to watch over the country's elite; boosted the J2 Bureau – the intelligence branch of the regular army; and, most importantly, with the help of the FBI and the Israeli Mossad established in 1957 a new intelligence agency. Known by its Persian acronym, SAVAK eventually grew into some 5,000 operatives and an unknown number of part-timer informers. Some claimed that one out of every 450 males was a SAVAK informer.[7] Headed for extended periods by General Nematollah Nasseri, another crony, SAVAK had the power to keep an eye on all Iranians – including high-ranking officers – censor the media, screen applicants for government jobs, even university appointments, and use all means available, including torture and summary executions, to deal with political dissidents. It soon created an Orwellian environment where intellectuals were not allowed to utter the name of Marx, who became "a nineteenth-century European social philosopher." In the words of a British journalist, SAVAK was the shah's "eyes and ears, and where necessary, his iron fist."[8] Its director – although nominally under the prime minister's supervision – met privately with the shah every morning. Frances FitzGerald, the well-known author and niece of the US ambassador, wrote of her experiences in Iran in a 1974 article entitled "Giving the Shah Everything He Wants":[9]

SAVAK has agents in the lobby of every hotel, in every government department, and in every university classroom. In the provinces, SAVAK runs a political intelligence-gathering service, and abroad it keeps a check on every Iranian student . . . Educated Iranians cannot trust anyone beyond a close circle of friends, and for them the effect is the same as if everyone else belonged. SAVAK intensifies this fear by giving no account of its activities. People disappear in Iran, and their disappearances go unrecorded . . . The Shah says that his government has no political prisoners. (Communists, he explains, are not political offenders but common criminals.) Amnesty International estimates that there are about 20,000 of them.

The shah's expansion of the state bureaucracy was equally impressive. In these years, he increased the number of fully fledged ministries from twelve to twenty – including the new ministries of energy, labor, social welfare, rural affairs, higher education, art and culture, tourism, and housing and urban construction. By 1975, the state employed more than 304,000 civil servants as well as some one million white-collar and blue-collar workers. The prime minister's office, which oversaw the Plan and Budget Organization as well as the religious foundations, employed 24,000. The ministries of education and higher education together employed 515,000, and administered 26,000 primary schools, 1,850 secondary schools, 750 vocational schools, and 13 universities. The interior ministry, with 21,000 employees, redrew the administrative map of the country, increasing the number of provinces from ten to twenty-three and subdividing them into 400 administrative districts, each with a mayor, village headman, or rural council appointed from the center. For the first time in history, the arm of the state reached not just into cities and towns but also into far-away villages and rural hamlets. By 1977, the state was directly paying one of every two full-time employees.

The state also financed indirectly a number of quasi-government institutions: the Central Bank; the Industrial and Mining Development Bank; the National Iranian Radio and Television Organization; the National Iranian Oil Company; and the National Film Company. By the mid-1970s, the state was trying to meet the ever-rising demand for popular films by producing more than fifty full-features a year. Although most were B movies made to compete with Indian Bollywood, a few, notably *Gav* (Cow) and *Tangsir*, contained social content and attained instant success among the intelligentsia. *Gav*, based on a short story by the radical playwright Ghulam-Hussein Saedi, depicted rural poverty. *Tangsir*, adapted from a popular short story written in the 1940s by Sadeq Chubak, then a Tudeh sympathizer, depicted the heroic struggle of a dispossessed peasant who took to arms to rectify injustices inflicted by local power-brokers, including clerics, money lenders, and government officials. The region of Tangsir in the south was famous for having caused the British a great deal of trouble during World War I. In later years, when a prominent film-maker was asked how come the best movies produced in this period were all financed by the state, he replied that film-makers, as intellectuals, had the responsibility to produce art containing social realism and social criticism.[10]

The third pillar, court patronage, experienced equally impressive growth. Established in 1958 as a tax-exempt charity, the Pahlavi Foundation began holding in trust for the nation the previous shah's landed estates. It then incorporated most of the fixed assets of the current shah as well as those of his sixty-four family members, many of whom received lucrative commissions for serving on corporate boards. The foundation received a further boost when it began to siphon off substantial sums from the annual oil revenues. At its height, the Pahlavi Foundation had assets worth in excess of $3 billion, with shares in 207 companies active in such diverse fields as mining, construction, automobile manufacturing, metal works, agrobusinesses, food processing, banking, insurance, and tourism (casinos, cabarets, and grand hotels). It also had shares in international corporations such as Krupp and General Electric. The shah's personal portfolio was estimated to be more than $1 billion. The royal family's total assets were estimated to be in excess of $20 billion.[11] The *New York Times* reported in 1979 that: "Behind the façade of charitable activities the foundation is apparently used in three ways: as a source of funds for the royal family, as a means of

exerting control over the economy, and as a conduit for rewards to supporters of the regime."[12] The opposition at home described the foundation
as a giant octopus whose tentacles tapped into almost all spheres of economic activity.

The shah used the military, bureaucracy, and court patronage to pack the
cabinet and parliament with his own placemen. He amended the constitution, giving himself the authority to appoint prime ministers. He also
increased the size of the Majles to 200 deputies and its term to four full
years. Of the eight men who headed cabinets between 1953 and 1977, all but
two were his personal favorites. The exceptions were General Zahedi and
Ali Amini. Zahedi, who was handpicked for the coup by the CIA and MI6,
was eased out after twenty months – even though his son had married the
shah's only daughter. The shah packed him off to Switzerland after spreading rumors that he had embezzled large sums. The British ambassador
reported that the shah wanted to break constitutional precedent and
make clear who was boss by replacing Zahedi during a parliamentary
recess.[13] To make it doubly clear, the shah announced that he personally
would preside over weekly cabinet meetings. Amini, a liberal scion of the
Ashtiyani family, had been foisted on the shah by the Kennedy administration in the hope that he would launch land reform. He was forced out as
soon as he tried to trim the military budget. The shah indicted some of
Amini's ministers for embezzlement.

All the other six premiers were the shah's nominees. They were mostly
young European-educated civil servants from prominent families that had
hitched their careers to the Pahlavi dynasty. Amir Hussein Ala (Mu'en al-
Vezareh) came from a long line of landed magnates in central Iran. His father,
Ala al-Saltaneh, had represented Nasser al-Din Shah in Britain. He himself
had studied at Westminster School, spent years in the diplomatic corps, and
served as court minister in 1950 and stop-gap premier in 1951 before
Mossadeq's election. The British reported that Ala "tends to overrate the
shah's virtues and does little to curb the latter's ambitions to rule the country
in much the same way as his father."[14] His wife was the daughter of the last
Qajar regent and had been one of the first women to discard the veil.
Manucher Eqbal was a French-educated physician who had moved from
hospital administration into government service. He had been dismissed as
governor of Azerbaijan by Mossadeq. His daughter was married to one of the
shah's half-brothers. Jafar Sharif-Emami was a German-trained railway engineer who had been arrested by the British during World War II. He spent
much of his life in government service. As president of the Senate for fifteen
years and as long-time deputy chair of the Pahlavi Foundation, he facilitated

Table 9 *Prime ministers, 1953–77*

	Cabinet	Birth	Father's occupation	Career	Education	Foreign languages
Zahedi Fazlollah	August 1953–April 1955	1890	Small landlord	Cossacks	Cossacks	Turkish
Ala Hussein	April 1955–June 1956	1884	Big landlord	Foreign office	Britain	English
Eqbal Manucher	June 1956–August 1960	1908	Small landlord	Medicine	France	French
Sharif-Emami Jafar	August 1960–June 1961	1910	Cleric	Engineer, civil servant	Germany	German
Amini Ali	June 1961–July 1962	1903	Big landlord	Lawyer, civil servant	France	French
Alam Asadallah	July 1962–March 1964	1919	Big landlord	Civil servant	France	French, English
Mansur Hassan	March 1964–January 1965	1924	Civil servant	Civil servant	France	French
Hoveida Abbas	January 1965–August 1977	1919	Civil servant	Civil servant	Beirut	French

lucrative contracts and thereby was dubbed Mr. Five Percent. Asadallah Alam came from the famous Baluchi family known as the "lords of the marshes." He was married to the daughter of Qavam al-Mulk of Shiraz. He had governed Kerman and Baluchestan before entering the court. A personal friend of the shah, Alam shared with him the call girls he imported from Paris.[15] Hassan-Ali Mansur was the son of Ali Mansur (Mansur al-Mamalek), the prime minister at the time of the Allied invasion. Educated in France, the younger Mansur had spent much of his life in government service. He was reputed to have told the Majles deputies that he did not care what they thought since he considered himself "His Majesty's servant." In 1965, he was assassinated by former members of the Fedayan-e Islam.

Mansur was succeeded by Amir Abbas Hoveida, his friend and brother-in-law. Hoveida, who also came from a family of civil servants, remained at the helm for a full twelve years – the longest term in modern Iran. He preferred to address the shah in French and English. In 1977, he was sacrificed to the religious opposition, which accused him of being a secret Bahai simply because his grandfather had been a Babi. Hoveida liked to boast that he was one of the shah's "new men." In the words of one foreign diplomat, the shah treated Hoveida and other ministers "as if they were office boys – and they loved it."[16] Every Nowruz, the shah held grand audiences in the royal palace with the leading dignitaries bowing before him and holding hands over their private parts – a gesture which to some was reminiscent of the days when ministers were household slaves and as such could be castrated by their royal masters.

These premiers used their influence to pack their cabinets and parliaments – so much so that both were deemed to be mere rubber stamps. The ministers – like the premiers – were mostly young Western-educated government officials.[17] Likewise, the Senators and Majles deputies were mostly professionals and career civil servants, with a smattering of landlords willing to follow the shah's leadership.[18] For most of these years, the Majles was divided into two major blocs: the majority formed first of Eqbal's National (*Melliyun*) Party, and then of Mansur and Hoveida's New Iran (*Iran Novin*) Party; and the minority formed of Alam's People's (*Mardom*) Party. The shah – with the help of SAVAK – would assign deputies their party affiliation. Not surprisingly, the two became known interchangeably as the "yes" and the "yes, sir" or "yes, of course" parties. In his 1961 memoirs *Mission for My Country* – ghost written by an American – the shah argued that he was fully committed to a multi-party system. "If I were a dictator rather than a constitutional monarch then I might be tempted to sponsor a single dominant party such as Hitler organized or such as you find today in Communist countries. But as constitutional monarch I can afford to encourage large scale party activity free from the strait-jacket of one party rule or the one party state."[19] In these years, the shah still liked to bill himself as a sincere "democrat" determined to "modernize" a highly "traditional society."

SOCIAL TRANSFORMATIONS (1953–77)

The shah used his newly gained power to bring about changes in the larger society. He began slowly with modest programs designed to complete those started by his father. He picked up pace after 1963, when he launched a White Revolution explicitly designed both to compete with and preempt a Red Revolution from below. He outdid his father by staging with much fanfare a multi-million dollar coronation in which he crowned not only himself but also his new wife, Farah Diba. Soraya, his second wife, had been discarded for failing to produce an heir – again reminiscent of Napoleon. Farah was named *Shahbanou* (Lady Shah) – a Sassanid title. To mark the occasion, he built on the main western entry into Tehran the gigantic Shahyad Monument which literally meant remember the Aryamehr Shah. What is more, he took full advantage of the oil boom to inaugurate with even more fanfare his new Great Civilization. He declared that Iran was at the gates of the Great Civilization; its future would be more glorious than its past – including the Achaemenid, Sassanid, and Pathian empires; its standard of living would soon surpass that of Europe; it would produce a way of life superior to both capitalism and communism; and indeed within a generation it would be the world's fifth most powerful country – after the USA, Soviet Union, Japan, and China. He also lectured Westerners on how they were not working hard enough, not paying enough for oil, not conserving valuable resources, not teaching the virtues of social responsibility, and, by not disciplining their youngsters, producing human monsters like those in the popular film *Clockwork Orange*.[20] Westerners retorted that the shah had become a "megalomaniac" with "Napoleonic illusions of grandeur." One secretary of the treasury in Washington described him as a "nut case."

Land reform constituted the centerpiece of the White Revolution. Initiated by Premier Amini in 1962, land reform was adopted by the shah in 1963 and touted as his most important achievement. Amini's initial plan limited landlords to one village. Excess land was to be transferred to share-croppers with tenancy rights. The watered-down version allowed landlords to pass villages to close relatives as well as to keep for themselves orchards, woodlands, plantations, mechanized farms, and agrobusinesses. Religious foundations were also allowed to keep their long-standing endowments (*awqafs*). Despite these dilutions, land reform accomplished what it was

Table 10 *Military expenditures, 1954–77*
(at 1973 prices and exchange rates)

Year	Expenditure ($ million)
1954	60
1955	64
1956	68
1957	203
1958	326
1959	364
1960	290
1961	290
1962	287
1963	292
1964	323
1965	434
1966	598
1967	752
1968	852
1969	759
1970	958
1971	944
1972	1,300
1973	1,800
1974	4,000
1975	5,500
1976	5,700
1977	7,200

Source: Stockholm International Peace Research Institute, *World Armaments and Disarmament: Year Book for 1977* (Cambridge: MIT Press, 1977), pp. 228–29.

designed to do, undercut the notables, even though some large landowners, including the Pahlavi family, managed to transform themselves into successful commercial farmers. Land reform made redundant such terms as *fudal*, *a'yan* (notables), *ashraf* (aristocracy), and *omdeh malek* (large landlords). It instead stratified the countryside into some 1,300 commercial enterprises each owning more than 200 hectares; some 640,000 landlords – many of them absentees – owning between 10 and 200 hectares; 1,200,000 families – most former sharecroppers with tenancy rights – owning less than 10 hectares; and more than 700,000 laborers – all former non-tenant peasants. Since 10 hectares was the minimum needed to survive in most regions, many smallholders were not better off than the landless laborers.

To receive land, peasants had to join rural cooperatives administered by the ministries of agriculture and rural affairs. In some areas the government set up health clinics and literacy classes. A European anthropologist visiting the Boir Ahmadis noted: "One is amazed at the high level of centralization achieved within the last decade. The government now interferes in practically all aspects of daily life. Land is contracted for cash by the government; fruits get sprayed, crops fertilized, animals fed, beehives set up, carpets woven, goods and babies born, populations controlled, women organized, religion taught and diseases controlled – all by the intervention of the government."[21] What is more, as the nomadic population shrank further, small tribal groups that had given Iran the appearance of being a social mosaic disappeared into oblivion. Similarly, terms such as *tireh* and *taifeh*, as well as *ilkhan* and *ilbeg*, became obsolete. They merely conjured up vague images of a bygone esoteric age.

While land reform transformed the countryside, five-year plans drawn up by the Plan and Budget Organization brought about a minor industrial revolution. They improved port facilities; expanded the Trans-Iranian Railway, linking Tehran to Mashed, Tabriz, and Isfahan; and asphalted the main roads between Tehran and the provincial capitals. They financed petrochemical plants; oil refineries; hydroelectric dams – named after members of the royal family; steel mills in Ahwaz and Isfahan – the Soviets constructed the latter; and a gas pipeline to the Soviet Union. The state also bolstered the private sector both by erecting tariff walls to protect consumer industries and by channeling low-interest loans via the Industrial and Mining Development Bank to court-favored businessmen. Old landed families – such as the Bayats, Moqadams, Davalus, Afshars, Qarahgozlus, Esfandiyaris, and Farmanfarmas – became capitalist entrepreneurs. *Le Monde* wrote that the shah – much like the kings of early nineteenth-century France – encouraged entrepreneurs to "enrich themselves," showering them with low-interest loans, exempting them from taxation, and protecting them from foreign competition.[22] Between 1953 and 1975, the number of small factories increased from 1,500 to more than 7,000; medium-sized factories from 300 to more than 800; and large factories – employing more than 500 workers – from fewer than 100 to more than 150. They included textile, machine tool, and car assembly plants in Tehran, Isfahan, Shiraz, Tabriz, Ahwaz, Arak, and Kermanshah. The smaller plants specialized in clothing, food processing, including beverages, cement, bricks, tiles, paper, and home appliances. The regime's showpieces were the Dezful Dam in Khuzestan, the steel mills in Isfahan, and the nuclear plant in Bushire. Key production figures indicate the extent of this industrial revolution.

Table 11 Industrial production, 1953–77

White Revolution

	1953	1977
Coal (tons)	200,000	900,000
Iron ore (tons)	5,000	930,000
Steel and aluminum (tons)	–	275,000
Cement (tons)	53,000	4,300,000
Sugar (tons)	70,000	527,000
Electricity (kw hours)	200 million	14 billion
Cotton textiles (meters)	110 million	533 million
Tractors	–	7,700
Motor vehicles	–	109,000

The state also pressed ahead with social programs. The number of educational institutions grew threefold after the launching of the White Revolution. Enrollment in kindergartens increased from 13,300 to 221,990; in elementary schools from 1,640,000 to 4,080,00; in secondary schools from 370,000 to 741,000; in vocational schools from 14,240 to 227,000; in colleges from 24,885 to 145,210; and in colleges abroad from 18,000 to 80,000. What is more, a Literacy Corps – modeled on the Cuban version – was declared to be an integral part of the White Revolution. It helped raise the literacy rate from 26 to 42 percent. Health programs increased the number of doctors from 4,000 to 12,750; nurses from 1,969 to 4,105; medical clinics from 700 to 2,800; and hospital beds from 24,100 to 48,000. These improvements, together with the elimination of famines and childhood epidemics, raised the overall population from 18,954,706 in 1956 – when the first national census was taken – to 33,491,000 in 1976. On the eve of the revolution, nearly half the population was younger than sixteen. The White Revolution also expanded to include women's issues. Women gained the right to vote; to run for elected office; and to serve in the judiciary – first as lawyers, later as judges. The 1967 Family Protection Law restricted men's power to get divorces, take multiple wives, and obtain child custody. It also raised the marriageable age for women to fifteen. Although the veil was never banned outright, its use in public institutions was discouraged. What is more, the Literacy and Health Corps established special branches designed to extend educational and medical facilities, especially birth control information, to women.

These changes produced a complex class structure.[23] At the apex was an upper class formed of a narrow circle of families linked to the Pahlavi court – the royal family itself, senior politicians and government officials, military

5.1 Set celebrating aspects of the White Revolution

5.2 Set commemorating Reza Shah

5.2 (cont.)

5.3 Stamp set commemorating the fiftieth anniversary of the Pahlavi dynasty

officers, as well as court-connected entrepreneurs, industrialists, and commercial farmers. Some came from old families; others were self-made men with court connections; yet others had married into the elite. Together they owned more than 85 percent of the large firms involved in insurance, banking, manufacturing, and urban construction. Although the vast majority came from Shi'i backgrounds, a few had Bahai connections, and some had joined the secretive Freemasons. This provided fuel for those who claimed that Iran was really controlled behind the scenes by the British through the Freemasons and by the Zionists through the Bahais who had located their headquarters in Haifa.

The middle layers were formed of two very distinct classes: the bazaar petty bourgeoisie which constituted a traditional middle class; and a modern middle class composed of white-collar employees and college-educated professionals. The propertied middle class constituted more than a million families – as much as 13 percent of the working population. It included not only bazaar shopkeepers and workshop owners, but also small manufacturers and absentee farmers owning between 50 and 100 hectares. It also included much of the ulama – both because of family links and because of historic links between mosque and bazaar. Despite economic modernization, the bazaar continued to control as much as half of the country's handicraft production, two-thirds of its retail trade, and three-quarters of its wholesale trade. It continued to retain craft and trade guilds as well as thousands of mosques, hayats (religious gatherings), husseiniehs (religious lecture halls), and *dastehs* (groups that organized Muharram processions). Ironically, the oil boom gave the traditional middle class the opportunity to finance religious centers and establish private schools that emphasized the importance of Islam. They were specifically designed to prepare the children of the bazaaris for the top universities. Thus the oil money helped nourish tradition.

The salaried middle class numbered more than 700,000 – some 9 percent of the working population. It included 304,000 civil servants in the ever-expanding ministries; some 200,000 teachers and school administrators; and in excess of 60,000 managers, engineers, and professionals. The total exceeded one million, including college students and other aspiring members of the class. In the past, the term intelligentsia – *rowshanfekr* – had been synonymous with the salaried middle class. But with the rapid expansion of the salaried class, the term had become more differentiated and specifically associated with intellectuals – writers, journalists, artists, and professors. The intelligentsia continued to be the bearers of nationalism and socialism.

The urban working class numbered as many as 1,300,000 – more than 30 percent of the labor force. It included some 880,000 in modern industrial factories; 30,000 plus oil workers; 20,000 gas, electrical, and power plant workers; 30,000 fishery and lumberyard workers; 50,000 miners; 150,000 dock workers, railwaymen, truck drivers, and other transport workers; and 600,000 workers in small plants. The total grows even larger if one adds the rapidly increasing army of shantytown poor formed of immigrants squeezed out of their villages by the lack of land. Migrants scraped out a living as construction workers, and, if there were no jobs on construction sites, as peddlers and hawkers. Tehran took in the largest influx of rural migrants, with population growth from 1.5 million in 1953 to more than 5.5 million in 1979. By the time of the revolution, 46 percent of the country's population lived in urban centers.

The rural population – some 40 percent of the labor force – consisted of three strata: prosperous farmers, hard-pressed smallholders, and village laborers. The first layer included former village headmen, bailiffs, and oxen-owning tenant sharecroppers who had benefited most from land reform. They numbered around 600,000 – less than 17 percent of the rural population. The second included some 1,100,000 sharecroppers who had received less than 10 hectares – the minimum needed in most regions. Many had no choice but to exchange their small plots for shares in state cooperatives. The third comprised peasants without sharecropping rights. Having received no land whatsoever, they survived as farm hands, shepherds, laborers, day commuters to nearby towns, and wage earners employed in the many small plants that flourished in the country-side during the early 1970s – small plants manufacturing carpets, shoes, clothes, and paper. Some migrated to the urban centers. Thus the White Revolution failed to provide land to the bulk of the rural population.

SOCIAL TENSIONS

These changes intensified social tensions in three major ways. First, they more than quadrupled the combined size of the two classes that had posed the most serious challenge to the Pahlavis in the past – the intelligentsia and the urban working class. Their resentments also intensified since they were grew systematically stripped of organizations that had in one way or another represented them during the interregnum – professional associations, trade unions, independent newspapers, and political parties. At the same time, land reform had undercut the rural notables who for centuries had controlled their peasants and tribesmen. Land reform had instead produced large numbers of independent farmers and landless laborers who could

Upper class

0.1%	Pahlavi family; military officers; senior civil servants, court-connected entrepreneurs

Middle classes

10% modern (salaried)	13% traditional (propertied)
professionals civil servants office employees college students	clerics bazaaris small-factory owners workshop owners commercial farmers

Lower classes

32% urban	45% rural
industrial workers small factory workers workshop workers construction workers peddlers unemployed	landed peasants near landless peasants landless peasants rural unemployed

Figure 1 Class structure (labor force in the 1970s)

easily become loose political cannons. The White Revolution had been designed to preempt a Red Revolution. Instead, it paved the way for an Islamic Revolution. Furthermore, the steady growth in population, compounded by the shortage of arable land, produced ever-expanding shanty-towns. By the mid-1970s, the regime faced a host of social problems of a magnitude unimaginable in the past.

Second, the regime's preferred method of development – the "trickle-down" theory of economics – inevitably widened the gap between haves and have-nots. Its strategy was to funnel oil wealth to the court-connected elite who would then set up factories, companies, and agrobusinesses. In theory, wealth would trickle down. But in practice, in Iran, as has been the case in many other countries, wealth tended to stick at the top, with less and less finding its way down the social ladder. Wealth, like ice in hot weather, melted in the process of being passed from hand to hand. The result was not surprising. In the 1950s, Iran had one of the most unequal income

Table 12 *Urban household expenditures (decile distribution in percent)*

Deciles (poorest to richest)	1959–60	1973–74
1st	1.7	1.3
2nd	2.9	2.4
3rd	4.0	3.4
4th	5.0	4.7
5th	6.1	5.0
6th	7.3	6.8
7th	8.9	9.3
8th	11.8	11.1
9th	16.4	17.5
10th	35.3	37.9

distributions in the Third World. By the 1970s, it had – according to the International Labor Office – one of the very worst in the whole world.[24] Although we have no hard data on actual income distribution, the Central Bank carried out surveys on household urban expenditures in 1959–60 and 1973–74 – a methodology that would inevitably underestimate real inequality. The 1959–60 survey showed that the richest 10 percent accounted for 35.2 percent of total expenditures; the poorest 10 percent only 1.7 percent of expenditures. The figures were worse in 1973–74. They showed that the richest 10 percent accounted for 37.9 percent; and the poorest 10 percent 1.3 percent of total expenditures. A leaked document from the Plan and Budget Organization showed that the income share of the richest 20 percent of the urban population had grown from 57 to 63 percent in the period between 1973 and 1975.[25] It also showed that the gap between urban and rural consumption had dramatically widened. Inequality was most visible in Tehran where the rich lived in their northern palaces and the poor in their shantytown hovels without public amenities – especially a decent transport system. A member of the royal family was rumored to have commented that "if people did not like being stuck in traffic jams why didn't they buy helicopters?" In the words of a Pentagon journal, the oil boom had brought "inequality" and "corruption to a boiling point."[26]

Finally, the White Revolution and the subsequent oil boom produced widespread resentments by drastically raising but not meeting public expectations. It was true that social programs made strides in improving educational and health facilities. But it was equally true that after two decades, Iran still had one of the worst infant mortality and doctor–patient rates in the Middle East. It also had one of the lowest percentages of the population in higher education. Moreover, 68 percent of adults remained illiterate, 60 percent of children did not complete primary school, and only 30 percent of applicants found university places within the country. Increasing numbers went abroad where they remained for good. By the 1970s, there were more Iranian doctors in New York than in any city outside Tehran. The term "brain drain" was first attached to Iran.

It was true that the White Revolution provided some farmers with land, cooperatives, tractors, and fertilizers. But it was equally true that the White Revolution did not touch much of the countryside. Most peasants received no or little land. Most villages were left without electricity, schools, piped water, rural roads, and other basic amenities. What is more, government-imposed prices on agricultural goods favored the urban sector at the expense of the countryside. This lowered incentives – even for those farmers who had benefited from land reform. This, in turn, stifled production at a time of rapid population growth. As a result, Iran, which in the 1960s had been a net exporter of food, was spending as much as $1 billion a year in the mid-1970s importing agricultural products. It is true that economic growth did benefit those who gained access to modern housing and such consumer goods as refrigerators, telephones, televisions, and private cars. But it is equally true that this growth tended to widen the gap not only between rich and poor, but also between the capital city and the outlying provinces. Of course, the state's center of gravity was very much located at the capital. The Industrial and Mining Bank compounded this imbalance by channeling 60 percent of its loans into the capital. By the mid-1970s, Tehran – with less than 20 percent of the country's population – had more than 68 percent of its civil servants; 82 percent of its registered companies; 50 percent of its manufacturing production; 66 percent of its university students; 50 percent of its doctors; 42 percent of its hospital beds; 40 percent of its cinema-going public; 70 percent of its travelers abroad; 72 percent of its printing presses; and 80 percent of its newspaper readers. One in ten of Tehran's residents had a car; elsewhere the figure was one in ninety.[27] In the words of a British economist: "Those who live in Tehran have the chance of better access to education, health facilities, the media, jobs and money – to say nothing of access to the decision-making processes. Not surprisingly people in villages or other towns are prepared to come to Tehran in the hope of better life, ignoring the problems of high rents, overcrowding and pollution."[28] Frances FitzGerald summed up the overall disparities: "Iran is basically worse off than a country like Syria that has had neither oil nor political stability. The reason for all this is simply that the Shah has never made a serious attempt at development . . . The wealth of the country has gone into private cars rather than buses, into consumer goods rather than public health, and into the salaries of soldiers and policemen rather than those of teachers."[29]

POLITICAL TENSIONS

Social tensions intensified political radicalism – not only among the intelligentsia and the modern middle class, but also among the ulama and the traditional middle class. The two outstanding figures articulating this radicalism were: Ali Shariati, a French-educated social scientist, highly popular among college and high school students; and Ayatollah Ruhollah Khomeini, who had been exiled after 1963 for accusing the shah of granting Americans "capitulations." For some, Shariati, who died in 1977, was the true ideologue of the Islamic Revolution. For others, Khomeini was not only the leader of the revolution, but also the *faqeh* (jurist) who formulated the concept of *Velayat-e Faqeh* (Jurist's Guardianship): the cornerstone of the future Islamic Republic. The 1979 revolution has often been labeled fundamentalist. In fact, it was a complex combination of nationalism, political populism, and religious radicalism.

Shariati was typical of the new generation of college-educated professionals coming from traditional middle-class backgrounds. He was born in rural Khurasan into a small landowning clerical family. Throughout his life he stressed his modest provincial roots. His father, a school teacher, had discarded his turban but continued to teach scripture in state schools in Mashed. He also founded the Center for the Propagation of Islamic Truth, set up the local chapter of the Movement of God-Worshipping Socialists, and staunchly supported Mossadeq during the oil crisis. Conservatives insinuated that the Shariatis were secret "Sunnis," "Wahhabis," and even "Babis." Graduating from Teachers College in Mashed, the younger Shariati taught in a village school; entered Mashed University to study Arabic and French; and translated from Arabic *Abu Zarr: Khodaparast-e Sosiyalist* (Abu Zarr: The God Worshipping Socialist) – a biography of one of the Prophet's less well-known Companions. This book, the first of many, argued that Abu Zarr had been the forerunner of socialism in world history. In eulogizing his son, the elder Shariati argued that he had "tried to live up to Abu Zarr's principles from the day he read the biography to the moment he died."[30] Others eulogized him as the "Abu Zarr of Iran."[31]

Winning a state scholarship to France, Shariati spent the turbulent early 1960s at the Sorbonne. He attended lectures given by Georges Gurvich, the Marxist sociologist, and Louis Massignon and Henri Corbin, French orientalists interested in Islamic mysticism. He translated Massignon's book on Salman Pak, whom he described as "the first Muslim, the first Shi'i, and the first Iranian to fight on behalf of Imam Ali." He participated in demonstrations for Algerian and Congolese independence – he was beaten up badly in one such demonstration. He wrote articles for the organ of the Confederation of Iranian Students – an organization formed by younger members of both Tudeh and the National Front. He translated Jean Paul Sartre's *What is Poetry?*, and Che Guevara's *Guerrilla Warfare*. He began translating Franz Fanon's *Wretched of the Earth* and a book on the Algerian war entitled *Le Meilleur Combat*. He praised the latter's author as a *Musulman-e Marksisti* (Muslim Marxist). He was also exposed to Christian Liberation Theology through the Catholic journal *L'Esprit*, which in those years ran many articles on the Christian–Marxist dialogue as well as on national liberation movements in the Third World.

Returning to Iran in 1965, Shariati spent the next decade teaching in Mashed and Tehran, where a group of religious philanthropists had recently established a famous lecture hall named the *Husseinieh-e Ershad*. His lectures were circulated widely both through booklets and through recorded tapes. They were later published in thirty-five book-length volumes. He was eventually arrested and forced to leave for England where he dropped dead at the age of forty-four, prompting some to suspect SAVAK of foul play.[32] By then Shariati was a household name. His prolific works have one dominant theme: that the true essence of Shi'ism is revolution against all forms of oppression, especially against feudalism, capitalism, and imperialism. According to Shariati, the Prophet Muhammad had been sent to establish not just a new religion but a dynamic society in permanent revolution moving toward a classless utopia. Imam Ali had opposed the early Caliphs not just because they had usurped authority but because they had betrayed the true mission by compromising with the powers-that-be. Imam Hussein had died in Karbala not just because of predestined fate but because of the burning desire to keep alive the true content of Islam. Similarly, the task of the contemporary intelligentsia was not just to write and contemplate, but to rediscover and revitalize the true essence of revolutionary Islam. According to him, Shi'ism had a coherent *jahanbeni* (world view) in which the main motor of human development was interchangeably *jebr-e tarikhi* (historical determinism), *harakat-e dialektiki* (dialectical movement), and *dialektik-e tarikhi* (historical dialectics).

Shariati injected radical meanings into stock scriptural terms. He transformed *ummat* (community) into dynamic society in permanent revolution; *towhid* (monotheism) into social solidarity; *imamat* (rule of the imam) into charismatic leadership; *jehad* (crusade) into liberation struggle; *mojahed* (crusader) into revolutionary fighter; *shahed* (martyr) into revolutionary hero; *momen* (pious) into genuine fighter; *kafer* (unbeliever) into passive observer; *sherk* (idol worship) into political submission; *entezar* (expectation of the Messiah) into expectation of the revolution; *tafsir* (scriptural commentary) into the skill of extracting radical meaning from sacred texts; and, perhaps most significant of all, *mostazafen* (the meek) into the oppressed masses – as in the wretched of the earth. He also transformed the Cain–Abel fable into a metaphor for the class struggle; and the Karbala paradigm into a morality lesson on revolutionary self-sacrifice. He coined the slogan: "Every Place, Karbala. Every Day, Ashura. Every Month, Muharram." He described Imam Hussein as an early-day Che Guevara; Fatemeh – the Prophet's daughter – as a long suffering mother; and Zaynab – Hussein's sister – as an exemplary woman who kept alive the revolutionary message. Not surprisingly, many credited Shariati with transforming Islam from a *din* (religion) and *mazhab* (faith) into a political *idologi* (ideology) known in the West interchangeably as Islamism, political Islam, or radical Islam.

In drastically reinterpreting Islam, Shariati did not shy away from denouncing the conservative and apolitical ulama. He accused them of using religion as a mass "opiate"; draining away its living soul and turning it into a dry dogma; obsessing with esoteric issues, mumbo-jumbo, and ritual cleanliness; collaborating with both the ruling class and the bazaar petty bourgeoisie; replacing the Red Shi'ism of the Imams with the Black Shi'ism of the Safavid dynasty; and, on the whole, being more concerned with theology, philosophy, and *feqh* (law) than with faith, action, and commitment. He drew sharp contrasts between Islam of the *mojtaheds* (clerical leaders) and Islam of the *mojaheds* (religious fighters):[33]

It is necessary to explain what we mean by Islam. By it we mean the Islam of Abu Zarr; not that of the caliphs; the Islam of justice and proper leadership, not that of the rulers, the aristocrats and the upper class; the Islam of freedom, progress and consciousness; not that of slavery, captivity and passivity; the Islam of the mojaheds, not that of the clergy; the Islam of virtue, personal responsibility and protest; not that of (religious) dissimulation, (clerical) intercession, and (divine) intervention; the Islam of struggle for faith, society, and scientific knowledge; not that of surrender, dogmatism, and uncritical imitation (taqlid) of the clergy.

Shariati's most radical views come in his last work, *Jehatger-ye Tabaqat-e Islam* (Islam's Class Bias).[34] He argues that the clergy have an organic relationship with the propertied classes since they derive their income from endowments, *khoms* (religious taxes), and *sahm-e imam* (imam's share). "Do you know," he asks rhetorically, "what the real problem of contemporary Islam is?" His answer is that Islam has consummated an unholy marriage with the *khordeh-e bourzhuazi* (petty bourgeoisie). In this marriage, the clergy makes religion comfortable for the bazaar and the bazaar makes the world comfortable for the clergy. Just as, in the age of feudalism, Islam justified the power of the landlords, so now, in the age of capitalism, it condones that of the bazaar merchants. He further takes on the clergy for giving themselves fancy new titles such as ayatollah and hojjat al-islam; for hiding from the people the fact that their leaders had been shepherds, craftsmen, and farmers; and for diluting Islam's radicalism into watered-down paternalism. He concludes that since the ulama have forfeited the task of propagating the true message of Islam, that mission has been passed on to the intelligentsia. "The task at hand," he declares, "is nothing less than the total liberation of Islam from the clergy and the propertied classes."

While Shariati's works appealed mostly to the young intelligentsia, Khomeini's pronouncements were directed predominantly to the ulama. Living in Najaf after 1963, Khomeini gradually developed his own interpretation of Shi'i Islam which can be best described as a form of clerical populism. He articulated his ideas first in a series of lectures to seminary students in 1970, and then published anonymously under the title *Velayat-e Faqeh: Hokumat-e Islami* (The Jurist's Guardianship: Islamic Government).[35] This work had little circulation outside the narrow circle of theology students until after the 1979 revolution. According to his new interpretation, the senior mojtaheds specializing in *feqh* (law) had the ultimate authority to rule the state. He came to this novel conclusion from conventional Shi'i premises: that God had sent the Prophets and the Imams to guide the community; that these Prophets and Imams had left behind the shari'a to keep the community on the right path; and that in the absence of the Twelfth Imam, his deputies in the world, the senior mojtaheds, became guardians of the shari'a. The traditional ulama had used the term *velayat-e faqeh* (jurist's guardianship) to mean the mojtaheds' jurisdiction over religious foundations and those in dire need of guidance – namely minors, widows, and the mentally incapacitated. Khomeini, however, expanded the term to encompass the whole population. He also interpreted the Koranic injunction "Obey God, the Prophet, and those who have authority" to mean the contemporary mojtaheds. As one of Khomeini's followers later admitted, this expanded meaning of *velayat-e faqeh* has no precedent either in the Koran, or in the shari'a, or in the teachings of the Twelve Imams.[36] Khomeini himself argued that his ideas would sound strange to some ears because for centuries monarchists, imperialists, and others had worked hard to falsify Islam.

Khomeini's break with tradition was not restricted to the issue of *velayat-e faqeh*. He argued that monarchy itself was a pagan (*taqut*) institution left over from the age of polytheism (*sherk*) and therefore incompatible with true Islam. He claimed that Moses had come to free people from pharaohs; that the Prophet Muhammad had deemed *malek al-mamalek* – which Khomeini associated with shah-in-shah – to be the most detestable of all titles; that the Ummayids, by establishing their Caliphate, had perpetuated Roman and Sassanid traditions; and that Imam Hussein, in raising the banner of revolt, had tried to liberate the people from hereditary monarchs. Muslims, Khomeini insisted, have the sacred duty to oppose all monarchies. They must not collaborate with them, have recourse to their institutions, pay for the bureaucrats, or practice dissimulation to protect themselves. On the contrary, they have the duty to rise up against them. Most kings have been criminals, oppressors, and mass murderers. In later years, Khomeini went further, arguing that all monarchs without exception had been corrupt. He even dismissed as thoroughly unjust the famous Anushirvan whom Iranians called "the Just."[37] For twelve centuries, the Shi'i ulama, including Khomeini, had accepted the monarchy – either as desirable, or, at least, as necessary to prevent worse calamities. They had deemed one day of anarchy to be worse than ten years of autocracy. The new Khomeini, however, broke with this tradition, arguing that Muslims had the sacred duty to carry out a root-and-branch destruction of the monarchy.

While Khomeini stressed *velayat-e faqeh* in seminary teachings, he scrupulously avoided the subject in public pronouncements. Instead, he hammered the regime on a host of political, social, and economic shortcomings.[38] He denounced the shah for supporting Israel against the Muslim world; allying with the West in the Cold War; undermining Islam by blindly imitating all things foreign and thereby spreading *gharbzadegi* (plague from the West); favoring cronies, relatives, Bahais, and *kravatis* (tie-wearers); wasting resources on the ever-expanding military; neglecting agriculture in order to turn the country into a lucrative dumping ground for American food exporters; failing to bring essential services, especially schools, clinics, electricity, and clean water, to the villages; neglecting to build low-income housing and thereby creating huge shantytowns; bankrupting the bazaars by failing to protect them from foreigners and court-connected entrepreneurs; and compounding urban problems by failing to combat crime, alcoholism, prostitution, and drug addiction. In making these denunciations, Khomeini increasing resorted to potent terms he had rarely used before – such as mostazafen, shahed, taqut, *tabaqeh* (class), and *enqelab* (revolution). He sprinkled his declarations with radical sound bites that were later adopted as revolutionary street slogans:

Islam belongs to the oppressed (*mostazafen*), not to the oppressors (*mostakbaren*)
Islam represents the slum-dwellers (*zaghehneshin*), not the palace-dwellers (*kakhneshin*)
Islam is not the opiate of the masses
The poor die for the revolution, the rich plot against the revolution
The oppressed (*mostazafen*) of the world, unite
Oppressed of the world, create a Party of the Oppressed
Neither East nor West, but Islam
We are for Islam, not for capitalism and feudalism
Islam will eliminate class differences
Islam originates from the masses, not from the rich
In Islam there will be no landless peasant
The duty of the clergy is to liberate the poor from the clutches of the rich

By the mid-1970s, tension between state and society had reached breaking point. The signs were there for all to see – although few at the time in the West and within the regime chose to see them. Khomeini's denunciations had become more vociferous. Some of his disciples were openly calling for the replacement of the monarchy with a republic – something completely unprecedented in Shi'i Iran. Shariati's ideas were spreading like wildfire among the young intelligentsia. Some of his followers had formed a guerrilla organization named *Mojahedin-e Khalq* (People's Mojahedin). The secular opposition had also grown more radical with its youth talking increasingly about lessons to be learnt from the "armed struggle" in Algeria, Vietnam, China, Cuba, and Latin America. In 1971, former youth members of Tudeh and the National Front launched their own guerrilla organization named *Fedayin-e Khalq* (People's Fedayin) – not to be confused with the religious fundamentalist Fedayan-e Islam. In the following years, the Fedayin and Mojahedin, together with smaller Marxist and Islamic groups, carried out a series of daring raids, bombings, assassinations, and attempted kidnappings of members of the royal family. Meanwhile, the Confederation of Iranian Students Abroad became a forum for the exiled opposition, and in Iran yearly on December 7 – the unofficial student day – general strikes broke out in many of the country's thirteen universities. The day commemorated the death of three students – two from the Tudeh and one from the National Front – who had been killed in 1953 protesting the visit of

Vice-President Nixon. The 1953 coup haunted Iran in more ways than one. The regime retaliated with more arrests, torture, executions, disappearances, and forced confessions. Eric Rouleau of *Le Monde* warned that economic development, especially the policy of "bourgeoisiefication," had ended up aggravating social tensions.[39] Yet another sign of this was an impasse in the two-party system. For two decades, the shah had choreographed the political stage through his two loyal parties. In 1974–75, however, the Mardom Party – the royal opposition – unexpectedly won a series of by-elections by running local candidates with few court links. These unforeseen victories unsettled the shah and SAVAK as well as the prime minister and his Iran-e Novin Party. The rumor mills gained even more momentum when in the midst of these events the leader of the Mardom Party was killed in a car accident. The two-party façade was clearly falling apart.[40] The political system was in dire need of a drastic remedy.

ONE-PARTY STATE

The remedy came in the shape of Samuel Huntington. This distinguished political scientist was best known in the early 1970s for his book *Political Order in Changing Societies* – at the time a must-read for any graduate course on political development.[41] According to Huntington, rapid "modernization" in the economic and social realms generates new demands, new pressures, and new tensions in the political realm. In other words, in the Third World political instability inevitably follows social modernization. To prevent revolution, Huntington argued that governments had to create one-party states in which the sole party would serve as an organic link with the country, mobilizing the population, transmitting orders from above to below, and, at the same time, channeling upward interests from below. It would also provide the state with cadres of disciplined and reliable foot soldiers. Not surprisingly, some heard in Huntington echoes of Lenin. Huntington's concepts gained currency when young PhDs returned from America and gained access to government thinktanks. Ironically, similar ideas were being circulated by a clique of ex-Tudeh members, who had been expelled from their party for collaborating with the regime, and had reentered politics under the patronage of Alam, the former premier and southern magnate who headed the Mardom Party. Politics make strange bedfellows.

The shah did a sudden about-face in March 1975. Dissolving the Mardom and Iran-e Novin Parties, he declared with much fanfare the establishment of the brand new Resurgence Party (*Hezb-e Rastakhiz*). He

announced that in future Iran would be a one-party state; that all facets of
political life would come under the supervision of the party; that all citizens
had the duty both to vote in national elections and to join the party; that
those reluctant to join must be "secret communists"; and that such "traitors"
would have the choice of either going to prison or leaving the country –
preferably for the Soviet Union. When European journalists pointed out
that such language differed from earlier pronouncements, he retorted:
"Freedom of thought! Freedom of thought! Democracy! Democracy?
What do these words mean? I don't want any part of them."[42] In typical
fashion, SAVAK acted quickly, removing from all libraries and bookstores
the shah's memoirs, *Mission for My Country*, which had waxed ecstatic
about the virtue of multi-party systems over those of one-party states.
Orwell would have had a good chuckle in his grave.

The Resurgence Party acted true to form. It elected a politburo with
Hoveida as its secretary-general; an executive committee of 50; and a central
committee of 150 – both committees were packed with former leaders from
the Iran-e Novin and Mardom Parties. It announced that it would observe
the principles of "democratic centralism," synthesize the best of "capitalism" and "socialism," establish "dialectical" links between government and
population, and assist the Great Guide (*Rahbar*) and Great Leader
(*Farmdandar*) in completing his White Revolution – now named the
Shah-People Revolution – and in leading his People towards the new
Great Civilization. In a handbook entitled the *Philosophy of Iran's
Revolution*, the party announced that the shah – the *Arya Mehr* (Aryan
Sun) – had eradicated from Iran once and for all the concept of class and
class conflict.[43] "The Shah-in-Shah," it declared, "is not just the political
leader of Iran. He is in the first instance the teacher and spiritual guide. He
is the helmsman who not only builds for his nation roads, bridges, dams,
and underground canals, but also guides the spirit, thought and hearts of his
people." The shah himself told an English-language newspaper that the
party's philosophy was based on the "dialectics and principles of the White
Revolution."[44] He added that no other country had such a close relationship between its rulers and its people. "No other nation," he boasted, "has
given its ruler such a *carte-blanche*." The terminology as well as the boast
revealed much about the shah at the peak of his power.

The Resurgence Party spent much of 1975 building a state-wide organization. It enrolled almost all the Majles deputies, and took over the main
state organizations – not just the radio/television network and the major
printing houses, but also the ministries of labor, education, higher education, industry, housing, tourism, health and social welfare, rural

cooperatives, art and culture. It convened a party congress, a labor syndicate's conference, and a May Day rally. It started a women's organization. It founded five major papers – *Rastakhiz*, its daily organ, *Rastakhiz-e Kargar* (Worker's Resurgence), *Rastakhiz-e Keshavarzan* (Farmer's Resurgence), *Rastakhiz-e Javan* (Youth's Resurgence), and *Andisheha-ye Rastakhiz* (Resurgent Concepts). Its local branches enrolled more than five million members, launched a voter-registration campaign, threatened dire consequences to those who refused to vote, and in June 1975 shepherded as many as seven million voters to the Majles elections. After the election, the party boasted that "Our success is unprecedented in the annals of political history."[45]

The formation of the Resurgence Party had two profound – and, one could say, disastrous – consequences for the regime. It intensified state control over the salaried middle class, the urban working class, and the rural farm cooperatives. The arm of the state further penetrated into these sectors of the population. Even more significant, the state now threatened to enter arenas it had kept out of in the past – the traditional middle class, especially the bazaars and the clerical establishment.[46] It rushed in where previous governments – including that of Reza Shah – had feared to tread. The Resurgence Party opened bazaar branches; dissolved guilds that for centuries had enjoyed some semblance of autonomy; created in their stead Chambers of Guilds; placed at their head court-connected businessmen; and forced many bazaaris to join not only these chambers but also the party. At the same time, it introduced a minimum wage for workers in small factories, including bazaar workshops, and obliged small businessmen to register employees with the labor ministry and pay monthly contributions for their health insurance. It talked openly of replacing the "flea-infested bazaars" and the old city centers with new highways and modern state-run markets operated like London's Covent Garden. The shah himself later stated that he had moved against the bazaars because they were "badly ventilated," "out-dated," and "fanatical."[47] The area around Imam Reza Shrine was flattened ostensibly to beautify Mashed. One shopkeeper informed a French journalist that he was convinced that the "oil bourgeoisie" planned to throttle the small businessman.[48] Another informed an American journalist: "If we let him, the shah will destroy us. The banks are taking over. The big stores are taking away our livelihoods. And the government will flatten our bazaars to make space for state offices."[49]

What is more, the Resurgence Party declared war on the bazaars in order to deal with inflation that hit the country in late 1975. It imposed price controls on basic commodities; flooded the market with large quantities of wheat, sugar, and meat; and invaded the bazaars with some 10,000 goons known as "inspectorate teams" to "wage a merciless crusade against profiteers, cheaters, hoarders, and unscrupulous capitalists."[50] Meanwhile, a so-called Guilds Court hastily set up by SAVAK meted out some 250,000 fines, banned 23,000 from their home towns, handed out 8,000 prison sentences ranging from two months to three years, and brought charges against another 180,000.[51] Almost every family in the bazaar had a member fall victim to the "anti-profiteering campaign." One shopkeeper complained to a French correspondent that he could not distinguish between a White and a Red Revolution.[52] Another informed an American correspondent that the "bazaar was being used as a smokescreen to hide the vast corruption rampant in government and in the bosom of the royal family."[53] The formation of the Resurgence Party had been an affront to the bazaars; the anti-profiteering campaign was a blatant war on the same bazaars. Not for the first time, the bazaars turned to their traditional allies, the ulama, for help and protection.

The Resurgence Party carried out a simultaneous assault on the clerical establishment. It proclaimed the shah to be a "spiritual" as well as a political leader – thus trespassing on hallowed ground; denounced the clergy as "black medieval reactionaries"; and, in declaring Iran to be on the road to the Great Civilization, supplemented the Muslim calendar, including Reza Shah's solar model, with a new imperial calendar which allocated 2,500 years for the presumed length of the Iranian monarchy and another 35 years for Muhammad Reza Shah. Thus Iran jumped overnight from the Muslim year 1355 to the imperial year 2535. Few regimes have been foolhardy enough to scrap their religious calendar. Moreover, the shah sent special investigators to scrutinize the accounts of religious endowments; announced that only state-sanctioned institutions could publish religious books; and expanded Tehran University's Theology College, as well as the Religious and Literacy Corps, so that more students could be sent into the villages to teach peasants "true Islam." In the words of one paper close to the ulama, the state was out to "nationalize" religion.[54]

Furthermore, the shah created a ministry for women's affairs; recruited women into the Religious and Literacy Corps; raised the marriageable age for women from fifteen to eighteen and for men from eighteen to twenty; expanded birth control clinics and permitted abortion in the first twelve weeks; and instructed the courts to be more diligent in enforcing the 1967 Family Protection Law. This law had contradicted the shari'a on a number of sensitive issues. It stipulated that men could not divorce their wives without giving valid reasons to family courts; that they could not enter

polygamous marriages without written permission from previous wives;
that wives had the right to petition for divorce; and that wives could work
outside the home without the permission of their husbands. In private, the
shah claimed powers even more threatening to the religious establishment.
He told Oriana Fallaci, an Italian journalist, that throughout his life he had
received "messages" and "visions" from the prophets, from Imam Ali, and
from God himself.[55] "I am accompanied," he boasted, "by a force that
others can't see – my mythical force. I get messages. Religious messages . . . if
God didn't exist, it would be necessary to invent him." It has often been said
that the shah eventually fell because he was too secular for his religious
people. If so, one would have drastically to redefine the term secular.

The ulama reacted sharply against the Resurgence Party. Fayzieh, the
main seminary in Qom, closed down in protest. Some 250 of its students
were conscripted into the army and one died soon after in prison. Many of
the leading mojtaheds issued fatwas declaring the Resurgence Party to be
against the constitutional laws, against the interests of Iran, and against the
principles of Islam.[56] Khomeini himself pronounced the party to be *haram*
(forbidden) on the ground that it was designed to destroy not just the
bazaars and the farmers but also the whole of Iran and Islam.[57] A few days
after the fatwa SAVAK rounded up his associates, including many who were
to play leading roles in the revolution to come. Never before in Iran had so
many clerics found themselves in prison at the same time.

Thus the Resurgence Party produced results that were diametrically
opposite to its original purpose. It had been created to stabilize the regime,
strengthen the monarchy, and firmly anchor the Pahlavi state in the wider
Iranian society. It had tried to achieve this by mobilizing the public,
establishing links between government and people, consolidating control
over office employees, factory workers, and small farmers, and, most
brazenly of all, extending state power into the bazaars and the religious
establishment. The result, however, was disastrous. Instead of bringing
stability, it weakened the regime, cut the monarchy further off from the
country, and thereby added to public resentments. Mass mobilization
brought mass manipulation; this, in turn, brought mass dissatisfaction.
Monopoly over organizations deprived social forces of avenues through
which they could channel grievances and aspirations into the political
arena. Increasing numbers gave up hope of reform and picked up incentives
for revolution. Drives for public participation led the government to replace
the dictum "those not actively against us are for us" with "those not actively
for us are against us." Dissenters, who in the past had been left alone so long
as they did not vociferously air their views, were now obliged to enroll in the

party, sign petitions in favor of the government, and even march in the streets singing praises for the 2,500-year-old monarchy. What is more, by unexpected barging into the bazaars and the clerical establishment, the regime undercut the few frail bridges that had existed in the past between itself and traditional society. It not only threatened the ulama but also aroused the wrath of thousands of shopkeepers, workshop owners, and small businessmen. In short, the Resurgence Party, instead of forging new links, destroyed the existing ones, and, in the process, stirred up a host of dangerous enemies. Huntington had been brought in to stabilize the regime; he ended up further destabilizing an already weak regime. The shah would have been better off following Sir Robert Walpole's famous motto "Let sleeping dogs lie."

CHAPTER 6

The Islamic Republic

Revolutions invariably produce stronger states.

De Tocqueville

We need to strengthen our state. Only Marxists want the state to wither away.

Hojjat al-Islam Rafsanjani

THE ISLAMIC REVOLUTION (1977–79)

There has been much speculation on whether the revolution could have been prevented if only this or that had been done: if the shah had been more resolute in crushing or reconciling the opposition; if he had not been suffering from cancer; if his forceful advisors had still been alive; if he had spent less on high-tech weaponry and more on crowd control gear; if his generals had shown a semblance of *esprit de corps*; if human rights organizations had not pestered him; if the CIA had continued to monitor the country closely after the 1950s; if the White House had ignored self-censoring diplomats and heeded the dire warning of skeptic academics; and if, in the final stages, Washington had been more consistent either in fully supporting him or in trying to reach out to Khomeini. Immediately after the debacle, Washington grappled with the question "Who lost Iran?" Some blamed President Carter, some the CIA, some the shah, some his generals.[1] Such speculation, however, is as meaningless as whether the *Titanic* would have sunk if the deckchairs had been arranged differently.

The revolution erupted not because of this or that last-minute political mistake. It erupted like a volcano because of the overwhelming pressures that had built up over the decades deep in the bowels of Iranian society. By 1977, the shah was sitting on such a volcano, having alienated almost every sector of society. He began his autocratic rule adamantly opposed by the intelligentsia and the urban working class. This opposition intensified over the years. In an age of republicanism, he flaunted monarchism, shahism,

155

and Pahlavism. In an age of nationalism and anti-imperialism, he came to power as a direct result of the CIA–MI6 overthrow of Mossadeq – the idol of Iranian nationalism. In an age of neutralism, he mocked non-alignment and Third Worldism. Instead he appointed himself America's policeman in the Persian Gulf, and openly sided with the USA on such sensitive issues as Palestine and Vietnam. And in an age of democracy, he waxed eloquent on the virtues of order, discipline, guidance, kingship, and his personal communication with God.

He not only intensified existing animosities but also created new ones. His White Revolution wiped out in one stroke the class that in the past had provided the key support for the monarchy in general and the Pahlavi regime in particular: the landed class of tribal chiefs and rural notables. His failure to follow up the White Revolution with needed rural services left the new class of medium-sized landowners high and dry. Consequently, the one class that should have supported the regime in its days of trouble stood on the sidelines watching the grand debacle. The failure to improve living conditions in the countryside – together with the rapid population growth – led to mass migration of landless peasants into the cities. This created large armies of shantytown poor – the battering rams for the forthcoming revolution. What is more, many saw the formation of the Resurgence Party in 1975 as an open declaration of war on the traditional middle class – especially on the bazaars and their closely allied clergy. It pushed even the quietist and apolitical clergy into the arms of the most vocal and active opponent – namely Khomeini. While alienating much of the country, the shah felt confident that his ever-expanding state gave him absolute control over society. This impression was as deceptive as the formidable-looking dams he took pride in building. They looked impressive – solid, modern, and indestructible. In fact, they were inefficient, wasteful, clogged with sediment, and easily breached. Even the state with its vast army of government personnel proved unreliable in the final analysis. The civil servants, like the rest of the country, joined the revolution by going on strike. They knew that the shah, the Pahlavis, and the whole institution of monarchy could be relegated to the dustbin of history without undermining the actual state. They saw the shah as an entirely separate entity from the state. They acted not as cogs in the state machinery but as members of society – indeed as citizens with grievances similar to those voiced by the rest of the salaried middle class.

These grievances were summed up in 1976 – on the half-century anniversary of the Pahlavi dynasty – by an exiled opposition paper published in Paris.[2] An article entitled "Fifty Years of Treason" written by Abul-Hassan

Bani-Sadr, the future president of the Islamic Republic, it indicted the regime on fifty separate counts of political, economic, cultural, and social wrongdoings. These included: the *coup d'état* of 1921 as well as that of 1953; trampling the fundamental laws and making a mockery of the Constitutional Revolution; granting capitulations reminiscent of nineteenth-century colonialism; forming military alliances with the West; murdering opponents and shooting down unarmed protestors, especially in June 1963; purging patriotic officers from the armed forces; opening up the economy – especially the agricultural market – to foreign agrobusinesses; establishing a one-party state with a cult of personality; highjacking religion and taking over religious institutions; undermining national identity by spreading "cultural imperialism"; cultivating "fascism" by propagating shah-worship, racism, Aryanism, and anti-Arabism; and, most recently, establishing a one-party state with the intention of totally dominating society. "These fifty years," the article exclaimed, "contain fifty counts of treason."

These grievances began to be aired in 1977 – as soon as the shah relaxed his more stringent police controls. He did so in part because Jimmy Carter in his presidential campaign had raised the issue of human rights across the world, in Iran as well as in the Soviet Union; in part because mainstream newspapers such as the London *Sunday Times* had run exposés on torture, arbitrary arrests, and mass imprisonments in Iran; but in most part because of pressure from human rights organizations, especially the highly reputable International Commission of Jurists. Anxious to cast off the label of "one of the worst violators of human rights in the world" – as Amnesty International had described him – the shah promised the International Commission of Jurists that the Red Cross would have access to prisons; that foreign lawyers would be able to monitor trials; that less dangerous political prisoners would be amnestied; and, most important of all, that civilians would be tried in open civilian courts with attorneys of their own choosing.[3] These concessions – however modest – chiseled cracks in the façade of this formidable-looking regime. The shah granted these concessions probably because he was confident he could weather the storm. In any case, he had deluded himself into thinking that he enjoyed overwhelming public support. He boasted privately to the representative of the International Commission of Jurists that the only people who opposed him were the "nihilists."[4]

The slight opening gave the opposition the space to air its voice. In the autumn of 1977, a stream of middle-class organizations formed of lawyers, judges, intellectuals, academics, and journalists, as well as seminary students, bazaar merchants, and former political leaders, appeared or reappeared, published manifestos and newsletters, and openly denounced the Resurgence Party. This stirring of unrest culminated in October with ten poetry-reading evenings near the Industrial University in Tehran, organized jointly by the recently revived Writers Association and the German-government funded Goethe House.[5] The writers – all well-known dissidents – criticized the regime, and, on the final evening, led the overflowing audience into the streets where they clashed with the police. It was rumored that one student was killed, seventy were injured, and more than one hundred were arrested. These protests persisted in the following months, especially on December 7 – the unofficial student day. Those arrested in these protests were sent to civilian courts where they were either released or given light sentences. This sent a clear message to others – including seminary students in Qom.

The situation worsened in January 1978 when the government-controlled paper *Ettela'at* dropped an unexpected bombshell. It ran an editorial denouncing Khomeini in particular and the clergy in general as "black reactionaries" in cahoots with feudalism, imperialism, and, of course, communism. It also claimed that Khomeini had led a licentious life in his youth, indulging in wine and mystical poetry, and that he was not really an Iranian – his grandfather had lived in Kashmir and his relatives used the surname Hendi (Indian).[6] The only explanation one can give for this editorial is that the regime was puffed up with its own power. One should never underestimate the role of stupidity in history. On the following two days, seminar students in Qom took to the streets, persuading local bazaars to close down, seeking the support of senior clerics – especially Grand Ayatollah Shariatmadari – and eventually marching to the police station where they clashed with the authorities. The regime estimated that the "tragedy" took two lives. The opposition estimated that the "massacre" killed 70 and wounded 500. In this, as in all clashes during the course of the next thirteen months, casualty estimates differed greatly. In the aftermath of the clash, the regime claimed that the seminary students had been protesting the anniversary of Reza Shah's unveiling of women. In fact, petitions drawn up by seminaries did not mention any such anniversary. Instead, they demanded apologies for the editorial; release of political prisoners; the return of Khomeini; reopening of his Fayzieh seminary; the cessation of physical attacks on university students in Tehran; freedom of expression, especially for the press; independence for the judiciary; the breaking of ties with imperial powers; support for agriculture; and the immediate dissolution of the Resurgence Party.[7] These remained their main demands throughout 1978. Immediately after the Qom incident, Shariatmadari asked the nation to observe the fortieth day after the deaths by staying away from work and attending mosque services.

The Qom incident triggered a cycle of three major forty-day crises – each more serious than the previous one. The first – in mid-February – led to violent clashes in many cities, especially Tabriz, Shariatmadari's hometown. The regime rushed in tanks and helicopter gunships to regain control of the city. The second – in late March – caused considerable property damage in Yazd and Isfahan. The shah had to cancel a foreign trip and take personal control of the anti-riot police. The third – in May – shook twenty-four towns. In Qom, the police violated the sanctity of Shariatmadari's home and killed two seminary students who had taken sanctuary there. The authorities claimed that these forty-day demonstrations had left 22 dead; the opposition put the figure at 250.

Tensions were further heightened by two additional and separate incidents of bloodshed. On August 19 – the anniversary of the 1953 coup – a large cinema in the working-class district of Abadan went up in flames, incinerating more than 400 women and children. The public automatically blamed the local police chief, who, in his previous assignment, had ordered the January shooting in Qom.[8] After a mass burial outside the city, some 10,000 relatives and friends marched into Abadan shouting "Burn the shah, End the Pahlavis." The *Washington Post* reporter wrote that the marchers had one clear message: "The shah must go."[9] The reporter for the *Financial Times* was surprised that so many, even those with vested interests in the regime, suspected that SAVAK had set the fire.[10] Decades of distrust had taken their toll.

The second bloodletting came on September 8 – immediately after the shah had declared martial law. He had also banned all street meetings, ordered the arrest of opposition leaders, and named a hawkish general to be military governor of Tehran. Commandoes surrounded a crowd in Jaleh Square in downtown Tehran, ordered them to disband, and, when they refused to do so, shot indiscriminately. September 8 became known as Black Friday – reminiscent of Bloody Sunday in the Russian Revolution of 1905–06. European journalists reported that Jaleh Square resembled "a firing squad," and that the military left behind "carnage." Its main casualty, however, was a feasible possibility of compromise.[11] A British observer noted that the gulf between shah and public was now unbridgeable – both because of Black Friday and because of the Abadan fire.[12] The French philosopher Michel Foucault, who had rushed to cover the revolution for an Italian newspaper, claimed that some 4,000 had been shot in Jaleh Square. In fact, the Martyrs Foundation – which compensates families

6 The statue of Shah Muhammad Reza Pahlavi lies on the ground near Khomeini's HQ during the revolution. Tehran, February 1979.

7 Woman passing soldiers during the revolution. Tehran, 1978.

of victims – later compiled the names of 84 killed throughout the city on that day.[13] In the following weeks, strikes spread from colleges and high schools to the oil industry, bazaars, state and private factories, banks, railways, port facilities, and government offices. The whole country, including the Plan and Budget Organization, the crème de la crème of the central government, had gone on strike.

The opposition showed more of its clout on December 11, 1978, during Ashura, the climactic day of Muharram, when its representatives in Tehran – speaking on behalf of Khomeini – reached an understanding with the government. The government agreed to keep the military out of sight and confined mostly to the northern wealthy parts of the city. The opposition agreed to march along prescribed routes and not raise slogans directly attacking the person of the shah. On the climactic day, four orderly processions converged on the expansive Shahyad Square in western Tehran. Foreign correspondents estimated the crowd to be in excess of two million. The rally ratified by acclamation resolutions calling for the establishment of an Islamic Republic, the return of Khomeini, the expulsion of the imperial powers, and the implementation of social justice for the "deprived masses."[14] In this as in all these demonstrations, the term *velayat-e faqeh* was intentionally avoided. The *New York Times* wrote that the message was loud and clear: "The government was powerless to preserve law and order on its own. It could do so only by standing aside and allowing the religious leaders to take charge. In a way, the opposition has demonstrated that there already is an alternative government."[15] Similarly, the *Christian Science Monitor* reported that a "giant wave of humanity swept through the capital declaring louder than any bullet or bomb could the clear message: 'The Shah Must Go.'"[16] Many treated the rally as a de facto referendum.

Khomeini returned from exile on February 1 – two weeks after the shah had left the country. The crowds that greeted Khomeini totaled more than three million, forcing him to take a helicopter from the airport to the Behest-e Zahra cemetery where he paid respects to the "tens of thousands martyred for the revolution." The new regime soon set the official figure at 60,000. The true figure was probably fewer than 3,000.[17] The Martyrs Foundation later commissioned – but did not publish – a study of those killed in the course of the whole revolutionary movement, beginning in June 1963. According to these figures, 2,781 demonstrators were killed in the fourteen months from October 1977 to February 1979. Most of the victims were in the capital – especially in the southern working-class districts of Tehran.[18] The *coup de grâce* for the regime came on February 9–11, when cadets and technicians, supported by Fedayin and Mojahedin, took on the Imperial Guards in the main air-force base near Jaleh Square. The chiefs of staff, however, declared neutrality and confined their troops to their barracks. *Le Monde* reported that the area around Jaleh Square resembled the Paris Commune, especially when people broke into armories and distributed weapons.[19] The *New York Times* reported that "for the first time since the political crisis started more than a year ago, thousands of civilians appeared in the streets with machine guns and other weapons."[20] Similarly, a Tehran paper reported that "guns were distributed to thousands of people, from ten-year-old children to seventy-year-old pensioners."[21] The final scene in the drama came on the afternoon of February 11, when Tehran Radio made the historic statement: "This is the voice of Iran, the voice of true Iran, the voice of the Islamic Revolution." Two days of street fighting had completed the destruction of the 53-year-old dynasty and the 2,500-year-old monarchy. Of the three pillars the Pahlavis had built to bolster their state, the military had been immobilized, the bureaucracy had joined the revolution, and court patronage had become a huge embarrassment. The voice of the people had proved mightier than the Pahlavi monarchy.

THE ISLAMIC CONSTITUTION (1979)

The main task at hand after the revolution was the drafting of a new constitution to replace the 1906 fundamental laws. This prompted a somewhat uneven struggle between, on the one hand, Khomeini and his disciples, determined to institutionalize their concept of *velayat-e faqeh*, and, on the other hand, Mehdi Bazargan, the official prime minister, and his liberal lay Muslim supporters, eager to draw up a constitution modeled on Charles de Gaulle's Fifth Republic. They envisaged a republic that would be Islamic in name but democratic in content. This conflict also indicated the existence of a dual government. On one side was the Provisional Government headed by Bazargan and filled by fellow veterans from Mossadeq's nationalist movement. Some cabinet ministers were members of Bazargan's Liberation Movement; others came from the more secular National Front. Khomeini had set up this Provisional Government to reassure the government bureaucracy – the ministries as well as the armed forces. He wanted to remove the shah, not dismantle the whole state. On the other side was the far more formidable shadow clerical government. In the last days of the revolution, Khomeini set up in Tehran a Revolutionary Council and a Central *Komiteh* (Committee). The former acted as a watchdog on the Provisional Government. The latter brought under its wing the local komitehs and their *pasdars* (guards) that had sprung up in the many mosques scattered throughout the country. It also purged from these units clerics closely associated with other religious leaders – especially Shariatmadari. Immediately after the fall of the shah, Khomeini established in Tehran a Revolutionary Tribunal to oversee the ad hoc courts that had appeared throughout the country; and in Qom a Central Mosque Office whose task was to appoint imam jum'ehs to provincial capitals. For the first time, a central clerical institution took control over provincial imam jum'ehs. In other words, the shadow state dwarfed the official one. Bazargan complained: "In theory, the government is in charge; but, in reality, it is Khomeini who is in charge – he with his Revolutionary Council, his revolutionary Komitehs, and his relationship with the masses."[22] "They put a knife in my hands," he added, "but it's a knife with only a handle. Others are holding the blade."

Bazargan's first brush with Khomeini came as early as March when the country prepared to vote either yes or no in a referendum on instituting an Islamic Republic. Bazargan wanted to give the public the third choice of a Democratic Islamic Republic. Khomeini refused with the argument: "What the nation needs is an Islamic Republic – not a Democratic Republic nor a Democratic Islamic Republic. Don't use the Western term 'democratic.' Those who call for such a thing don't know anything about Islam."[23] He later added: "Islam does not need adjectives such as democratic. Precisely because Islam is everything, it means everything. It is sad for us to add another word near the word Islam, which is perfect."[24] The referendum, held on April 1, produced 99 percent yes votes for the Islamic Republic. Twenty million – out of an electorate of twenty-one million – participated. This laid the ground for elections to a 73-man constituent body with the newly coined name of *Majles-e Khebregan* (Assembly of Experts) – a term with religious connotations. In August, the country held elections for these delegates. All candidates were closely vetted by the Central Komiteh, the Central Mosque Office, and the newly formed Society for the Militant Clergy of Tehran (*Jam'eh-e Rouhaniyan-e Mobarez-e Tehran*). Not surprisingly, the elections produced landslide victories for Khomeini's disciples. The winners included fifteen ayatollahs, forty hojjat al-islams, and eleven laymen closely associated with Khomeini. The Assembly of Experts set to work drafting the Islamic Constitution.

The final product was a hybrid – albeit weighted heavily in favor of one – between Khomeini's *velayat-e faqeh* and Bazargan's French Republic; between divine rights and the rights of man; between theocracy and democracy; between *vox dei* and *vox populi*; and between clerical authority and popular sovereignty. The document contained 175 clauses – 40 amendments were added upon Khomeini's death.[25] The document was to remain in force until the return of the Mahdi. The preamble affirmed faith in God, Divine Justice, the Koran, Judgment Day, the Prophet Muhammad, the Twelve Imams, the return of the Hidden Mahdi, and, most pertinent of all, Khomeini's concept of *velayat-e faqeh*. It reaffirmed opposition to all forms of authoritarianism, colonialism, and imperialism. The introductory clauses bestowed on Khomeini such titles as Supreme Faqeh, Supreme Leader, Guide of the Revolution, Founder of the Islamic Republic, Inspirer of the Mostazafen, and, most potent of all, Imam of the Muslim Umma – Shi'is had never before bestowed on a living person this sacred title with its connotations of Infallibility. Khomeini was declared Supreme Leader for life. It was stipulated that upon his death the Assembly of Experts could either replace him with one paramount religious figure, or, if no such person emerged, with a Council of Leadership formed of three or five faqehs. It was also stipulated that they could dismiss them if they were deemed incapable of carrying out their duties. The constitution retained the national tricolor, henceforth incorporating the inscription "God is Great."

The constitution endowed the Supreme Leader with wide-ranging authority. He could "determine the interests of Islam," "set general guidelines for the Islamic Republic," "supervise policy implementation," and "mediate between the executive, legislative, and judiciary." He could grant amnesty and dismiss presidents as well as vet candidates for that office. As commander-in-chief, he could declare war and peace, mobilize the armed forces, appoint their commanders, and convene a national security council. Moreover, he could appoint an impressive array of high officials outside the formal state structure, including the director of the national radio/television network, the supervisor of the imam jum'eh office, the heads of the new clerical institutions, especially the Mostazafen Foundation which had replaced the Pahlavi Foundation, and through it the editors of the country's two leading newspapers – *Ettela'at* and *Kayhan*. Furthermore, he could appoint the chief justice as well as lower court judges, the state prosecutor, and, most important of all, six clerics to a twelve-man Guardian Council. This Guardian Council could veto bills passed by the legislature if it deemed them contrary to the spirit of either the constitution or the shari'a. It also had the power to vet candidates running for public office – including the Majles. A later amendment gave the Supreme Leader the additional power to appoint an Expediency Council to mediate differences between the Majles and the Guardian Council.

Khomeini had obtained constitutional powers unimagined by shahs. The revolution of 1906 had produced a constitutional monarchy; that of 1979 produced power worthy of Il Duce. As one of Khomeini's leading disciples declared, if he had to choose between democracy and *velayat-e faqeh*, he would not hesitate because the latter represented the voice of God.[26] Khomeini argued that the constitution in no way contradicted democracy because the "people love the clergy, have faith in the clergy, and want to be guided by the clergy." "It is right," he added, "that the supreme religious authority should oversee the work of the president and other state officials, to make sure that they don't make mistakes or go against the law and the Koran."[27] A few years later, Khomeini explained that Islamic government – being a "divine entity given by God to the Prophet" – could suspend any laws on the ground of *maslahat* (protecting the public interest) – a Sunni concept which in the past had been rejected by Shi'is. "The government of Islam," he argued, "is a primary rule having precedence over secondary

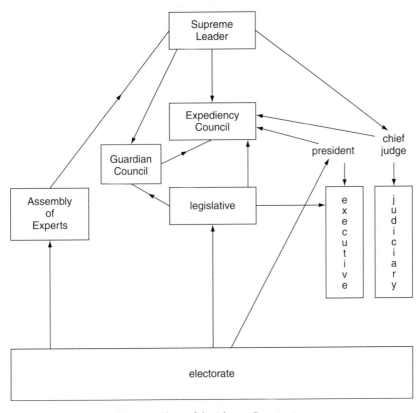

Figure 2 Chart of the Islamic Constitution

rulings such as praying, fasting, and performing the hajj. To preserve Islam, the government can suspend any or all secondary rulings." [28] In enumerating the powers of the Supreme Leader, the constitution added: "The Supreme Leader is equal in the eyes of the law with all other members of society."

The constitution, however, did give some important concessions to democracy. The general electorate – defined as all adults including women – was given the authority to choose through secret and direct balloting the president, the Majles, the provincial and local councils as well as the Assembly of Experts. The voting age was initially put at sixteen years, later lowered to fifteen, and then raised back to sixteen in 2005. The president, elected every four years and limited to two terms, was defined as the "chief executive," and the "highest official authority after the Supreme Leader." He presided over the cabinet, and appointed its ministers as well as all ambassadors, governors, mayors, and directors of the National Bank, the National Iranian Oil Company, and the Plan and Budget Organization. He was responsible for the annual budget and the implementation of external as well as internal policies. He – it was presumed the president would be a male – had to be a Shi'i "faithful to the principles of the Islamic Revolution."

The Majles, also elected every four years, was described as "representing the nation." It had the authority to investigate all affairs of state and complaints against the executive and judiciary; approve the president's choice of ministers and to withdraw this approval at any time; question the president and cabinet ministers; endorse all budgets, loans and international treaties; approve the employment of foreign advisors; hold closed meetings, debate any issue, provide members with immunity, and regulate its own internal workings; and determine whether a specific declaration of martial law was justified. It could – with a two-thirds majority – call for a referendum to amend the constitution. It could also choose the other six members of the Guardian Council from a list drawn up by the judiciary. The Majles was to have 270 representatives with the stipulation that the national census, held every ten years, could increase the overall number. Separate seats were allocated to the officially recognized religious minorities: the Armenians, Assyrians, Jews, and Zoroastrians.

Local councils – on provincial as well as town, district, and village levels – were to assist governors and mayors in administering their regions. The councils were named *showras* – a radical-sounding term associated with 1905–06 revolutions in both Iran and Russia. In fact, demonstrations organized by the Mojahedin and Fedayin pressured the Assembly of Experts to incorporate them into the constitution. Finally, all citizens, irrespective of race, ethnicity, creed, and gender, were guaranteed basic human and civil liberties: the rights of press freedom, expression, worship, organization, petition, and demonstration; equal treatment before the law; the right of appeal; and the freedom from arbitrary arrest, torture, police surveillance, and even wiretapping. The accused enjoyed habeas corpus and had to be brought before civilian courts within twenty-four hours. The law "deemed them innocent until proven guilty beyond any doubt in a proper court of law."

The presence of these democratic clauses requires some explanation. The revolution had been carried out not only under the banner of Islam, but also in response to demands for "liberty, equality, and social justice." The country had a long history of popular struggles reaching back to the Constitutional Revolution. The Pahlavi regime had been taken to task for trampling on civil liberties and human rights. Secular groups – especially lawyers and human rights organizations – had played their part in the revolution. And, most important of all, the revolution itself had been carried out through popular participation from below – through mass meetings, general strikes, and street protests. Die-hard fundamentalists complained that these democratic concessions went too far. They privately consoled themselves with the notion that the Islamic Republic was merely a transitional stage on the way to the eventual full Imamate.

The constitution also incorporated many populist promises. It promised citizens pensions, unemployment benefits, disability pay, decent housing, medical care, and free secondary as well as primary education. It promised to encourage home ownership; eliminate poverty, unemployment, vice, usury, hoarding, private monopolies, and inequality – including between men and women; make the country self-sufficient both agriculturally and industrially; command the good and forbid the bad; and help the "mostazafen of the world struggle against their *mostakaben* (oppressors)." It categorized the national economy into public and private sectors, allocating large industries to the former but agriculture, light industry, and most services to the latter. Private property was fully respected "provided it was legitimate." Despite generous guarantees to individual and social rights, the constitution included ominous Catch-22s: "All laws and regulations must conform to the principles of Islam"; "The Guardian Council has the authority to determine these principles"; and "All legislation must be sent to the Guardian Council for detailed examination. The Guardian Council must ensure that the contents of the legislation do not contravene Islamic precepts and the principles of the Constitution."

The complete revamping of Bazargan's preliminary draft caused consternation not only with secular groups but also with the Provisional

Government and Shariatmadari who had always held strong reservations about Khomeini's notion of *velayat-e faqeh*. Bazargan and seven members of the Provisional Government sent a petition to Khomeini pleading with him to dissolve the Assembly of Experts on the grounds that the proposed constitution violated popular sovereignty, lacked needed consensus, endangered the nation with *akhundism* (clericalism), elevated the ulama into a "ruling class," and undermined religion since future generations would blame all shortcomings on Islam.[29] Complaining that the actions of the Assembly of Experts constituted "a revolution against the revolution," they threatened to go to the public with their own original version of the constitution. It is quite possible that if the country had been given such a choice it would have preferred Bazargan's version. One of Khomeini's closest disciples later claimed that Bazargan had been "plotting" to eliminate the Assembly of Experts and thus undo the whole Islamic Revolution.[30]

It was at this critical moment that President Carter permitted the shah's entry to the USA for cancer treatment. With or without Khomeini's knowledge, this prompted 400 university students – later named Muslim Student Followers of the Imam's Line – to climb over the walls of the US embassy and thereby begin what became the famous 444-day hostage crisis. The students were convinced that the CIA was using the embassy as its headquarters and planning a repeat performance of the 1953 coup. The ghosts of 1953 continued to haunt Iran. As soon as Bazargan realized that Khomeini would not order the pasdars to release the hostages, he handed in his resignation. For the outside world, the hostage affair was an international crisis par excellence. For Iran, it was predominantly an internal struggle over the constitution. As Khomeini's disciples readily admitted, Bazargan and the "liberals" had to go "because they had strayed from the Imam's line."[31] The hostage-takers hailed their embassy takeover as the Second Islamic Revolution.

It was under cover of this new crisis that Khomeini submitted the constitution to a referendum. He held the referendum on December 2 – the day after Ashura. He declared that those abstaining or voting no would be abetting the Americans as well as desecrating the martyrs of the Islamic Revolution. He equated the ulama with Islam, and those opposing the constitution, especially lay "intellectuals," with "satan" and "imperialism." He also warned that any sign of disunity would tempt America to attack Iran. Outmaneuvered, Bazargan asked his supporters to vote yes on the ground that the alternative could well be "anarchy."[32] But other secular groups, notably the Mojahedin, Fedayin, and the National Front, refused to participate. The result was a foregone conclusion: 99 percent voted yes. The turnout, however, was noticeably less than in the previous referendum – especially in the Sunni regions of Kurdestan and Baluchestan as well as in Shariatmadari's home province, Azerbaijan. In the previous referendum, twenty million had voted. This time, only sixteen million did so. In other words, nearly 17 percent did not support the constitution. The ulama got their theocratic constitution, but at the cost of eroding the republic's broad base.

CONSOLIDATION (1980–89)

The Islamic Republic survived despite the conventional wisdom that its demise was imminent as well as inevitable. At the outset, few envisaged its survival. After all, history had not produced many fully fledged theocracies – either inside or outside the Middle East. Many lay people – royalists, leftists, secular nationalists, and members of the intelligentsia – tended to look down upon the clergy as out of place in the contemporary world. They certainly did not consider them capable of running a modern state. What is more, political émigrés throughout history have had the tendency – first noted by the "European social philosopher of the nineteenth century" – to see the smallest sign of discontent, such as a strike, a protest, or a disgruntled voice, as indisputable evidence of the coming deluge. They gave the regime a few months – at most, a few years.

The new state, however, not only survived but consolidated its power. It ceased to be an isolated and autonomous entity hovering over society – as it had been under the Pahlavis. Instead it became an arena in which various interest groups competed and jockeyed for influence. It became part and parcel of the larger society. It took over the previous state intact, merely purging the top echelons, and then gradually but steadily expanded its ranks. It continued the five-year plans with their ambitious projects – all except initially the Bushire nuclear plant. The central bureaucracy grew from twenty ministries with 304,000 civil servants in 1979 to twenty-six ministries with 850,000 civil servants in 1982. It further grew to more than a million civil servants in 2004.[33] The new ministries included intelligence, revolutionary guards, heavy industries, higher education, reconstruction crusade, and Islamic guidance. In 1979, Bazargan had called upon the revolution to liberate the country from the shackles of bureaucracy, which he identified as the main legacy of the Pahlavi era.[34] The Islamic Revolution, however, like others, expanded the bureaucracy. As in the Pahlavi decades, the expansion was made possible by the steady inflow of oil revenues, which, despite fluctuations, brought an average of $15 billion a year throughout the 1980s and as much as $30 billion a year in the early 2000s.

8 Stamps from the Islamic Republic

8.1 Stamps honouring the forerunners of the Islamic Revolution. They depict (from left to right) Fazlollah Nuri, Ayatollah Modarres, Kuchek Khan, and Navab Safavi.

8.2 Stamp for Ayatollah Kashani.

8.3 Two stamps for Ayatollah Beheshti and the seventy-two martyrs.

8.3 (cont.)

The Iran–Iraq War gave the state an immediate impetus to expand. Initiated by Saddam Hussein – most probably to regain control over the crucial Shatt al-Arab waterway – the war lasted eight full years. Iran pushed Iraq out in May 1983, then advanced into enemy territory with the slogans "War, War Until Victory," and "The Road to Jerusalem Goes Through Baghdad." Iran resorted to trench warfare and the strategy of full mobilization – reminiscent of World War I. At the time, it was thought that Iran suffered more than a million dead. But government spokesmen later gave the figure of 160,000

8.4 Stamps issued by the Bazargan government for al-e Ahmad, Shariati, Mossadeq, and Dehkhoda.

8.5 Anniversary stamps for the Islamic Revolution issued in the course of the 1980s.

8.5 (cont.)

Table 13 *Oil revenues, 1977–94*

Year	Revenue ($ billion)
1977–78	23
1978–79	21
1979–80	19
1980–81	13
1981–82	12
1982–83	19
1983–84	19
1984–85	12
1985–86	15
1986–87	6
1987–88	10
1988–89	9
1989–90	10
1990–91	17
1991–92	16
1992–93	15
1993–94	19

Source: Data compiled from C. Benia, "Global Oil and the Oil Policies of the Islamic Republic," in C. Benia and H. Zanganeh, *Modern Capitalism and Islamic Ideology in Iran* (London: Macmillan, 1992), p. 127.

killed in battle.[35] Others add that another 30,000 died later from war-related wounds, that 16,000 civilians were killed in the bombing of cities, and that more than 39,000 suffered permanent injuries – many of them from gas and chemical attacks in the trenches. It is also estimated that another 23,000 suffered PTSD – post-traumatic stress disorder, known in World War I as "shell shock." Not surprisingly, the war had long-lasting consequences.

In the course of the war, the militias were transformed into a fully fledged military force named the *Sepah-e Pasdaran-e Enqelabi* (Army of Revolutionary Guards). With their own ministry, the Revolutionary Guards numbered as many as 120,000 men and contained their own small naval and air units. They also controlled some 200,000 young and old volunteers in a support force known as the *Basej-e Mostazafen* (Mobilization of the Oppressed). The new regime retained much of the previous military as its main professional fighting force, only purging the higher echelons. It also instituted a religious variant of the communist commissar system, using some 270 chaplains to keep watch on key

divisions.[36] The regular armed forces totaled 370,000. They were administered by the war ministry, now once more renamed the defense ministry. Of
course, SAVAK and the Imperial Guards were both abolished. The former
was replaced with the much larger intelligence ministry; the latter with the
Qods (Jerusalem) Force of some 2,000–5,000 select Revolutionary Guards.
In other words, the armed forces now totaled more than half a million –
370,000 regular soldiers, 120,000 Revolutionary Guards, and some
200,000 support volunteers. The war with Iraq, like the hostage crisis,
provided the regime with a highly potent rallying cry. Even those with
strong reservations about the regime were willing to rally behind the
government in a time of national emergency. It became a patriotic as well
as a religious-inspired revolutionary war. The movie industry produced a
number of full-length features such as *The Horizon* and *The Imposed War*,
glorifying martyrdom in the front line.

The war expanded the state in many other ways. The economics ministry
issued ration cards for all basic goods to provide the poor with necessities. It
introduced price controls, opened food cooperatives, and restricted imports.
It even tried to nationalize all foreign trade. The industries ministry took
over factories abandoned by sixty-four entrepreneurs.[37] In the midst of the
revolution, a komiteh in the Central Bank had circulated a list of 177
millionaires who had supposedly absconded with fabulous sums.[38] Even
though the list may have been embellished, it named the obvious suspects –
former aristocrats including the Aminis, Alams, Imamis, Zolfeqaris,
Davalus, Dibas, and Farmanfarmas, who had entered the business world
by taking advantage of court connections and low-interest state loans. Their
flight from Iran had pre-dated that of the shah. The revolution put the final
nail into the coffin of the notables. The government nationalized their
enterprises in order to keep their employees working. The list is a real who's
who of the late Pahlavi era – ministers such as Jamshid Amouzegar and
Houshang Ansari, as well as generals such as Jahanbani, Tofanian, and
Oveissi. It also included self-made businessmen, some of whom, such as
Habeb Elqanian and Hojaber Yazdani, had Jewish or Bahai origins.
Ironically, leading figures from the old regime escaped the full wrath of
the revolution. The state ended up with more than 2,000 factories – many
of them operating in the red.[39]

The justice ministry extended its reach across the whole legal system –
from the Supreme Court, to regional courts, all the way down to local and
revolutionary courts. According to conventional interpretations of the
shari'a, local judges should have the final say in court decisions.
According to the new structure, however, the final say resided in the

hands of the central state with its appeal system. In fact, the revolution did not dismantle the Pahlavi judiciary. It merely replaced secular-trained jurists with seminary-educated ones, and codified more features of the shari'a into state laws – especially into the Law of Retribution.

Similarly, the ministry of Islamic guidance launched a "Cultural Revolution" to combat "cultural imperialism." Proponents declared it the Third Islamic Revolution. This type of linguistic rhetoric derived its pedigree from the previous regime which had declared a new revolution every time it had added a new clause to land reform. The new regime undid the Family Protection Law, lowering the marriage age for girls back to thirteen and allowing husbands to divorce wives without court permission. It purged both women from the judiciary and secular teachers from the educational system. It removed Bahais from government positions, closed down their temples, and arrested and even executed their leaders. It enforced on all a strict "Islamic code of public appearance" – men were discouraged from wearing ties, women were obliged to wear either scarves and long coats or preferably the full chadour. Transgressors against these rules were fined and even physically punished. The regime also encouraged the public to take pilgrimages – not only to the conventional sites but also to the wishing well of Jamkaran near Qom where the Twelfth Imam had supposedly been sighted in more recent decades. Jamkaran – an invented tradition – became a popular pilgrimage site.

The regime censored newspapers, books, movies, and the airwaves; rewrote textbooks to eliminate favorable depictions of the monarchy and secular heroes; banned the use of European personal names; and removed from public places any references to previous monarchs – even distant ones. The famous Shah Mosque built by the Safavids in Isfahan was renamed the Imam Mosque. Streets and public squares bearing references to the Pahlavis were given new designations. Towns that had been renamed by Reza Shah reverted to their previous designations – for example, Pahlavi reverted back to Enzeli, Rezaieh to Urmiah; and Shahi to Aliabad.

The regime also waged a concerted media campaign in praise of the clergy. For example, a series of postage stamps highlighted their role thoughout history as well as in the recent revolution. They featured Fazlollah Nuri, the mojtahed hanged by the constitutionalists in 1909; Ayatollah Modarres, Reza Shah's outspoken opponent; Kuchek Khan, the Jangali leader, who was portrayed wearing a turban; Navab Safavi, the Fedayan-e Islam founder who assassinated a number of politicians and tried to kill Mossadeq; Ayatollah Kashani, the former Mossadeq supporter who turned against him in 1953; and Ayatollah Beheshti, the chairman of the Assembly of Experts who was blown up by the Mojahedin in 1982. The official announcement claimed that this bomb had killed Beheshti and "his seventy-two companions." Only four stamps – all designed during Bazargan's brief administration – honored laymen: Mossadeq; Dehkhoda – the famous writer from the 1906 revolution; and Shariati and Al-e Ahmad – the early proponents of the return to Islam. Moreover, anniversary stamps for the revolution became increasingly more abstract and stylized as human figures receded from the scene. The overall aim was to Islamicize Iran. Extremists even advocated removing Nowruz from the official calendar, and converting the ancient ruins of Persepolis into a public urinal. For them, any sign of respect for pre-Islamic Iran smacked of paganism – *sherk*, *jahlileh*, and *taquti*.

The Islamic Republic not only expanded the ministries but created numerous semi-public religious foundations. The Mostazafen Foundation – successor to the Pahlavi Foundation – more than doubled its original assets when the new regime confiscated the property of some fifty millionaires.[40] Because of the war with Iraq, its official name was expanded into the Foundation for the Oppressed and Disabled (*Bonayad-e Mostazafen va Janbazan*). By the late 1980s, its assets, totaling more than $20 billion, encompassed some 140 factories, 470 agrobusinesses, 100 construction firms, 64 mines, and 250 commercial companies. It also owned Coca-Cola – renamed Zam Zam Cola – and the former Hyatt and Hilton hotels, as well as *Ettela'at* and *Kayhan*. Likewise, the other foundations – all with specific missions – began with confiscated properties and grew with government subsidies and foreign exchange currencies far below the official rates. The Alavi Foundation, Martyrs Foundation, Pilgrimage Foundation, Housing Foundation, Foundation for War Refugees, and Foundation for Imam Khomeini's Publications together employed in excess of 400,000 people.[41] Their combined budgets were as much as half that of the central government. What is more, the long-existing shrines such as those of Imam Reza in Mashed, Fatemeh in Qom, and Abdul 'Azim in Ray together owned as much as $8 billion of real estate. They were states within the state – or rather, clerical fiefdoms accountable only to the Supreme Leader.

The regime enjoyed good rapport with the bazaars – so much so that two prominent American social scientists have described the regime as a "bourgeois" republic.[42] The Chamber of Commerce was packed with import-exporters who had impeccable records for giving alms. Its chairman served as minister of commerce. Other ministers had relatives in the bazaar and the clerical establishment. The Council of Guilds – which the shah had closed down – was revived as the Islamic Association of Bazaar Guilds. It expanded to include wage earners in both stores and workshops. Its leaders, who had been imprisoned in 1965 for assassinating the prime minister, formed a parliamentary group named the Islamic Coalition Society. Its chairman, Habibollah Asgar-Owladi, was the brother of the commerce minister. Among his colleagues were the director of the Mostazafen Foundation, the warden of Evin Prison, and the director of a conglomerate dealing in cement, sugar and cotton.[43] Rafsanjani, a pistachio grower and future president of the republic, had also been a member of the group in earlier years. Other well-connected bazaaris had lucrative contracts and import licenses with much coveted foreign currencies. The Guardian Council was filled with conservative judges who vetoed not only the nationalization of foreign trade but also a reform bill proposing to place a ceiling on land-ownership. Moreover, the Majles, which had been a debating chamber for notables in the distant past and a club for the shah's placemen in more recent years, was now filled with the propertied middle class. For example, more than 70 percent of the deputies in the First Islamic Majles came from that class. Their fathers included 63 clergymen, 69 farm owners, 39 shop-keepers, and 12 merchants.[44]

Furthermore, Khomeini went out of his way to stress that Islam consid-ered property to be sacred, that the clergy would respect private ownership, and that the constitution guaranteed the private sector a special role in the economy. In 1981 he launched an Eight Point Declaration instructing the authorities to respect people's "movable and immovable possessions, including homes, stores, workshops, farms, and factories."[45] In an address to a delegation of merchants and guild leaders, he praised them for financing mosques and seminaries, upholding Islam throughout history, and playing a key role in the recent revolution. "Previous rulers," he continued, "did not dare to set foot in the bazaars. But things are very different now. The president and the bazaaris are all brothers."[46] In his last will and testament, he advised future generations to respect property on the grounds that free enterprise turns the "wheels of the economy" and prosperity would produce "social justice" for all, including the poor. "Islam," he proclaimed, "differs sharply from communism. Whereas we respect private property, commu-nism advocates the sharing of all things – including wives and homosex-uals."[47] Ali Khamenei, his successor as Supreme Leader, continued in the same vein, arguing that Islam respects the bazaar, that the Koran praises commerce, and that socialists, not Muslims, associate business with theft, corruption, greed, and exploitation. "The bazaar," he declared, "helped the Islamic Revolution and continues to be the bastion supporting the Islamic Republic."[48] In the words of the London *Economist*: "The bazaar enjoys a close relationship with the regime, benefiting from business contracts in exchange for funding individual mosques and conservative parliamentary and presidential candidates."[49]

The new regime reached out beyond the bazaars into the countryside. Even though it placed no ceiling on landownership, it distributed more than 850,000 hectares of confiscated agrobusiness land to some 220,000 peasant families in Gurgan, Mazanderan, and Khuzestan.[50] The new farmers formed more than 10,000 cooperatives. The regime assisted farmers in other ways. It raised agricultural prices – helping the country become self-sufficient in cereal production; channeled the Reconstruction Crusade into the provinces; launched an ambitious literacy campaign among the peasantry; and extended roads, electricity, piped water, and, most important of all, health clinics, into the villages. This strategy – which continued into the next decade – transformed the countryside, turning peasants into farmers. Soon most farmers had access not only to roads, schools, clinics, electricity, and piped water, but also to such consumer goods as radios, refrigerators, telephones, televisions, motorbikes, even pickup trucks. One key indicator illustrates the dramatic changes in everyday life: on the eve of the revolution, life expectancy at birth had been less than 56; by the end of the century, it was near 70.

The regime brought other benefits to the working class. It spent a quarter of the annual budget in subsidies to the poorer population – direct subsidies for bread, rice, sugar, cheese, fuel, and cooking oil, as well as indirect subsidies for electricity, sanitation, and piped water. It set up a Worker's House, and passed a Labor Law, which, while not legalizing strikes and free unions, gave factory workers significant concessions: 6-day, 48-hour workweeks, paid Fridays, a minimum wage, 12-day annual holidays, and some semblance of job security. Worker's House published the paper *Kar va Kargar* (Work and Worker), and organized annual May Day rallies with slogans reminiscent of the Tudeh Party. Some statistics show the fundamental changes taking place throughout the country: the percentage of children in school rose from 60 to 90; infant mortality per 1,000 dropped from 104 to 25; the annual population growth hit an all-time high of 3.2 percent – increasing the total population from 34 million in 1976 to 50 million in 1989, and to nearly 70 million in 2000; and, most important of all, the literacy rate doubled, almost eradicating illiteracy among the age group between six and twenty-nine. This meant that for the first time in history most of the population, including Azeris, Kurds, Gilakis, and Mazanderanis, could converse and read in Persian.[51]

Finally, the Islamic Republic consolidated itself by using the stick as well as the carrot. It unleashed a reign of terror worthy of the Jacobins when the Mojahedin – supported by President Bani-Sadr – tried to overthrow the government in June 1981 and instead ended up assassinating numerous prominent figures including the speaker of the Assembly of Experts, the chair of the Supreme Court, the chief of the revolutionary courts, the head of the gendarmerie, the editor of *Kayhan*, four cabinet ministers, ten deputy ministers, twenty-eight Majles deputies, two imam jum'ehs, and the new president – Muhammad Rajai. They also wounded Khomeini's two closest advisors: Hojjat al-Islam Ali Khamenei, the future Supreme Leader; and Hojjat al-Islam Ali-Akbar Hasehmi Rafsanjani, the speaker of the Majles and also future president. Khamenei used the anniversary of Mossadeq's death to declare ominously: "We are not liberals, like Allende, whom the CIA can snuff out."[52]

In the twenty-eight months between February 1979 and June 1981, revolutionary courts had executed 497 political opponents as "counter-revolutionaries" and "sowers of corruption on earth."[53] They included Hoveida, the former premier; 6 cabinet ministers – one of whom was accused of nourishing "cultural imperialism"; 3 chiefs and 90 operatives of SAVAK; 33 Bahais and 1 Jewish businessman accused of spying for Israel; 35 generals, 25 colonels, 20 majors, and 125 non-commissioned officers. In the next four years from June 1981 until June 1985, revolutionary courts executed more than 8,000 opponents. Although they targeted mainly the Mojahedin, they also went after others – even some who opposed the Mojahedin. The victims included Fedayins and Kurds as well as Tudeh, National Front, and Shariatmadari supporters. Many – including Shariatmadari, Bazargan supporters, and Tudeh leaders – were forced to appear on television and recant their previous views. Thus the toll taken among those who had participated in the revolution was far greater than that among the royalists. This revolution – like others – had devoured its own children. The regime also took the unprecedented step of defrocking Shariatmadari on the trumped-up charge of plotting to kill Khomeini.

One final bloodletting came in 1988, immediately after Khomeini ended the war by accepting a UN-mediated ceasefire. He announced that he had no choice but to "drink the poisoned chalice." In four short weeks, special courts set up in the main prisons hanged more than 2,800 prisoners – Amnesty International described them as "prisoners of conscience."[54] Former Mojahedin were executed on suspicion they harbored secret sympathies for the organization. Leftists were executed for "apostasy" on the grounds they had turned their backs on God, the Prophet, the Koran, and the Resurrection. Their bodies were dumped into a desolate area known as *Kafarestan* (Land of the Unbelievers) and *Lanatabad* (Land of the Damned). This extraordinary bloodbath has one plausible explanation. Khomeini, in his dying years, was eager to leave behind disciples baptized in a common bloodbath. The killing would test their mettle, weeding out the halfhearted from the true believers, the weak-willed from the fully committed, and the wishy-washy from the resolute. It would force them to realize that they would stand or fall together. What is more, it would sever ties between religious populists within his movement and secular radicals outside. Some of his followers had toyed with the dangerous notion of working with the Tudeh Party to incorporate more radical clauses into the Labor Law as well as into the Land Reform Law. To unify his disciples further against the West, Khomeini issued his famous and unprecedented fatwa against Salman Rushdie. He declared that Rushdie, a Muslim-born Indian living in Britain, could lawfully be killed on the grounds that his book *Satanic Verses* satirized the Prophet and therefore proved that he was an "apostate." The 1988 bloodbath had its intended effect. Within months, Grand Ayatollah Hussein Montazeri, who since the revolution had been groomed to be the next Supreme Leader, resigned in protest and went into retirement in Qom – where he became a non-person. By the time Khomeini died a few months later, in June 1989, he could feel confident that he was leaving his republic in secure hands.

THERMIDOR (1989–2005)

The transfer of power took place smoothly. On his deathbed, Khomeini appointed a twenty-five-man Constitutional Reform Council which named Khamenei as the next Supreme Leader and drew up amendments to the original constitution. Since the senior mojtaheds had given lukewarm support to the revolution and the groomed heir, Montazeri, had strayed from the straight path, they dropped the original prerequisite that the leadership of the republic had to be in the hands of either a paramount faqeh or a council of senior faqehs. They decided that the Supreme Leader could be a seminary-trained cleric with the right qualifications – "honesty," "piety," "courage," "administrative abilities," and "versed in the political issues of the age." One delegate even argued that the *velayat-e faqeh* did not require a *faqeh*.[55] In designating Khamenei as Supreme Leader, they, together with the official press, began to address him and his close colleagues, including Hojjat al-Islam Rafsanjani, as ayatollahs. The republic has often been dubbed the regime of ayatollahs. It could more aptly be called that of hojjat al-islams. The Leader ceased to be addressed also as the Supreme Faqeh – he became simply the Supreme Leader.

The Reform Council amended the constitution in many other ways. The *Majles-e Melli* (National Assembly) became the *Majles-e Islami* (Islamic Assembly). The Assembly of Experts – increased to eighty-six members – obtained the authority to convene at least once a year, and to determine whether the Supreme Leader was "mentally and physically capable of carrying out his arduous duties." The Assembly of Experts itself was to be elected by the public every six years. The Reform Council also transformed the Expediency Council into a permanent body with members appointed by the Supreme Leader as well as representatives from the three branches of government, the armed forces, the intelligence service, and the Guardian Council. In other words, the Expediency Council became an upper house of some forty power-brokers. In July 1989 – seven weeks after Khomeini's death – the Reform Council submitted its amendments to a national referendum. In the same elections, Rafsanjani ran against a relatively unknown to replace Khamenei as president. The results were a foregone conclusion. The amendments passed with 97 percent voting yes. Rafsanjani won with 94 percent. The turnout, however, was less than 55 percent – a 20 percent drop since the last referendum.

The duumvirate of Khamenei and Rafsanjani initiated a Thermidor. In a televised sermon, Khamenei informed the nation that Imam Ali had been a successful plantation owner, who, when not out fighting for Islam, had stayed home meticulously cultivating his property. He added that Imam Ali had taken care of his appearance and had worn the best clothes possible when preaching.[56] Imam Ali, a former member of the *mostazafen*, became a plantation owner. Meanwhile, Rafsanjani forthrightly declared that "it was time to put away childish things," that many were guilty of "excesses, crudities, and irresponsible behavior," and that it was high time the revolution went on its proper and healthy course.[57] They took immediate measures to liberalize the economy, although they avoided the label "liberal" – a term closely associated in the public mind with secular intellectuals, Bazargan, and the West. What is more, Khomeini had often denounced liberalism as an integral part of the "Western plague." The two new leaders abolished rationing; relaxed price controls; and tried to balance the budget. They also tried to trim the bureaucracy, and, although they failed, they managed to reduce the total number of ministries from twenty-five to twenty-one by merging the ministries of heavy industry with industries, higher education with education, revolutionary guards with defense, and reconstruction with Islamic guidance. In addition, they imported consumer goods as well as essentials to relieve shortages; stopped the anti-hoarding campaigns; returned some real estate to previous owners; printed less paper money; narrowed the gap between the official and the black-market price of the dollar; revitalized the national stock exchange; started five free trade zones; lowered business taxes; and, most important of all, reduced the defense budget – which had been as high as 17 percent of the gross national product in the shah's last years – to less than 2 percent of GNP.[58] Thus resources continued to flow into development programs: education, health, electrification, rural roads, urban renewal, city parks, and the Tehran subways, as well as into capital-intensive projects such as steel, car manufacturing, and petrochemicals – even the nuclear program was restarted. These programs retained their impetus even though the price of oil continued to fluctuate widely.

The regime's most visible success was its promotion of birth control. In 1989, the government, having previously encouraged population growth, reversed gears and declared that Islam favored families with only two children. It opened birth control clinics – especially for women; distributed condoms and pills; cut subsidies to large families; introduced sex education into the school curriculum; and held mandatory classes for newlyweds. It also discouraged polygamy by encouraging women to have husbands sign prenuptial contracts agreeing not to take second wives and to divide property equally in case of divorce. Between 1989 and 2003, the annual population growth fell from an all-time high of 3.2 percent to 1.2. In the same period, the fertility rate – the average number of children born to a woman in her lifetime – plummeted from 7 to 3. The UN expects the figure will go down to 2 by 2012 – this would give the country a zero population growth. The UN has praised Iran for having the most successful population control program in the whole world. The campaign owed its success to the government's ability to reach the rural population through the mass media, literacy campaigns, and village health clinics.[59] It was also helped by the rising marriage age which averaged thirty for men and twenty-six for women.

Khamenei and Rafsanjani, however, parted company when the latter, after a state visit to Peking, toyed with the Chinese model of economic development. He talked of cutting subsidies for food, fuel, and gasoline; trimming financial support for the clerical foundations; bringing these foundations under state supervision; privatizing companies that had been nationalized in 1979; and, most important of all, attracting foreign and expatriate capital by allowing free flow of profits; permitting citizens living abroad to hold foreign citizenship; convening conferences for foreign and expatriate investors; granting territorial concessions to foreign oil companies, such as the contract worth $1 billion to the American Conoco. He also talked of diluting the Labor Law to make factory ownership more profitable; and drafting a new Investment Law to allow foreigners to own as much as 45 percent of companies. These proposals aroused the opposition not only of Khamenei and the Guardian Council, but also of the majority in the Majles and the dominant figures in the bazaar.

Ironically, Rafsanjani also ran up against the US government, which, in the aftermath of the hostage crisis, continued to see Iran as a major regional threat both to America and Israel. Congress passed the Iran Sanctions Act which threatened to penalize foreign as well as American oil companies that dared to invest more than $20 million in Iran. The drying up of foreign investment, together with another fall in oil prices – from $20 per barrel in 1991 to $12 in 1994 – added to Iran's external debt, strained the currency, and thereby triggered an economic recession. The rial, which had already fallen from 7 to the dollar before the revolution to 1,749 to the dollar in 1989, plummeted to 6,400 to the dollar in 1995. Meanwhile, unemployment reached 30 percent, and the price of sugar, rice, and butter rose threefold – and that of bread sixfold. Exiles predicted the imminent demise of the Islamic Republic.

The economic crisis, however, paved the way not to revolution but to reform. In 1997, Rafsanjani ended his two-term presidency and was barred by the constitution from running again. In an untypical miscalculation, the Guardian Council permitted Hojjat al-Islam Sayyed Muhammad Khatemi, a relatively unknown and mild-mannered former minister of culture, to run against the conservative, flamboyant, and well-known Speaker of the Majles. In addition to having been prominent in national politics since 1978, the conservative candidate had the backing of much of the establishment: the Association of Militant Clergy, the main ecclesiastical body; the Chamber of Commerce, Association of Farmers, and Association of Guilds and Trades; the Islamic Coalition Society; the Office of Imam Jum'ehs; and the heads of the large foundations, the main seminaries, and, of course, the Revolutionary Guards. Most observers, including the London *Economist*, expected a shoo-in. Khatemi's organized support was limited to the Society of Militant Clergy – an offshoot of the Association of Militant Clergy; the Islamic Student Association; the newly created Labor Party attached to the Worker's House; the *Kargozaran-e Sazandegi* (Construction Executives) – a party formed recently by Rafsanjani; *Zan* (Women), a newspaper edited by Rafsanjani's daughter; the semi-legal Liberation Movement; and the Mojahedin Organization of the Islamic Revolution – a circle of intellectuals and technocrats radical in economic policies but relatively liberal in cultural matters.

Khatemi's main asset was his liberal reputation. The fact that he was a sayyed also helped. As minister of culture under Rafsanjani, he had tried to loosen censorship and had been accused by *Ettela'at* and *Kayhan* of disseminating "corrupt and immoral films and books." Complaining that overly stringent censorship had produced a "stagnant and retrograde climate," he resigned quietly from his ministerial post in 1992 and took up the directorship of the National Library. He also taught Western political thought at Tehran University. His demeanor was more like that of a university professor than a revolutionary cleric. He ran his campaign for the presidency on the themes of nourishing "civil society," curing the "sick economy," and replacing the "clash of civilizations" with a "dialogue of civilizations." He hammered away on the importance of having an open society with individual liberties, free expression, women's rights, political pluralism, and, most important of all, rule of law. He visited supermarkets, used city buses, and traveled in a small private car with his wife in the driver's seat. His campaign managers went out of their way to stress that he knew German, having supervised the Iranian mosque in Hamburg before the revolution. They also stressed that the philosophical books he had written had much praise for such Western thinkers as Hume, Kant, Descartes, Locke, Voltaire, and Montesquieu. "The essence of Iranian history," he declared, "is the struggle for democracy."[60]

He won hands-down with 70 percent of the vote in a campaign in which 80 percent of the electorate participated. In the previous presidential campaign, only 50 percent had voted. His support cut across regions and class lines – even Revolutionary Guards and Qom seminarians voted for him. But his core support came from the modern middle class, college students, women, and urban workers. The reformers immediately launched the newspaper *Khordad* (May), named after the month when they had won the presidential election. They soon became known as the *Khordad* Movement. Khatemi's brother, a medical doctor, founded the paper *Moshakerat* (Participation) and the Islamic Iran Participation Party. *Khordad* and *Moshakerat* soon outsold the long-established *Kayhan* and *Ettela'at*.

These reform newspapers, together with others that followed, changed the whole tenor of public discussion. In previous decades, the key terms in public discourse had been *emperialism, mostazafen, jehad, mojahed, shahed* (martyrdom), *khish* (roots), *enqelab* (revolution), and *gharbzadegi* (Western intoxication). Now the key terms were *demokrasi, pluralism, moderniyat, azadi* (liberty), *barabari* (equality), *jam'eh-e madani* (civil society), *hoquq-e beshar* (human rights), *mosakerat-e siyasi* (political participation), *goft-e gou*

Table 14 *Presidents, 1980–2007*

	Term	Birthplace and date	Education	Profession	Father's profession	Political past	Foreign languages
Bani-Sadr, Sayyed Abul-Hassan	Jan 1980–June 1981	Hamadan, 1933	Tehran University	Intellectual	Ayatollah	National Front	Arabic, French
Rajai, Muhammad Ali	July–August 1981	Qazvin, 1933	Teachers college	Math teacher	Small shopkeeper	Prison 1963, 1975–78	None
Khamenei, Sayyed Ali	August 1981–July 1989	Mashed, 1934	Seminary, Mashed, Qom	Hojjat al-Islam	Minor cleric	Prison 1963, 1975	Turkish, Arabic
Rafsanjani, Hashemi Ali-Akbar	July 1989–May 1997	Rafsanjan, 1934	Seminary, Qom	Hojjat al-Islam and Business	Business	Prison, 1963, 1975	Arabic
Khatemi, Sayyed Muhammad	May 1997–July 2005	Ardakan, 1943	Seminary and Tehran University	Hojjat al-Islam	Ayatollah		Arabic, German
Ahmadinejad, Mahmud	July 2005–	Village near Tehran, 1956	Tehran Industrial Univ.	University lecturer	Blacksmith		None

(dialogue), and the brand new word *shahrvandi* (citizenship). This was a cultural turn almost as significant as that of the 1979 revolution. The new intellectuals – many of whom had started political careers as militant revolutionaries – cited freely not only Rousseau, Voltaire, and Montesquieu, but also Hume, Kant, and Descartes. In some ways, the clock had been turned back to the Constitutional Revolution. But these intellectuals were oblivious to any irony since they – like most of their compatriots – had little appreciation of early twentieth-century history. Their public discourse placed as much stress on Iran as on Islam, on pre-Muslim Persia as on Shi'i Islam, and on national celebrations such as Nowruz and nationalization of the oil company as on Muharram and Ramadan. Nationalism appeared to have attained a happy synthesis between pre-Islamic Iran and Islam – at least, Shi'i Islam.

The reformers followed up the 1997 triumph with three equally spectacular victories. They obtained 75 percent of the vote in local elections in 1999, when 334,000 candidates – including some 5,000 women – competed for 115,000 seats on provincial, town, and village councils. In parliamentary elections in 2000, they won 80 percent of the vote and obtained 195 of the 290 Majles seats. Khatemi's brother topped the list in Tehran. And in 2001, Khatemi won a second term as president increasing his vote by two million and receiving 80 percent of all votes cast. More than 67 percent of the electorate participated. The president was now able to fill the cabinet with his own supporters. *The Economist* commented: "Iran, although an Islamic state, imbued with religion and religious symbolism, is an increasingly anti-clerical country. In a sense it resembles some Roman Catholic countries where religion is taken for granted, without public display, and with ambiguous feelings towards the clergy. Iranians tend to mock their mullahs, making mild jokes about them; they certainly want them out of their bedrooms. In particular, they dislike their political clergy."[61] The clergy, it added, complained that more than 70 percent of the population did not perform their daily prayers and that less than 2 percent attended Friday mosques.[62] In other words, the reformers, with enthusiastic popular support, had won control not only over local assemblies but also over the legislative and executive branches of the national government. The conservative core was confined to less than 25 percent of the electorate. This can be described as their solid "base."

Khatemi used these victories to open up both foreign relations and internal politics. He avoided the sensitive issue of state dominance over the economy – in part because he did not want to lose labor support, and in part because Rafsanjani had learnt through hard experience that tampering with the privileges of the foundations and the bazaars was tantamount to hitting the third rail of Iranian politics. He, therefore, skirted around this main economic obstacle, and instead continued to funnel revenues – which, fortunately for him, rapidly increased as the price of a barrel of oil went from $10 in 1997 to $65 in 2003. The state continued to be able to expand development programs for education, electrification, housing, rural construction, and nuclear installations. By 2000, 94 percent of the population had access to medical facilities and safe water; 97 percent of those between six and twenty-nine were literate; the mortality rate was the best in the Middle East; and women formed 63 percent of university students, 54 percent of college enrollment, and 45 percent of doctors. The government also put aside a portion of the oil revenues for emergencies.

In foreign affairs, Khatemi launched a campaign to improve relations with the outside world. He paid state visits to Tokyo, Moscow, Madrid, Rome, and Paris, where, at the Pantheon, he laid wreaths for Rousseau, Zola, and Victor Hugo. He assured international lawyers that the courts would no longer resort to stoning and would be sparing in imposing corporal punishments. He hosted a conference on dialogue between civilizations, and a human rights delegation from the European Union. He told CNN how much he admired the West, especially America. "The secret of American civilization," he opined, "lies on Plymouth Rock."[63] He even expressed "regret" for the student takeover of the US embassy. He invited foreigners to invest in Iran – especially in oil exploration, oil refining, and oil pipelines. He announced – in a clear break with precedent – that Iran would accept a two-state solution for Palestine if the Palestinians themselves agreed to such a settlement. He relaxed restrictions on the Bahais, and persuaded Khamenei quietly to amnesty a group of Jews who had been framed for spying for Israel. He also assured Britain that Iran had no intention of implementing the fatwa against Rushdie.

In return, Britain reestablished full diplomatic relations which had been broken since 1979. President Clinton loosened the economic embargo, permitting the export of medical and farm goods and the import of rugs and pistachios. His secretary of state came close to apologizing for the 1953 coup. At the UN, fifteen European countries refrained from introducing motions critical of Iran. The UN itself dropped Iran from its list of human rights violators. The World Bank – without US approval – lent Iran $232 million for medical services and sewage lines. European, Russian, and Japanese firms – again without American approval – agreed to invest $12 billion in the oil, gas, and automobile industries. Euros flowed into the stock exchange in Tehran. And the International Monetary Fund (IMF) gave Iran high marks in 2003 for its fiscal reforms – especially for balancing the budget.

In internal politics, liberals in the Majles passed more than a hundred reform bills. These included the explicit ban on all forms of torture and physical coercion, including sleep deprivation, blindfolding, and solitary confinement; the right of political prisoners to have legal counsel, access to their families, and trial by judges with at least ten years' experience; the establishment of a special press court independent of the judiciary to deal with issues of libel and censorship; the right of all accused to jury trials with strict separation between judges and prosecutors; and the presidential authority to remove activist judges who blatantly interfere in politics and overextend their judicial powers. They tried to transfer the authority to supervise elections and vet candidates from the Guardian Council to the interior ministry. "The constitution," they argued, "gave the Guardian Council the authority to oversee elections – not to fix and interfere with them." Some deputies openly talked of the need for a referendum to strengthen the democratic features of the constitution.

The liberal deputies also made a pitch for women's support. They allowed women to study abroad on state scholarships; colleagues to wear headscarf instead of the full chadour; and schoolgirls to wear colourful clothes. They even passed bills directly contradicting traditional interpretations of the shari'a. They eliminated all distinctions between men and women, between Muslims and non-Muslims, in accepting witnesses in court and awarding monetary compensations for damages. They increased the marriageable age for girls to fifteen. They reopened the judiciary to women. They gave them equal rights in divorce courts and permitted them to have custody rights over children under the age of seven. Never before in the Middle East had a freely elected parliament so blatantly challenged basic tenets of the shari'a. What is more, they ratified the UN Convention on Elimination of All Forms of Discrimination against Women – the USA has still refused to ratify this highly egalitarian convention. The liberal cause was further bolstered when Shiren Ebadi, a human rights lawyer, won the Nobel Peace Prize, and Ayatollah Youssef Sanai, one of Khomeini's favorite disciples, came out in full support of women's rights. He ruled that the law should not differentiate between the sexes, and that women should have the right to become presidents, chief judges, and even Supreme Leaders.

The reformers managed to end political assassinations at home and abroad. They purged from the intelligence ministry a group of operatives who had carried out "serial killings" of dissidents – their ringleader "committed suicide" before he could implicate his superiors. They relaxed the controls placed on Montazeri, the ayatollah who had been groomed to succeed Khomeini. They sent parliamentary committees into prisons, removing some wardens, releasing more political inmates, and improving the conditions of others. They imposed restraints on *basej* vigilantes who harassed middle-class youth, especially girls, for listening to music, watching videos, having satellite dishes, not covering their heads fully, and having private parties. One party-goer joked: "In the old days, when we heard the door bell we froze in fear. Now we know someone is late."[64] European reporters noted that whereas the basej had grown sparse in the northern middle-class suburbs they continued to be a problem in the southern slums: "In the working class suburbs they remain popular for their piety and their patriotism and for bringing the rich kids down a peg or two."[65]

The reformers also channeled state funds into non-government organizations: local clubs, theaters, and cultural centers; newspapers – the number of dailies increased from five to twenty-six and their combined daily circulation rose from 1.2 million to 3.2 million. The number of journals rose from 778 to 1,375; and the number of book titles from 14,500 to 23,300 with a total circulation of 118 million – in 1986 the number of book titles had been as few as 3,800 with a circulation of fewer than 28 million.[66] *Hamshahri* (Citizen), a daily owned by the mayor's office in Tehran with a circulation of 460,000, became the first paper in Iran to survive through advertisements. The consumer market had finally come to Iran. The liberals scored their most celebrated cultural success in the international film community by winning prizes at Cannes and Venice. Films such as *Two Women, The Hidden Half, Gilaneh, Marriage of the Blessed, A Taste of Cherry, A Time for Drunken Horses, A Moment of Innocence,* and *Once Upon a Time Cinema* dealt with social issues, especially the plight of women, children, the poor, and war veterans. One of the most celebrated directors was a former Revolutionary Guard. Of course, the movie industry was heavily subsidized by the state.

The conservatives hit back. The Guardian Council vetoed most of the reform bills on the grounds they violated the shari'a and the constitution. The judiciary closed down an increasing number of papers, eventually banning more than sixty publications in what became known as the "great newspaper massacre." It also brought charges of "apostasy" against the new intellectuals. One historian was taken to task for arguing that Islam needed a Protestant Reformation. A journalist was imprisoned for writing that he could not find traces of *velayat-e faqeh* in the Koran or in the teachings of the Twelve Imams. Another was arrested for noting that the veil pre-dated Islam and originated instead in ancient pagan civilizations.

Yet another was incarcerated for publishing a public opinion poll which showed that the majority of Iranians wanted to improve relations with the USA even though they distrusted Washington. One paper was even banned for reprinting a New Deal cartoon of FDR's hand pressing down on white-bearded Supreme Court judges. *Zan*, edited by Rafsanjani's daughter, was banned for a cartoon showing a husband pleading with a mugger to go after his wife with the caption that according to the shari'a her "blood money" would be only half that of his. The Liberation Movement was outlawed on the grounds it did not sincerely believe in the concept of *velayat-e faqeh*. The mayor of Tehran – a Rafsanjani protégé – was tried on trumped-up charges of financial corruption. Moreover, the Revolutionary Guards – supported by vigilantes – broke up a protest meeting in Tehran University injuring more than a hundred and ransacking the student dormitories. Khatemi took the opportunity of December 7 both to celebrate that day and to warn that such clashes would undermine democracy and pave the way for the emergence of extremism.[67] Furthermore, the Guardian Council barred more than 2,000 candidates, including 87 deputies, from the forthcoming Majles elections. The barred deputies complained: "Our revolution brought freedom and independence in the name of Islam. But now our national rights are being trampled upon in the name of Islam."[68]

The reformers suffered yet another blow from an unexpected quarter – the United States. It came in the form of the "axis of evil" speech delivered by President Bush in January 2002. In naming Iran as a major threat to world peace, he accused it of aspiring to build nuclear weapons and of financing international terrorism directed at the United States. He also accused its "unelected leaders" of depriving the Iranian people of their freedoms. His national security advisor followed, denouncing Iran as a "totalitarian" nightmare. The speech came as a bolt from the blue since the state department and Iran had been working closely but quietly behind the scenes over Afghanistan – in overthrowing the Taliban and installing a new government in Kabul. The speech took the state department as much as Iran by surprise. A Western correspondent in Tehran reported: "Khatemi blames Bush's axis of evil speech for plunging Iran into an extended crisis that has played into the hands of his conservative opponents and has frozen hopes of domestic reform."[69] A British intelligence analyst argued that the speech had been counterproductive since it "played into the hands of the conservatives, bolstered their anti-Americanism, and helped silence the reformers."[70] An American journalist reported: "President Bush came to the rescue of the conservatives by naming Iran as part of the axis of evil. This threw the reformers on the defensive."[71] The *New York Times* reported:

"Ever since President Bush designated Iran part of the international terrorist network open to American attack, conservatives in Iran have been buoyed, trying to use a resurgence of disgust with America to quash reform at home. This has made it harder for President Khatemi to preserve his reformist agenda for promoting democracy."[72] One of the new Iranian intellectuals visiting Harvard complained that the speech "emboldened the conservatives to crack down further on those promoting change."[73] Another noted that the speech "energized the conservatives and infused a sense of urgency into their efforts to regain power."[74] Most serious of all, the speech, together with the other setbacks, divided the whole reform movement. Some, notably Khatemi, continued to insist that it was still possible to bring about reform from within the system. Others talked of the need for a more militant campaign – even a referendum. Yet others, disillusioned by the prospects of reform, withdrew from active politics. The liberal euphoria had evaporated.

This gave the conservatives the opportunity to win a series of elections – for municipal councils in 2003, for the Majles in 2004, and for the presidency in 2005. In all three campaigns, the conservative Militant Clergy Association and the Islamic Coalition Society ran against the liberal Militant Clergy Society, Islamic Iran Participation Party, Construction Executives, and Worker's House. The conservatives won in part because they retained their 25 percent base; in part because they recruited war veterans to run as their candidates; in part because they wooed independents on the issue of national security; but in most part because large numbers of women, college students, and other members of the salaried middle class stayed home. Turnout in the Majles elections fell below 51 percent – one of the worst since the revolution. In Tehran, it fell to 28 percent.

In the presidential elections, Mahmud Ahmadinejad – a relatively unknown candidate – won on the double platform of strengthening national security and fulfilling the populist promises of the Khomeini era. Describing himself as champion of the *mostazafen* as well as an *osulgar* (principalist) and *abadgar* (developer) – two recently coined terms – Ahmadinejad promised to raise wages and salaries, especially for teachers and government workers; alleviate poverty; tackle unemployment and poor housing; distribute bonuses to newlyweds; deliver "social justice" to the masses, particularly to war veterans; and, most emphatically of all, remove the cancerous sore of corruption which many felt endangered the whole body politic. He claimed that the masses were being "plundered" by "new capitalists" (*sarmayedaran-e now*) as well as by remnants of the "one thousand families." He denounced the stock exchange as a "den of gambling." He even accused his main opponent, Rafsanjani, of having converted the oil ministry into a family fiefdom and turned himself into one of the richest men in the country. The populist rhetoric was helped by television coverage of Ahmadinejad's own apartment showing that he lived a simple lower-middle-class life. Also helpful was the fact that Ahmadinejad's father had been a blacksmith – the same occupation as that of Kaveh, one of the lead heroes in the *Shahnameh*. Class identity was alive and well in Iran – despite all the changes brought about by the Islamic Revolution. With the reformers divided, Ahmadinejad swept the elections – although with a much lower turnout than in the previous two presidential contests. The conservatives had won not so much by expanding their limited core base as by dividing the reformers and discouraging them from voting. Electoral politics had come to Iran in all its complex aspects.

CONTEMPORARY IRAN

Iran entered the twenty-first century as a major regional power – certainly in the Persian Gulf, if not in the entire Middle East. With some 70 million people, it is the largest country in the region. It plays a key role in the Organization of Petroleum Exporting Countries, is the world's third largest producer of oil, and has the globe's third or perhaps even second largest proven reserves of gas and oil. It will remain important so long as the hydrocarbon age lasts. It has produced over the past century a strong centralized state – one whose arm reaches from the capital into the outlying provinces, touching in one way or another almost every citizen. It also controls a mass citizen army, which, although unequipped to wage offensive war, would be highly effective for defensive purposes. Iran cannot be dismissed as a "failed" state – unlike some in the region. Thanks mainly to oil revenues, it has brought citizens a respectable standard of living: low infant mortality, reasonable longevity, high literacy, impressive college enrollment – including for women – and for many of its citizens access not only to electricity, piped water, and modern transportation, but also to such consumer goods as refrigerators, telephones, radios, televisions, and cars. It now contains a large salaried middle class and an educated working class as well as a traditional entrepreneurial middle class. In many ways, the country is no longer part of the Third World.

What is more, Iran is bound together with a sense of national identity derived not only from its Shi'i and pre-Islamic heritages, but also from the shared experiences of the past century – the imperial threat from the West, the Constitutional Revolution, the nationalist movement led by Mossadeq, the traumatic 1953 coup, the Pahlavi era, and, of course, the dramatic experiences of both the Islamic Revolution and the total war with Iraq. Iranian identity has been forged not only by common history, common geography, common language, and common religion, but also by common experience in the recent past – including nine presidential and seven parliamentary elections since 1979. History has turned subjects, peasants, and often non-Persian speakers into fully fledged Iranian citizens. This national identity is questioned only in the peripheral Sunni regions inhabited by Kurds, Turkmans, and Baluchis. Unlike many states in the region, Iran is not the product of imperial map-making.

Iran's emergence as a regional power has brought it into a collision course with the other major power in the region – the United States, especially with the latter's recent occupation of Iraq and Afghanistan as well as establishment of military bases in the Caucasus and Central Asia, not to mention the earlier ones in Turkey and the Gulf sheikhdoms. Their relations are further complicated by the fact that Shi'is in the region – in Iraq, Afghanistan, and Lebanon – look toward Iran as their main protector against local and external threats. The USA–Iran rivalry has recently focused on the highly explosive issue of nuclear technology. Iran vehemently insists on the right to develop such technology, citing international law, the need to find energy alternatives, and the inalienable right of developing countries to enter the modern world by harnessing what it sees to be the cutting edge of science. It adds that it has no intention of expanding its current nuclear program to producing weapons. The USA insists with equal vehemence that Iran should not be trusted with nuclear technology – some even argue not with any nuclear know-how – because its real intention is to develop weapons of mass destruction. Such weapons, the USA claims, will not only violate international law, but will also change the whole balance of power in the region and pose an imminent threat to Israel, Saudi Arabia, and the Gulf sheikhdoms – not to mention the American presence in the Middle East. The forthcoming decade will probably answer the question as to how this explosive issue will be worked out: by one side or the other backing down; by a negotiated compromise in which the two powers learn to live together in the same dangerous neighborhood; or by ongoing brinkmanship which could easily escalate into a catastrophe on the magnitude of Europe's Thirty Years War.

Notes

INTRODUCTION

1. Conventional demographers estimate the total population in 1900 to have been fewer than 10 million. They do so by projecting back the 1956 census – the first national census carried out in Iran. These back projections, however, overlook the drastic losses suffered in the 1917–21 period brought about by war, famine, cholera, and the flu pandemic. For a somewhat exaggerated discussion of these losses see M. G. Majd, *The Great Famine and Genocide in Persia, 1917–1919* (New York: University Press of America, 2003). For a conventional back projection see C. Issawi, *Economic History of Iran, 1800–1914* (Chicago: Chicago University Press, 1971), pp. 26–34. Morgan Shuster, who as a chief financial advisor had direct interest in the topic, estimated the total population in 1912 to be more than 12 million. See M. Shuster, *The Strangling of Persia* (New York, 1912). Similarly, J. Balfour, a British financial advisor, estimated the 1917–20 losses to have been as much as 2 million. He placed the 1920 population at more than 13 million. See J. Balfour, *Recent Happenings in Persia* (London, 1922), p. 20.
2. A. Mounsey, *A Journey through the Caucasus and the Interior of Persia* (London, 1872), p. 329.
3. F. Hale, *From Persian Uplands* (London, 1920), p. 30.
4. F. M. Javanshir (F. Mizani), *Hemaseh-ye Dad* (Epic for Justice) (Tehran, 1980).
5. A. Shariati, *Majmu'eh-e Asar* (Collected Works) (Aachen: Husseinien-e Ershad Publications, 1977), Vol. XXII.
6. S. Najafabadi, *Shahed-e Javid* (Eternal Martyr) (Tehran, 1981).
7. A. Rezai, *Nahzat-e Husseini* (Hussein's Movement) (Springfield, Mo.: Liberation Movement of Iran Publications, 1975).
8. E. J. Hobsbawm, "From Social History to the History of Society," *Daedalus*, vol. 100 (Winter 1971), pp. 20–45.

1 "ROYAL DESPOTS": STATE AND SOCIETY UNDER THE QAJARS

1. G. Curzon, *Persia and the Persian Question* (London, 1892), I, p. 433.
2. R. Sheikholeslami, *The Structure of Central Authority in Qajar Iran, 1871–96* (Atlanta: Scholars Press, 1997), pp. 191–92.

196

3. A. Ashraf and A. Banuazizi, "Classes in the Qajar Period," in *Encyclopedia Iranica* (Costa Mesa, Calif.: Mazda, 1999), Vol. V, pp. 667–77.

4. A. Lambton, *Islamic Society in Persia* (Oxford, 1954), pp. 1–32; Lambton, "Justice in the Medieval Persian Theory of Kingship," *Studia Islamica*, Vol. 17 (1962), pp. 91–119.

5. M. Ansari, "Land and the Fiscal Organization of Late Qajar Iran," Unpublished Paper Presented at a Conference on the Economic History of the Middle East at Princeton University, 1974, p. 3.

6. M. Shuster, *The Strangling of Persia* (New York, 1912), pp. 277–81.

7. Curzon, *Persia and the Persian Question*, II, pp. 480–85.

8. M. Mirzayi, *Tarekh-e Berigard va Diviziyun-e Qazaq* (Short History of the Cossack Brigade and Division) (Tehran, 2004).

9. Military Attaché, "Memorandum on the Persian Army," FO 371/Persia 1907/34–2762.

10. J. Morier, *A Journey through Persia, Armenia, and Asia Minor* (London, 1812), p. 242.

11. Curzon, *Persia and the Persian Question*, I, p. 602.

12. P. Sykes, *Ten Thousand Miles in Persia* (New York, 1902), p. 259.

13. M. Amin al-Dowleh, *Khaterat-e Siyasi* (Political Memoirs) (edited by H. Farmanfarmayan) (Tehran, 1962), p. 77.

14. *Ibid.*, p. 258

15. A. Mostowfi, *Tarekh-e Idari va Ijtem'i-ye Dowreh-ye Qajariyya ya Sharh-e Zendegani-ye Man* (Administrative and Social History of the Qajar Era or Narrative of My Life), 3 vols. (Tehran, 1943–45), I, pp. 99–100.

16. W. Floor, "Change and Development in the Judicial System of Qajar Iran," in *Qajar Iran: Political, Social and Cultural Change, 1800–1925* (edited by E. Bosworth and C. Hillenbrand) (Edinburgh: Edinburgh University Press, 1983), p. 130.

17. J. Malcolm, *The History of Persia* (London, 1829), II, pp. 438–54.

18. A. Saidi-Sirjani (ed.), *Vaqay'-e Ettefaqiyeh* (Events that Occurred) (Tehran, 1982), pp. 1–243.

19. M. Dowlatabadi, *Tarkekh-e Mo'aser*, vol. I (Contemporary History) (Tehran, 1957), p. 327.

20. A. Piemontese, "An Italian Source for the History of Qajar Persia," *East and West*, Vol. 19, Nos. 1–2 (March–June 1969), p. 170.

21. Curzon, *Persia and the Persian Question*, I, pp. 391–432.

22. H. Qodsi (Azam al-Vazeh), *Ketab-e Khaterat-e Man*, Vol. I (Book of My Memoirs)(Tehran, 1963), p. 36.

23. A. Amanat, *Pivot of the Universe: Nasir al-Din Shah Qajar and the Iranian Monarchy* (Berkeley: University of California Press, 1997), pp. 19–20.

24. Curzon, *Persia and the Persian Question*, I, p. 411.

25. Mostowfi, *Administrative and Social History*, I, p. 259.

26. M. Bamdad, *Tarekh-e Rajal-e Iran* (History of Iranian Statesmen), 6 vols. (Tehran, 1968).

27. A. Ashraf, "Social Hierarchy in the Qajar Era," *Ketab-e Agah*, Vol. I (1981), pp. 71–98.

28. S. Benjamin, *Persia and the Persians* (Boston, 1887), p. 441.
29. L. Diba, *Royal Persian Paintings: The Qajar Epoch* (London: Tauris, 1998), p. 92.
30. Benjamin, *Persia and the Persians*, p. 384.
31. The numbers seventy-two and seventy-three – like twelve – have potent meaning in Islam as well as in Judaism and Christianity. They mark the numbers of sons Seth took with him into Noah's ark – each son representing the future "nations" of the world; the languages created to sabotage the Tower of Babel; the names Yahweh has; the Jewish elders whom Moses consulted both before the Exodus and before climbing the mountain to see God; the apostles Christ sent out into the world; the Medina delegates with whom Muhammad negotiated before initiating his *Hejira* (migration); the companions who participated in the Hejira; and the "branches" that eventually formed the flourishing tree of Islam. For true believers, the number 72–73 signifies the presence of God's hidden hand.
32. E. Sykes, *Through Persia on a Side-Saddle* (London, 1901), p. 154.
33. P. Chelkowski (ed.), *Ta'ziyeh: Ritual and Drama in Iran* (New York: New York University Press, 1979), p. 20.
34. Benjamin, *Persia and the Persians*, p. 379.
35. Curzon, *Persia and the Persian Question*, II, p. 499.
36. A. Piemontese, "The Statutes of the Qajar Order of Knighthood," *East and West*, Vol. 19, Nos. 3–4 (September–December 1969), pp. 431–73.
37. M. Hume-Griffith, *Behind the Veil in Persia* (London, 1909), p. 46.
38. A. Kasravi, *Tarekhcheh-e Shir-u-Khorshid* (Short History of the Lion and Sun) (Tehran, 1934), pp. 1–33.
39. J. Luft, "The Qajar Rock Reliefs," *Iranian Studies*, Vol. 36, Nos. 1–4 (2001), pp. 31–49.
40. E. Stack, *Six Months in Persia*, 2 vols. (New York, 1882), I, p. 105; W. Ousely, *Travels in the Various Countries of the East*, Vol. II (London, 1819), p. 115.
41. E. Browne, *Literary History of Persia* (Cambridge: Cambridge University Press, 1914), Vol. II, p. 143.
42. Malcolm, *History of Persia*, II, pp. 324–25.
43. P. Cox, "The Qashqai Tribes," FO 371/1912–1447.
44. Sykes, *Ten Thousand Miles in Persia*, p. 399.
45. M. I'temad al-Saltaneh, *Mir'at-e al-Buldan-e Nasseri* (Mirror of the Nasseri Lords) (Tehran, 1877), p. 270.
46. H. Garrod, "Tour of Tribal Areas of Fars," FO 371/Persia 1944/34–40180.
47. C. Gault, "Report on the Bakhtiaris," FO 371/Persia 1944/34–6816.
48. Stack, *Six Months in Persia*, II, p. 280.
49. L. Sheil, *Glimpses of Life and Manners in Persia* (London, 1858), p. 100.
50. Benjamin, *Persia and the Persians*, pp. 170–73, 471.
51. J. Fraser, *Historical and Descriptive Narrative Account of Persia* (Edinburgh, 1834), p. 303.
52. J. Fraser, *A Winter's Journey from Constantinople to Tehran*, Vol. II (London, 1838), p. 289.

53. F. Forbes-Leites, *Checkmate* (New York, 1927).

54. P. Sykes, *Ten Thousand Miles in Persia* (New York, 1902), p. 400.

55. Mostowfi, *Administrative and Social History*, III, p. 67.

56. M.-J. Good, "Social Hierarchy and Social Change in a Provincial Iranian Town," PhD thesis, Harvard University (1976), p. 58.

57. Sykes, *Ten Thousand Miles in Persia*, p. 400.

58. H. Rabino, *Mazandaran and Astarabad* (London, 1928), pp. 20–30; India Office, *Who's Who in Persia* (Simla: Government Press, 1923).

59. C. Davies, "A History of the Province of Fars during the Later Part of the Nineteenth Century," PhD thesis, Oxford University (1985).

60. A. Sha'bani, *Hezar Famil* (Thousand Families) (Tehran, 1987).

61. R. Binning, *A Journal of Two Years' Travel in Persia*, 2 vols. (London, 1857), II, pp. 47–8.

62. Rabino, *Mazandaran and Astarabad* , pp. 20–30.

63. C. Gault, "A Report on the Isfahan Province," FO 371/Persia 1945/34–6218.

64. Rabino, *Mazandaran and Astarabad*, p. 99.

65. C. and E. Burgess, *Letters from Persia, 1828–1855* (edited by B. Schwartz) (New York, 1942), p. 48.

66. C. MacGregor, *Narrative of a Journey through the Province of Khurasan*, 2 vols. (London, 1879), I, p. 277.

67. Burgess, *Letters from Persia*, p. 65.

68. Stack, *Six Months in Persia*, II, p. 250.

69. N. Daryabandari, *Ketab-e Mostatab-I Ashpazi*, 2 vols. (Book of Good Cooking) (Tehran, 1990).

70. G. Thaiss, "Religious Symbolism and Social Change," in *Scholars, Saints, and Sufis* (edited by N. Keddie) (Berkeley: University of California Press, 1972), pp. 349–66.

71. Davies, "A History of the Province of Fars," p. 389.

72. W. Ouseley, *Travels in Various Countries of the East*, Vol. III (London, 1812), p. 401.

73. M. Imami, "The First Tehran Census," *'Ulom-e Ejtema-yi*, Vol. 1, No. 3 (February 1970), pp. 76–94.

74. Malcolm, *History of Persia*, II, p. 429.

75. M. Tahvildar-e Isfahan, *Juqrafiya-ye Isfahan* (The Geography of Isfahan) (Tehran, 1963), pp. 88–90.

76. Sheil, *Glimpses of Life and Manners in Persia*, p. 325.

77. A. Kasravi, *Tarekh-e Pansad Saleh-e Khuzestan* (Five-Hundred-Year History of Khuzestan) (Tehran 1950), pp. 131–51.

78. A. Shamim, *Iran dar Dowreh-e Saltanat-e Qajar* (Iran during the Qajar Dynasty) (Tehran, 1963), p. 296.

79. A. Kasravi, *Tarekh-e Mashruteh-e Iran* (History of the Iranian Constitution) (Tehran, 1961), pp. 130–35, 171–73, 109–97, 490–94. The Sheikhi community was also important in Kerman. Percy Sykes, traveling through Kerman in 1900, estimated the town's population at around 49,000 consisting of 37,000 Shi'is, 6,000 Sheikhis, 3,000 Bahais, 60 Azalis, 1,700 Zoroastrians, 12,000

Sufis, 70 Sunnis, 70 Jews, and 20 Hindus. He estimated the nationwide Sheikhi population to be 50,000, concentrated in Tabriz, Kerman, and Hamadan. Sykes, *Ten Thousand Miles in Persia*, pp. 195–96.

80. Benjamin, *Persia and the Persians*, p. 379.
81. A. Lambton, *Landlord and Peasant in Persia* (Oxford: Oxford University Press, 1954), pp. 161–62.
82. J. Malcolm, *Sketches of Persia* (London, 1845), p. 156.
83. Gault, "Report on the Bakhtiaris."
84. *Ibid.*
85. Mostowfi, *Administrative and Social History*, I, p. 20.
86. C. A. De Bode, *Travels in Luristan and Arabistan*, Vol. I, (London, 1845), p. 181.
87. F. Barth, *Nomads of South Persia: The Basseri Tribe of the Khamseh Confederacy* (Boston: Little, Brown, 1961), p. 88.

2 REFORM, REVOLUTION, AND THE GREAT WAR

1. A. Ashraf, *Mavaneh-e Tarekhi-ye Rashad-e Sarmayehdari dar Iran* (Historical Obstacles to Capitalist Development in Iran) (Tehran, 1980).
2. N. Mozaffari, "Crafting Constitutionalism: Ali Akbar Dehkhoda and the Iranian Constitutional Revolution," PhD thesis, Harvard University (2001), p. 112.
3. H. Taqizadeh, "The term *Mashruteh*," *Ettela'at-e Mahaneh*, Vol. 7, No. 5 (October 1952), 3–4.
4. T. Atabaki, "Disgruntled Guests: Iranian Subaltern on the Margins of the Tsarist Empire," *International Instituut voor Sociale Geschiedenis*, Vol. 48 (2003), pp. 401–26.
5. I. Bishop, *Journeys in Persia and Kurdistan*, Vol. I (London, 1891), p. 267.
6. G. Curzon, *Persia and the Persian Question*, 2 vols. (London: Longmans, 1892), I, pp. 1–5.
7. *Ibid.*, II, p. 404.
8. *Ibid.*, II, p. 604.
9. M. Ansari, "Fiscal Organization and Financial Stringency in Iran, 1800–1925," unpublished paper, University of Chicago (1974), p. 19.
10. Curzon, *Persia and the Persian Question*, I, p. 480.
11. C. Issawi, *Economic History of Iran, 1800–1914*, (Chicago: Chicago University Press, 1971), p. 370.
12. A. Kasravi, *Tarekh-e Mashruteh-e Iran* (History of the Iranian Constitution) (Tehran, 1961), pp. 49–58.
13. British Government, *Correspondence Respecting the Affairs of Persia* (London: Government Printing House, 1909), Vol. I, No. 1, pp. 1.
14. M. Tafreshi-Husseini, *Ruznameh-e Akhbar-e Mashruteyat va Enqelab-e Iran* (Daily News on the Iranian Revolution and Constitution) (Tehran, 1973), p. 2.
15. M. Malekzadeh, *Tarekh-e Enqelab-e Mashruteyat-e Iran* (History of the Constitutional Revolution in Iran), 6 vols. (Tehran, 1949), II, p. 41.

16. Kasravi, *History of the Iranian Constitution*, p. 85.
17. A. Najmabadi, *The Daughters of Quchan* (Syracuse: Syracuse University Press, 1998).
18. British Government, *Correspondence Respecting the Affairs of Persia*, Vol I, No. 1, pp. 3–4.
19. Kasravi, *History of the Iranian Constitution*, p. 110.
20. Tafreshi-Husseini, *Daily News*, p. 40.
21. M. Heravi-Khurasani, *Tarekh-e Paydayesh-e Mashrutiyat-e Iran* (History of the Genesis of the Iranian Constitution) (Tehran, 1953), p. 50.
22. British Government, *Correspondence Respecting the Affairs of Persia*, Vol. 1, No. 1, p. 4.
23. E. Browne, *The Persian Revolution of 1905–1909* (London: Frank Cass, 1910), p. 137.
24. For the electoral law as well as the fundamental laws see *ibid.*, pp. 353–400.
25. E. Browne, *Press and Poetry of Modern Persia* (Cambridge: Cambridge University Press, 1914), p. 56.
26. Z. Shaji'i, *Nemayandegan-e Majles-e Showra-ye Melli* (Members of the National Consultative Assembly) (Tehran, 1965), p. 176.
27. British Legation, "Report on the National Assembly," FO 371/Persia 1907/34–301.
28. H. Siyah, *Khaterat-e Hajji Siyah* (Hajji Siyah's Memoirs) (Tehran, 1945), pp. 565–67.
29. Mostowfi, *Administrative and Social History*, Vol. II p. 75. See also India Office, *Who's Who in Persia* (Simla: Government Control Press, 1923), II.
30. British Legation, "Memorandum on the New Cabinet," FO 371/Persia 1907/34–312.
31. W. Olson, *Anglo-Iranian Relations during World War I* (London: Cass, 1984), pp. 14–16.
32. Mostowfi, *Administrative and Social History*, I, pp. 563.
33. Iranian Government, *Mozakerat-e Majles-e Showra-ye Melli* (Parliamentary Debates), First Majles, pp. 385–400.
34. Malekzadeh, *History of the Constitutional Revolution*, IV, p. 59.
35. H. Razavani (ed.), *Lavayeh-e Aqa-e Sheikh Fazlollah Nuri* (Sheikh Fazlollah Nuri's Documents) (Tehran, 1983), pp. 30–31.
36. H. Qodsi, *Ketab-e Khaterat-e Man* (Book of My Memoirs) (Tehran, 1963), p. 157.
37. Heravi-Khurasani, *History of the Genesis of the Iranian Constitution*, p. 126.
38. A. Dehkhoda, "Charivari," *Sur-e Israfil*, 30 December 1907.
39. India Office, *Who's Who in Persia*, p. 341.
40. British Legation, "Annual Report for 1908," FO 371/Persia 1909/956–2836.
41. H. Berberian, *Armenians and the Iranian Constitutional Revolution of 1905–1911* (Boulder: Westview Press, 2001).
42. M. Shuster, *The Strangling of Persia* (New York, 1912), p. 45.
43. N. Hamdani, *Pedaram Sattar Khan* (My Father Sattar Khan) (Tehran, 1960), p. 73.

44. J. Hone and P. Dickenson, *Persia in Revolution* (London, 1910), p. 27.
45. India Office, *Who's Who in Persia*, p. 201.
46. A. Amir, "Iranian Cabinets from the Time of the Constitutional Revolution to the Present," *Ettela'at-e Haftegi*, Vol. 1, No. 10–Vol. 2, No. 6 (March 1948–August 1950).
47. British Minister, "Monthly Report for June 1910," FO 371/Persia 1919/34–950.
48. British Minister, "Annual Report for Persia (1912)," FO 371/Persia 1913/34–1728.
49. British Consul, "Report on the Bakhtiari Tribe," FO 371/ Persia 1944/34–40181.
50. British Government, *Further Correspondence Respecting the Affairs of Persia* Vol. III (London: Government Printing House, 1914), pp. 135–36.
51. British Government, *Correspondence Respecting the Affairs of Persia*, Vol. I, p. 39; *Further Correspondence Respecting the Affairs of Persia*, Vol. I, p. 20.
52. British Minister, "Annual Report for Persia (1925)," FO 371/Persia 1926/34–11500.
53. British Minister, "General Situation Report," FO 371/Persia 1914/34–2059.
54. British Government, *Correspondence Respecting the Affairs of Persia*, I, pp. 39, 189; *Further Correspondence Respecting the Affairs of Persia*, I, pp. 152, 169.
55. Shuster, *Strangling of Persia*, p. 56.
56. British Government, *Further Correspondence Respecting the Affairs of Persia*, III, p. 137.
57. British Government, *Further Correspondence Respecting the Affairs of Persia*, I, p. 152.
58. British Political Resident, "Report on the Qashqai Tribe," FO 371/Persia 1912/34–1447.
59. British Political Resident, "Report on the Persian Gulf," FO 371/Persia 1912/34–1418.
60. British Minister, "Annual Report for Persia (1913)," FO 371/Persia 1914/34–2173.
61. British Minister, *Correspondence Respecting the Affairs of Persia*, II, No. 2, p. 146.
62. British Minister, Letter to the Foreign Minister (23 September 1912), FO 371/Persia 1912/34–1447.
63. D. Fraser, *Persia and Turkey in Revolt* (London: Blackwood, 1910), p. 36.
64. British Consul General, "Memorandum on the Sheikh of Mohammerah," FO 371/Persia 1909/34–715.
65. British Minister, "Annual Report for Persia (1912)," FO 371/Persia 1913/34–1728.
66. Fraser, *Persia and Turkey in Revolt*, p. 258.
67. British Consul, "Report on the Bakhtiari Tribe," FO 371/Persia 1944/34–40181.
68. British Minister, "Annual Report for Persia (1912)," FO 371/Persia 1913/34–1728.
69. British Minister, "Report on the Bakhtiari Khans," FO 371/Persia 1914/34–2073.

70. H. Taqizadeh, "List of Members of the Second Majles," *Kaveh*, 15 July 1918.
71. Z. Shaji'i, *Nemayandegan-e Majles-e Showra-ye Melli* (Deputies in the National Assembly) (Tehran, 1964), p. 176.
72. Moderate Party, *Maramnameh-e Firqeh* (Party Program) (Tehran, n.d.)
73. British Government, *Correspondence Respecting the Affairs of Persia*, II, p. 55.
74. British Government, *Correspondence Respecting Recent Affairs of Persia*, II, p. 56.
75. T. Atabaki, "The Ottomans' Secret Service Activities in Iran," unpublished paper, St Antony's College (1998), pp. 1–14.
76. British Minister, "General Situation Report on Persia," FO 371/Persia 1914/34–2059.
77. Olson, *Anglo-Iranian Relations*, p. 153.
78. British Minister, "Annual Report for Persia (1922)," FO 371/Persia 1923/34–10848. This annual report also covers the period from 1913 to 1922.
79. H. Balfour, *Recent Happenings in Persia* (London, 1922), p. 25
80. M. Donohoe, *With the Persian Expedition* (London: Arnold, 1919), p. 120.
81. H. Nicolson, *Curzon: The Last Phase* (London: Constable, 1934), p. 3.
82. A. Wynn, *Persia in the Great Game* (London: Murray, 2003), p. 316.
83. D. Gilmour, *Curzon* (London: Papermac, 1995), p. 515.
84. British Government, *Documents on British Foreign Policy, 1919–1934* (London: Government Printing House, 1948), First Series, Vol. IV, pp. 1125–26.
85. Nicolson, *Curzon*, p. 129.
86. India Office, "Mesopotamia Police Report (27 May 1929)," FO 371/Turkey 1929/44–5074.
87. M. Farrukh, *Khaterat-e Siyasi-ye Farrukh* (The Political Memoirs of Farrukh) (Tehran, 1969), pp. 15–17.
88. British Minister, "Annual Report for Persia (1922)," FO 371/Persia 1923/34–10848.
89. British Minister, *Documents on British Foreign Policy*, Vol. XIII, pp. 657, 720.
90. British Minister, *Documents on British Foreign Policy*, Vol. XIII, pp. 274–75.
91. General Dickson, *Documents on British Foreign Policy*, Vol. XIII, p. 585.
92. British Minister, "Memorandum on Persia," *Documents on British Foreign Policy*, Vol. XIII, p. 721.

3 THE IRON FIST OF REZA SHAH

1. British Government, *Documents on British Foreign Policy, 1919–1934* (London: Government Printing House, 1948), first series, III, p. 745.
2. E. Ironside, *High Road to Command* (London: Leo Caper, 1972), p. 161.
3. India Office, "Persian Situation in 1921," *India Office*/Political and Secret Library/10/907.
4. British Minister, "Annual Report for Persia (1922)," FO 371/ Persia 1925/34–10848.
5. British Government, *Documents on British Foreign Policy*, XIII, p. 731.
6. British Minister, "Annual Report for Persia (1922)," FO 371/Persia 1925/34–10848.

7. British Minister, "Annual Report for Persia (1922)," FO 371/Persia 1925/34–10848.
8. J. Shahri, *Tehran-e Qadem* (Old Tehran) (Tehran, 1978), p. 43.
9. British Minister, "Annual Report for Persia (1925)," FO 371/Persia 1926/34–11500; E.P. Elwell-Sutton, *Persian Oil* (London: Lawrence and Wishart, 1955), p. 74; J., Bharier, *Economic Development in Iran, 1900–1970* (London: Oxford University Press, 1971), p. 158.
10. A. Millspaugh, *The American Task in Persia* (New York: Century, 1925), p. 23.
11. *Ibid.*, p. 186.
12. *Ibid.*, p. 126.
13. British Minister, "Annual Report for Persia (1923)," FO 371/Persia 1925/34–10848.
14. British Minister, "Annual Report for Persia (1935)," FO 371/Persia 1936/34–20052.
15. British Minister, "Annual Report for Persia (1922)," FO 371/Persia 1925/34–10848.
16. War Office, "Memorandum on Persian Forces (August 1941)," FO 371/Persia 1941/34–27206.
17. British Minister, "Persian Attitudes to the War," FO 371/Persia 1940/34–24582.
18. British Minister, "Annual Report for Persia (1937)," *India Office*/Political and Secret Library/12/3472A.
19. D. Amini, *Poliys dar Iran* (Police in Iran) (Tehran, 1947).
20. British Minister, "Annual Report for Persia (1937)," *India Office*/ Political and Secret Library/12/3472A.
21. British Legation, "Biographies of Leading Personalities in Persia," FO 371/Persia 1940/34–24582.
22. In 1927, all the governor-generals without exception were either military officers or senior civil servants with titles. See British Minister, "Annual Report for Persia (1927)," FO 371/ Persia 1928/34–13069.
23. British Consul, "Report on Isfahan Province," FO 371/Persia 1945/34–45426.
24. D. Wilber, *Reza Shah Pahlavi* (Princeton: Exposition Press, 1975), pp. 243–44.
25. British Legation, "Report on Seizures of Land by the Shah," FO 371/Persia 1932/34–16077.
26. British Legation, "Acquisition of Land by the Shah," FO 371/Persia 1935/34–18992.
27. British Minister, "Annual Report for Persia (1927)," FO 371/Persia 1928/34–13069.
28. British Legation, "Biographies of Leading Personalities in Persia," FO 371/Persia 1940/34–24582.
29. British Minister, "Annual Report for Persia (1934)," FO 371/Persia 1935/34–18995.
30. M. Bahar, *Tarekh-e Mokhtasar-e Ahzab-e Siyasi-ye Iran* (Short History of Political Parties in Iran) (Tehran, 1944), p. 306.
31. Shaji'i, *Deputies in the National Assembly*, p. 176.

32. Presidential Office, *Asnad az Entekhabat-e Majles-e Showra-ye Melli dar Dowreh-e Pahlavi-e Aval* (Documents on Elections for the National Consultative Assembly in the First Pahlavi Era) (Tehran, 1999), pp. 37–44.

33. Presidential Office, *Documents on Elections*, p. 53.

34. British Minister, "Annual Report for Persia (1926)," FO 371/Persia 1927/34–12296.

35. H. Kasravi, "Trials," *Parcham*, 28 July 1942.

36. British Legation, "Biographies of Leading Personalities in Persia," FO 371/Persia 1940/34-24582.

37. A. Matin-Daftari, "Memoirs from Previous Elections," *Khvandaniha*, 5 April 1956.

38. British Minister, "Annual Report for Persia (1927)," FO 371/Persia 1928/34–13069.

39. British Legation, "Biographies of Leading Personalities in Persia," FO 371/Persia 1929/34-13483.

40. F. Farmanfarma, *Khaterat-e Mohabes* (Prison Memoirs) (edited by M. Ettehadieh) (Tehran, 1976).

41. British Legation, "Biographies of Leading Personalities in Persia," FO 371/Persia 1929/34-13483.

42. British Minister, "Annual Report for Persia (1927)," FO 371/Persia 1928/34–13069.

43. C. Schayegh, "Modern Civilization is Paradoxical: Science, Medicine, and Class in the Formation of Semi-Colonial Iran, 1900–1940s," PhD thesis, Columbia University (2003), p. 201.

44. H. Filmer, (J. Childs), *The Pageant of Persia* (London, 1936), p. 368.

45. *Ibid.*, p. 378.

46. Anonymous, "Education in Iran," *Iranshahr*, Vol. 3, No. 1 (December 1924), pp. 56–58.

47. Millspaugh, *The American Task in Persia*, pp. 100–12.

48. D. Menashri, *Education and the Making of Modern Iran* (Ithaca: Cornell University Press, 1992), p. 110.

49. B. Moazemi, "The Making of the State, Religion and the Islamic Revolution in Iran (1796–1979)," PhD thesis, New School University (2003), p. 270.

50. British Minister, "Annual Report for Persia (1934)," FO 371/Persia 1935/34–18995.

51. British Minister, "Annual Report for Persia (1933)," FO 371/Persia 1934/34–17909.

52. K. Bayat, "The Cultural Academy and Changes of Place Names in Iran," *Nashreh-e Danesh*, No. 11 (1990–91), pp. 12–24.

53. H. Kazemzadeh, "The Formation of the National Heritage Society," *Iranshahr*, Vol. 3, No. 10 (August 1925), pp. 12–14.

54. M. Husseini, "Prisons and Imprisonment in Iran," *Ganjieh*, Vol. 1, Nos. 2–3 (Fall–Winter 1991), pp. 44–58.

55. Gh. Forutan, *Hezb-e Tudeh dar Sahneh-ye Iran* (The Tudeh Party on the Iranian Scene) (n.p., n.d.), p. 242.

56. A. Dashti, *Ayyam-e Mahbas* (Prison Days) (Tehran, 1954).
57. F. Richards, *A Persian Journey* (London: Jonathan Cape, 1932), p. 190.
58. F. Bohrer (ed.), *Sevruguin and the Persian Image: Photography of Iran, 1870–1930* (Seattle: University of Washington Press, 1999), p. 29.
59. Iranian Government, "Registered Doctors in Tehran," *Muzakert-e Melli* (Parliamentary Debates), 14th Majles, 1 January 1945.
60. B. Good, "The Social History of Maragheh: Health Care, Stratification, and Reform," PhD Thesis, Harvard University (1976), p. 49.
61. Shahri, *Old Tehran*, p. 151.
62. *Ibid.*, pp. 1–10.
63. British Minister, "Annual Report for Persia (1928)," FO 371/Persia 1929/34–13799.
64. British Minister, "Annual Report for Persia (1937)," *India Office*/Political and Secret Library/12/3472A.
65. A. Millspaugh, *Americans in Persia* (Washington, DC: Brookings Institution Press, 1946), pp. 34, 84.
66. A. Lambton, "The Situation in Iran (May 1941)," *India Office*/Political and Secret Library/12/3405.
67. Ambassador, Letter to the Secretary of State (26 June 1945), *Foreign Relations of the United States* (Washington, DC: Government Printing Office, 1958–79), 1945, Vol. VIII, p. 385.
68. British Minister, "Annual Report for Persia (1924)," FO 371/Persia 1925/34–10848.
69. British Minister, "Annual Report for Persia (1927)," FO 371/Persia 1928/34–13079
70. British Consul, "Report on the Events in Mashad," FO 371/Persia 1935/34–18997.
71. British Legation, "Report on the Situation in Iran (5 January 1935)," FO 371/34–18992.
72. British Minister, Letter of 7 February 1936, FO 371/Persia 1936/34-20048.
73. British Minister, Letter of 7 February 1936, FO 371/Persia 1936/34-20048.
74. British Minister, "Annual Report on Persia (1937)," *India Office*/Political and Secret Library/12–3472A.
75. A. Kasravi, "The Case for the Accused," *Parcham*, 16 August 1942.
76. A. Kasravi, "Concerning Reza Shah Pahlavi," *Parcham*, 23–25 June 1942.
77. Millspaugh, *Americans in Persia*, p. 5.
78. A. Lambton, "The Situation in Iran (May 1941)," *India Office*/Political and Secret Library/12/3405.
79. British Minister, "Annual Report on Persia (1937)," *India Office*/Political and Secret Library/12/3472A.

4 THE NATIONALIST INTERREGNUM

1. British Minister, "Annual Report for Persia (1941)," *India Office*/Political and Secret Library/12/3472A.
2. United Nations, *Supplement to the World Report: Economic Conditions in the Middle East* (New York: UN Publishing House, 1953), p. 79.

3. War Office, "Memorandum on the Reorganization of the Persian Army," FO 371/Persia 1941/34-27251. British Ambassador, "Conversations with the Shah," FO 371/Persia 1942/34-31385. The shah told Bullard that "his people had no ideals" and that he could give them ideals through a large army.

4. *Ibid.*

5. *Ibid.*

6. British Minister, 16 December 1943, FO 371/Persia 1943/34-35077.

7. Foreign Office, "The Merits and Demerits of the Shah," FO 371/Persia 1943/38-35072.

8. H. Kuhi-Kermani, *Az Shahrivar 1320 to Faje'eh-e Azerbaijan* (From August 1941 to the Azerbaijan Tragedy) (Tehran, 1944), I, p. 118.

9. Iranian Government, *Muzakerat-e Majles* (Parliamentary Debates), 13th Majles, 29 November 1941–16 June 1942.

10. British Minister, 10 July 1943, FO 371/Persia 1943/34-35072.

11. British Consul in Kermanshah, Monthly Diary (October), FO 371/Persia 1942/34-31402.

12. British Minister, 7 June 1943, FO 371/Persia 1943/34-55070.

13. British Minister, "Annual Report for Persia (1941)," *India Office*/Political and Secret Library/12-3472A.

14. British Minister, 10 April 1942, FO 371/Persia 1942/34-31285.

15. R. Bullard, *Letters from Persia* (London: Tauris, 1991), p. 147.

16. India Office, *Who's Who in Persia* (1922).

17. A. Sepehr, "Qavam al-Saltaneh after August 1941," *Salnameh-e Donya*, Vol. 15 (1959), pp. 55–56.

18. N. Shabstari, "Qavam al-Saltaneh," *Vazifeh*, 25 February 1946.

19. British Minister, 31 August 1943, FO 371/Persia 1943/34-35073.

20. British Minister, "Monthly Reports for February (1943)," FO 371/Persia 1943/34-35070.

21. British Embassy, "Leading Personalities in Persia (1947)," FO 371/Persia 1947/34-62035.

22. Shaji'i, *Deputies in the National Assembly*, p. 176.

23. Foreign Office, Comment on 10 April 1942 Memorandum, FO 371/Persia 1942/34-31385.

24. British Consul in Tabriz, 9 July 1943, FO 371/Persia 1943/34-35098.

25. British Embassy, "Leading Personalities of Persia (1947)," FO 371/Persia 1947/34-62035.

26. British Consul in Isfahan, 15 April 1943, FO 371/Persia 1943/34-31412.

27. British Consul in Isfahan, "Report on Isfahan," FO 371/Persia 1945/34-45476.

28. Editorial, "End of the Tehran Elections," *Mardom*, 6 February 1944.

29. I. Iskandari, *Khaterat-e Siyasi* (Political Memoirs), Vol. II (edited by B. Amir-Khosravi and F. Azarnow) (France: 1986), pp. 1–5, 12–13. See also I. Iskandari, *Yadmandeh-ha* (Memoirs) (Germany, 1986), pp. 98–99.

30. Comments in the FO, 23 October 1941, FO 371/Persia 1941/42-27155.

31. Tudeh Party, "Party Program," *Rahbar*, 5-7 September 1944.

32. *New York Times*, 15 June 1945.

33. British Ambassador, 13 June 1946, FO 371/Persia 1946/34-52664.
34. American Ambassador, 31 May 1946, *Foreign Relations of United States* (Washington, DC, 1946), VII, p. 490.
35. British Cabinet, "Notes on the Report of the Parliamentary Delegation to Persia," FO 371/Persia1946/34-52616.
36. British Embassy, 29 May 1946, FO 371/Persia 1946/34-52714.
37. British Embassy, 18 April 1946, FO 371/Persia 1946/34-52673.
38. British Embassy, "Political Activity for the Majles Election," FO 371/Persia 1943/34-35074.
39. British Consul in Mashed, "Six Monthly Reports (July–December 1943)," FO 371/Persia 1944/34-40184.
40. British Labour Attaché, "The Tudeh Party and the Iranian Trade Unions," FO 371/Persia 1947/34-61993.
41. British Military Attaché, 10 June 1946, FO 371/Persia 1946/34-52710.
42. British Consul in Isfahan, 4 February 1944, FO 371/Persia 1944/34-40163.
43. British Ambassador, "Memorandum on the Present Situation in Persia," *India Office*/L/P&S/12-3491A.
44. Tudeh Party, "Petition in Support of Tudeh Candidates in the Majles Elections," *Mardom*, 6 December 1943.
45. *The Times*, 24 October 1947.
46. British Ambassador, 25 October 1944, FO 371/Persia 1944/34-6058.
47. Iskandari, *Political Memoirs*, II, pp. 87–98.
48. J. Hassanov, "South Azerbaijan – 1945," unpublished paper on documents on Iran in the Baku Archives.
49. British Consul in Khorramshahr, "Report on Tudeh Activities in the Oil Industry," *F.o. 371*/Persia 1946/34-52714.
50. M. Mossadeq, "Proposal for Reform of the Electoral Law," *Ayandeh*, Vol. 3 (1944), pp. 61–63.
51. M. Mossadeq, Speech, *Parliamentary Debates*, 14th Majles, 2 June 1944.
52. British Embassy, "Leading Personalities in Persia (1952)," *F.O. 416*/Persia 1952/105.
53. J. Emami, *Parliamentary Debates*, 16th Majles, 3 November 1951.
54. Foreign Office, "Memorandum," *FO 371*/Persia 1957/127074.
55. M. Mossadeq, "Speech to the Nation," *Bakhtar-e Emruz*, 27 July 1953.
56. British Ministry of Fuel, Memorandum on Persian Oil, FO 371/Persia 1951/98608.
57. British Foreign Ministry, Memorandum on the Persian Oil Crisis, FO 371/Persia 1951/91471.
58. British Ambassador, "Memorandum to London," FO 371/Persia 1951/91606.
59. British Ambassador, "Comparison between Persian and Asian Nationalisms in General," FO 371/Persia 1951/91464.
60. *Washington Post*, 11 July 1951.
61. FO 248/Persia 1951/1527.
62. FO 248/Persia 1951/1528.
63. Foreign Office, Memorandum, FO 371/Persia 1952/98608.

64. D. Acheson, *Present at the Creation* (New York: Norton, 1969), pp. 680–81.
65. FO 371/Persia 1952/98602.
66. D. Wilber, "Overthrow of Premier Mossadeq of Iran," unpublished CIA report, 1954. See also http://cryptome.org/cia-iran-all.htm.
67. S. Marigold, "The Streets of Tehran," *The Reporter*, 10 November 1953.
68. *New York Times*, 20 August 1953.
69. President Eisenhower, "Address to the Nation," *Declassified Documents/1978/White House/Doc. 318.*

5 MUHAMMAD REZA SHAH'S WHITE REVOLUTION

1. H. Beblawi and G. Luciani (eds.), *The Rentier State* (London: Helm, 1987).
2. Foreign Relations Senate Committee, *US Military Sales to Iran* (Washington, DC: US Printing Office, 1976), p. 5.
3. US Congressional Joint Committee, *Economic Consequences of the Revolution in Iran* (Washington, DC: US Printing Office, 1980), p. 76.
4. E. Bayne, *Persian Kingship in Transition* (New York: American Universities Field Staff, 1968), p.186.
5. J. Kraft, "The Crisis in Iran," *The New Yorker*, 18 December 1978.
6. *Ibid.*
7. F. FitzGerald, "Giving the Shah Everything He Wants," *Harper's Magazine*, November 1974.
8. R. Graham, *Iran: The Illusion of Power* (New York: St. Martin's Press, 1979), p. 143.
9. FitzGerald, "Giving the Shah Everything He Wants."
10. B. Maghsoudlou, *In Sou-e Zahan, An Sou-e Mardmak* (This Side of the Mind, That Side of the Pupil) (Tehran, 1998), p. 307.
11. W. Branigin, "Pahlavi Fortune: A Staggering Sum," *Washington Post*, 17 January 1979.
12. A. Crittenden, "Bankers Say Shah's Fortune is Well Above a Billion," *New York Times*, 10 January 1979.
13. British Ambassador, 19 April l955, FO 371/Persia 1955/114807.
14. British Embassy, "Leading Personalities in Persia (1947)," FO 416/105.
15. A. Alam, *The Shah and I* (New York: St. Martin's Press, 1992).
16. W. Holden, "Shah of Shahs, Shah of Dreams," *New York Times Magazine*, 26 May 1974.
17. Z. Shajii, *Vezarat va Vaziran dar Iran*, Vol. 1 (Ministries and Ministers in Iran) (Tehran, 1975).
18. Z. Shajii, *Nemayandegan-e Majles-e Showra-ye Melli* (Deputies in the National Majles Tehran, 1964).
19. M. Pahlavi, *Mission for My Country* (London: Hutchinson, 1961), p. 173.
20. A. Taheri, "Historic Interview with His Imperial Majesty," *Kayhan International*, 10 November 1976.
21. R. Loeffler, "From Tribal Order to Bureaucracy: The Political Transformation of the Boir Ahmadi," unpublished paper, 1978.

22. E. Rouleau, "L'Iran a l'heure de l'enbourgeoisement," *Le Monde*, 4–9 October 1973.

23. These statistics have been obtained mainly from the national censuses carried out in 1956, 1966, and 1976. See Plan and Budget Organization, *Salnameh-e Amar-e Keshvar* (Annual National Statistics) (Tehran, 1956, 1966, 1976).

24. International Labor Office, "Employment and Income Policies for Iran," unpublished report, Geneva, 1972, Appendix C, p. 6.

25. Kraft, "Crisis in Iran."

26. A. Mansur, "The Crisis in Iran," *Armed Forces Journal International*, January 1979, pp. 33–34.

27. F. Kazemi, *Poverty and Revolution in Iran* (New York: New York University Press, 1980), p. 25

28. Graham, *Iran*, p. 25.

29. FitzGerald, "Giving the Shah Everything He Wants."

30. T. Shariati (Introduction) to A. Shariati, *Abu Zarr: Khodaparast-e Sosiyalist* (Abu Zarr: The God Worshipping Socialist) (Tehran, 1989), p. iii.

31. Anonymous, "Commemoration of Dr. Shariati's Emigration," *Ettela'at*, 17 May 1978.

32. Husseinieh-e Ershad, *Majmueh-e Asrar az Baradar Shahed Ali Shariati* (The Collected Works of Martyred Brother Ali Shariati), 35 vols.(Solon, Ohio: Muslim Student Association, 1977).

33. A. Shariati, *Darsha-ye Islamshenasi* (Lessons on Islam) (Houston: Muslim Student Association, n.d), Lesson II, pp. 98–99.

34. Husseinieh-e Ershad, *Collected Works*, X.

35. R. Khomeini, *Velayat-e Faqeh: Hokumat-e Islami* (The Jurist's Guardianship: Islamic Government) (Tehran, 1978).

36. M. Kadivar, *Andisheh-e Siyasi dar Islam* (Political Thought in Islam) (Tehran, 1998); *Nazariyeh-ha-ye Dowlat dar Feqh-e Shiah* (Ideas of Government in Shi'i Law) (Tehran, 1998); and *Hokumat-e Velay'e* (Guardianship Government) (Tehran, 1998).

37. R. Khomeini, Speech, *Ettela'at*, 2 December 1985.

38. Front for the Liberation of the Iranian People, *Majmu'eh az Maktab, Sukhanrani-ha, Payham-ha va Raftari-ha-ye Imam Khomeini)* (Collection from Imam Khomeini's Teachings, Speeches, Messages, and Activities) (Tehran, 1979).

39. Rouleau, "L'Iran a l'heure de l'embougeoisement."

40. K. Musavi, "The Beginnings of the Rastakhiz Party," unpublished paper, St. Antony's College, Oxford, 1982.

41. S. Huntington, *Political Order in Changing Societies* (New Haven: Yale University Press, 1968).

42. FitzGerald, "Giving the Shah Everything He Wants," p. 82.

43. Resurgence Party, *The Philosophy of Iran's Revolution* (Tehran, 1976).

44. Taheri, "Historic Interview…" *Kayhan International*, 10 November 1976.

45. P. Vieille and A. Bani-Sadr, *L'analyse des elections nonconcurrentielles* (Analysis of the Non-Competitive Elections) (Paris, 1976), p. 1.

46. P. Azr, "The Shah's Struggle against the Guilds," *Donya*, Vol. 2 (December 1975), pp. 10–14.

47. M. Pahlavi, *Answer to History* (New York: Stein and Day, 1982), p. 156.

48. P. Balta, "Iran in Revolt," *Ettela'at*, 4 October 1979.

49. J. Kendall, "Iran's Students and Merchants Form an Unlikely Alliance," *New York Times*, 7 November 1979.

50. A. Masoud, "The War against Profiteers," *Donya*, No. 3 (January 1976), pp. 6–10.

51. Balta, "Iran in Revolt."

52. E. Rouleau, "Iran: Myth and Reality," *The Guardian*, 31 October 1976.

53. N. Cage, "Iran: Making of a Revolution," *New York Times*, 17 December 1978.

54. Anonymous, "The *Nationalization* of Religion," *Mojahed*, No. 29 (March 1975), pp. 6–10.

55. O. Fallaci, *Interviews with History* (Boston: Houghton Mifflin, 1976), pp. 262–87.

56. A. Rouhani, "Proclamation," *Mojahed*, No. 30 (May 1975), p. 7.

57. R. Khomeini, "Proclamation," *Mojahed*, No. 29 (March 1975), pp. 1–11.

6 THE ISLAMIC REPUBLIC

1. For a good summary of such discussions, see S. Bakhash, "Who Lost Iran?," *New York Review of Books*, 14 May 1981; and W. Daughterly, "Behind the Intelligence Failure in Iran," *International Journal of Intelligence and Counter-Intelligence*, Vol. 14, No. 4 (Winter 2001), pp. 449–84.

2. Editorial, "Fifty Years of Treason," *Khabarnameh* (Newsletter), No. 46 (April 1976).

3. Amnesty International, *Annual Report for 1974–75* (London: Amnesty International, 1975); International Commission of Jurists, *Human Rights and the Legal System in Iran* (Geneva: International Commission of Jurists, 1976); W. Butler, "Memorandum on Proposed Amendments on the Iranian Military Court Rules of Procedure," unpublished letter to the International Commission of Jurists, 1977.

4. W. Butler, "Private Audience with the Shah of Iran on May 30, 1977," unpublished memorandum to the International Commission of Jurists.

5. N. Pakdaman, "Ten Nights of Poetry Readings: An Evaluation of an Event at the Beginning of the Iranian Revolution," *Kankash*, No. 12 (Fall 1995), pp. 125–206.

6. Editorial, "Iran and the Black and Red Reactionaries," *Ettela'at*, 7 January 1978.

7. Center of Qom Seminaries, "Declaration," *Mojahed*, No. 53 (January 1978).

8. After the revolution, a group of freelance religious fanatics were found guilty of the arson. See Sh. Nabavi, "Abadan, 19th August, Cinema Rex," *Cheshmandaz*, No. 20 (Spring 1999), pp. 105–27.

9. W. Branigin, "Abadan Mood Turns Sharply Against the Shah," *Washington Post*, 26 August 1978.

10. A. McDermouth, "Peacock Throne Under Pressure," *Financial Times*, 12 September 1978.

11. J. Gueyras, "Liberalization is the Main Casualty," *The Guardian*, 17 September 1978.
12. D. Harney, *The Priest and the King: An Eyewitness Account of the Iranian Revolution* (London: Tauris, 1999), p. 25.
13. E. Baqi, "Figures for the Dead in the Revolution," *Emruz*, 30 July 2003.
14. Document, "Resolution Passed by Acclamation in the Ashura Rally," *Khabarnameh*, 15 December 1978.
15. R. Apple, "Reading Iran's Next Chapter," *New York Times*, 13 December 1978.
16. T. Allway, "Iran Demonstrates," *Christian Science Monitor*, 12 December 1978.
17. A. Ashraf and A. Banuazizi, "The State, Classes and Modes of Mobilization in the Iranian Revolution," *State, Culture and Society*, Vol. 1, No. 3 (Spring 1985), p. 23.
18. Baqi, "Figures for the Dead in the Revolution."
19. P. Balta, "L'action decisive des groupes de guerilla," *Le Monde*, 13 February 1979.
20. Y. Ibrahim, "Scores Dead in Tehran," *New York Times*, 11 February 1979.
21. *Kayhan*, 11 February 1979.
22. O. Fallaci, "Interview with Mehdi Bazargan," *New York Times*, 21 October 1979.
23. *Ettela'at*, 1 March 1979.
24. O. Fallaci, "Interview with Khomeini," *New York Times*, 7 October 1979.
25. Islamic Republic, *Qanon-e Asasi-ye Jomhuri-ye Islami-ye Iran* (The Constitution of the Islamic Republic of Iran) (Tehran: Government Printing House, 1989), pp. 1–79.
26. H. Montazeri, *Ettela'at*, 8 October 1979.
27. Fallaci, "Interview with Khomeini."
28. R. Khomeini, "Government is an Absolute Authority Entrusted by Divinity to the Prophet," *Kayhan-e Hava'e*, 19 January 1988.
29. *Ettela'at*, 19 September 1979; see also A. Entezaam, "Letter to the Court," *Ettela'at*, 30 June 1980.
30. *Ettela'at*, 8 March 1980.
31. *Kayhan*, 7 November 1979. See also "Interview with Sheikh Ali Tehrani," *Iran Times*, 20 July 1984.
32. *Ettela'at*, 24 November 1979.
33. Islamic Republic of Iran, "Government Employees," www.sci.or.ir/english/sel/f3/F19.HTM.
34. M. Bazargan, "The State Should be Given Back to the Nation," *Ettela'at*, 10 May 1979.
35. Government spokesmen broke down the 160,000 dead into: 79,664 pasdars, 35,170 from regular military, 5,061 gendarmers, 2,075 from the Construction Crusade, 1,006 from the revolutionary komitehs, 264 from the police, and 11,000 civilians – most of the latter were killed in air attacks. The official figures did not reveal how many died later from gas and chemical attacks. For the official figures see *Iran Times*, 23 September 1988.
36. *Iran Times*, 16 April 1982.

37. *Iran Times*, 4 January 1980.
38. Anonymous, "Millions Plundered," *Iranshahr*, Vol. 1, No. 6 (December 1978).
39. Anonymous, "The Economy is too Dependent on Oil," *Economist*, 16 January 2003.
40. S. Maloney, "Politics, Patronage, and Social Justice: Parastatal Foundations and Post-Revolutionary Iran," PhD thesis, fletcher School, 2000.
41. J. Amuzegar, *Iran's Economy under the Islamic Republic* (London: Tauris, 1993), p. 100.
42. L. Binder, "Iran's Unfinished Revolution," in *Economic Consequences of the Revolution in Iran* (Washington, DC: Joint Economic Committee of the US Congress, 1980), pp. 22–46; M. Fischer, "Islam and the Revolt of the Petit Bourgeoisie," *Deadalus*, Vol. 111, No. 2 (Winter 1982), pp. 101–25.
43. A. Keshavarzian, "Bazaar under Two Regimes," PhD thesis, Princeton University, 2003.
44. Islamic Majles, *Ashnai-ye Ba Majles-e Showra-ye Islami*, Vol. 11 (Guide to the Islamic Majles) (Tehran, 1992), p. 205.
45. R. Khomeini, "Eight Point Declaration," *Ettela'at*, 16 December 1981.
46. R. Khomeini, "Address to Merchants," *Ettela'at*, 17 January 1981.
47. R. Khomeini, "Complete Text of the Last Will and Testament," *Kayhan-e Hava'e*, 14 June 1989.
48. A. Khamenei, Speech, *Iran Times*, 18 December 1988.
49. Economist Intelligence Unit, *Iran Risk Analysis* (London: The Economist, 2003), p. 10.
50. A. Schirazi, *Islamic Development Policy: The Agrarian Question in Iran* (London: Lynne Rienner, 1993), pp. 194–95.
51. B. Houchard, *Atlas d'Iran* (Paris: Reclus, 1998), p. 60.
52. A. Khamenei, Speech, *Ettela'at*, 6 March 1981.
53. For figures on executions, see E. Abrahamian, *Tortured Confessions: Prisons and Public Recantations in Modern Iran* (Berkeley: University of California Press, 1999), pp. 124–29.
54. Amnesty International, *Iran: Violations of Human Rights* (London: Amnesty Press, 1991), p. 12. See also Human Rights Watch, "Pour Mohammadi and the 1988 Prison Massacres," *Human Rights Watch Report*, December 2005.
55. A. Janati, Speech, *Kayhan-e Hava'e*, 24 May 1989.
56. A. Khamenei, "The Economy and Society," *Kayhan-e Hava'e*, 11 October 1989.
57. H. Rafsanjani, "Put Away Childish Things," *Iran Times*, 21 October 1988.
58. Anonymous, "A Survey of Iran: The Children of the Revolution," *The Economist*, 18 January 1997.
59. J. Larsen, "Iran's Birth Rate Plummeting at Record Pace," *The Humanist*, January–February 2003; H. Hoodfar, "Devices and Desires," *Middle East Report*, September–October 1994.
60. M. Khatemi, "Address to Students," *National Radio Agency*, 23 December 2001.
61. *The Economist*, 9 February 2000.
62. *The Economist*, 16 January 2003.

63. M. Khatemi, "Trust is Basis of Dialogue among Civilizations," *Ettela'at*, 9 January 1998.
64. W. Samii, "Iran Report: White House Backs ILSA Renewal," *Radio Free Europe*, 11 June 2001.
65. J. Borger, "Iran's Moral Enforcers Beat a Retreat," *Guardian Weekly*, 3 May 1998.
66. BBC, 21 March 2001.
67. M. Khatemi, "Address to Students," *IRNA*, 23 December 2001.
68. G. Esfandiari, "Reformist Fire Unprecedented Criticism," *Radio Free Europe*, 18 February 2004.
69. C. de Bellaigue, "Big Deal in Iran," *New York Review of Books*, 28 February 2004.
70. D. Neep, "Dealing with Iran," www.rusi.org.
71. W. Mason, "Iran's Simmering Discontent," *World Policy Journal*, Vol. 19, No 1 (Spring 2002), pp. 71–80.
72. N. MacFarquhar, "Millions in Iran Rally Against the US," *New York Times*, 12 February 2002.
73. B. Slavin, "New Attitudes Color Iranian Society," *USA Today*, 1 March 2005.
74. K. Yasin, "US Hard-Line Helped Bring About Reformists' Demise in Iran," *Eurasia Insight*, 10 March 2004.

Bibliography

For the sake of brevity, the bibliography lists recent rather than older works; and dispenses with Iranian publishers as well as with nineteenth-century European ones that no longer exist. The unpublished British documents are in the Public Record Office and India Office in the United Kingdom under the files FO 371, FO 248, FO 416, L/P, and S/12.

Amin al-Dowleh, M., *Khaterat-e Siyasi* (Political Memoirs) (edited by K. Farmanfarmayan) (Tehran, 1962).

Amirahmadi, H., "Transition from Feudalism to Capitalist Manufacturing and the Origins of Dependency Relations in Iran," PhD thesis, Cornell University (1982).

Ansari, M., "Land and the Fiscal Organization of Late Qajar Iran," Unpublished Paper Presented at a Conference on the Economic History of the Middle East, Princeton University, 1974.

Ashraf, A., "Social Hierarchy in the Qajar Era," *Ketab-e Agah*, Vol. 1 (1981), pp. 71–98.

Ashraf, A. and Banuazizi, A., "Classes in the Qajar Period," in *Encyclopaedia Iranica* (Costa Mesa, Calif.: Mazda, 1991), Vol. v, pp. 667–77.

Ashuri, D., *Farhang-e Siyasi* (Political Dictionary) (Tehran, 1979).

Ayin, A., *Vazhehnameh-e Siyasi-Ijtemayi* (Dictionary of Political and Social Terms) (Tehran, 1980).

Bamdad, M., *Tarekh-e Rajal-e Iran* (History of Iranian Statesmen), 6 vols. (Tehran, 1968).

Benjamin, S., *Persia and the Persians* (Boston, 1887).

Binning, R., *A Journal of Two Years' Travel in Persia*, 2 vols. (London, 1857).

Bruk, S. I., "The Ethnic Composition of the Countries of Western Asia," *Central Asian Review*, Vol. 7, No. 4 (1960), pp. 417–20.

Burgess, C. and E., *Letters from Persia, 1828–1855* (edited by B. Schwartz) (New York, 1942).

Carr, E. H., *What is History?* (London: Penguin, 1962).

Chelkowski, P., *Ta'ziyeh: Ritual and Drama in Iran* (New York: New York University Press, 1979).

Curzon, G., *Persia and the Persian Question*, 2 vols. (London: Longmans, 1892).

Davies, C., "A History of the Province of Fars during the Later Nineteenth Century," PhD thesis, Oxford University (1985).

Diba, L., *Royal Persian Paintings: The Qajar Epoch* (London: Tauris, 1998).

Dowlatabadi, Y., *Hayat-e Yahya* (My Life) (Tehran, 1982).

Field, H., *Contribution to the Anthropology of Iran* (Chicago: Field Museum of Natural History, 1939).

Forbes-Leites, F., *Checkmate* (New York, 1927).

Good, M.-J., "Social Hierarchy and Social Change in a Provincial Iranian Town," PhD thesis, Harvard University (1976).

Grigor, T., "Cultivat(ing) Modernities: The Society for National Heritage, Political Propaganda, and Public Architecture in Twentieth-Century Iran," PhD thesis, Massachusetts Institute of Technology (2004).

Hale, F., *From Persian Uplands* (London, 1920).

I'temad al-Saltaneh, M., *Mir'at-e al-Buldan-e Nasseri* (Mirror of the Nasseri Lands) (Tehran, 1877).

Javanshir, F. M. (F. M Mizani), *Hemaseh-ye Dad* (Epic of Justice) (Tehran, 1980).

Kasravi, A., *Tarekhcheh-e Shir-u-Khorshid* (Short History of the Lion and Sun) (Tehran 1934).

    Tarekh-e Hejdah Saleh-e Azerbaijan (Eighteen-Year History of Azerbaijan) (Tehran, 1967).

    Tarekh-e Mashruteh-e Iran (History of the Iranian Constitution) (Tehran, 1961).

    Tarekh-e Pansad Saleh-e Khuzestan (Five-Hundred-Year History of Khuzestan) (Tehran, 1950).

    Zendegani-ye Man (My Life) (Tehran, 1946).

Kermani, Nazem al-Islam, *Tarekh-e Bedari-ye Iraniyan* (History of the Iranian Awakening), 3 vols. (Tehran, 1946).

Landor, A., *Across Coveted Lands* (New York, 1903).

MacGregor, C., *Narrative of a Journey through the Province of Khurasan*, 2 vols. (London, 1879).

Majd, M. G., *The Great Famine and Genocide in Persia, 1917–1919* (New York: University Press of America, 2003).

Malcolm, J., *History of Persia*, 2 vols. (London, 1829).

Malekzadeh, M., *Tarekekh-e Enqelab-e Mashruteyat-e Iran* (History of the Constitutional Revolution in Iran), 6 vols. (Tehran, 1949).

Moazemi, B., "The Making of the State, Religion and the Islamic Revolution in Iran (1796–1979)," PhD thesis, New School University (2003).

Mostowfi, A. *Tarekh-e Idari va Ijtema'i-ye Dowreh-e Qajariyya ya Shahr-e Zendegani-ye Man* (Administrative and Social History of the Qajar Era or a Narrative of My Life), 3 vols. (Tehran, 1943–45). 8.

Najafabadi, S., *Shahed-e Javid* (Eternal Martyr) (Tehran, 1981).

Piemontese, A., "An Italian Source for the History of Qajar Persia," *East and West*, Vol. 19, Nos. 1–2 (March–June 1969), pp. 147–75.

    "The Statutes of the Qajar Orders of Knighthood," *East and West*, Vol. 19, Nos. 3–4 (September–December 1969), pp. 431–73.

Qodsi, H. (Azam al-Vazeh), *Ketab-e Khaterat-e Man* (Book of My Memoirs) (Tehran, 1963).

Rabino, H., *Mazandaran and Astarabad* (London, 1928).

Rezai, A., *Nahzat-e Husseini* (Hussein's Movement) (Springfield, Mo.: Liberation Movement of Iran Publication, 1975).

Schayegh, C., "Modern Civilization is Paradoxical: Science, Medicine, and Class in the Formation of Semi-Colonial Iran, 1910–1940s", PhD thesis, Columbia University (2003).

Shaji'i, Z., *Nemayandegan-e Majles-e Showra-ye Melli* (Deputies in the National Assembly) (Tehran, 1964).

Vezarat va Veziran dar Iran (Ministries and Ministers in Iran) (Tehran, 1975).

Shariati, A., *Majmu'eh-e Asar* (Collected Works), 36 vols. (Aachen: Husseinieh-e Ershad Publications, 1977).

Stack, E., *Six Months in Persia*, 2 vols. (New York, 1882).

Tahvildar-e Isfahan, M., *Jughrafiya-ye Isfahan* (The Geography of Isfahan) (Tehran, 1963).

Further reading

GENERAL

Avery, P., *Modern Iran* (London: Benn, 1965).

Bakhash, S., "Historiography of Modern Iran," *American Historical Review*, Vol. 96, No. 5 (December 1991), pp. 1479–96.

Beck, L., *The Qashaqa'i of Iran* (New Haven: Yale University Press, 1986).

Bharier, J., *Economic Development in Iran, 1900–1970* (Oxford: Oxford University Press, 1971).

Bosworth, E. and Hillenbrand, C. (eds.), *Qajar Iran: Political, Social and Cultural Change, 1800–1925* (Edinburgh: Edinburgh University Press, 1983).

Cole. J., *Modernity and the Millennium: The Genesis of the Baha'i Faith in the Nineteenth Century* (New York: Columbia University Press, 1998).

Daniel, E., *The History of Iran* (London: Greenwood Press, 2001).

Fisher, W. B., *Cambridge History of Iran: The Land of Iran* (Cambridge: Cambridge University Press, 1968), Vol. I.

Garthwaite, G., *Khans and Shahs: A Documentary History of the Baktiyari in Iran* (Cambridge: Cambridge University Press, 1983).

The Persians (Oxford: Blackwell, 2004).

Hourcade, B., Mazurek, H., Taleghani, M., and Papol-Yazdi, M., *Altas d'Iran* (Paris: RECLUS, 1998).

Issawi, C., *Economic History of Iran, 1800–1914* (Chicago: Chicago University Press, 1971).

Kashani-Sabet, F., *Frontier Fictions: Land, Culture, and Shaping the Iranian Nation, 1804–1946* (Princeton: Princeton University Press, 2000).

Keddie, N., *Iran: Religion, Politics and Society* (London: Cass, 1980).

(ed.), *Religion and Politics in Iran* (New Haven: Yale University Press, 1983).

Koohi-Kamali, F., *The Political Development of the Kurds in Iran* (New York: Palgrave, 2003).

Limbert, J., *Iran: At War with History* (London: Croom Helm, 1987).

Meshkoob, Sh., *Iranian Nationality and the Persian Language* (Washington, DC: Mage, 1992).

Sanasarian, E., *Religious Minorities in Iran* (Cambridge: Cambridge University Press, 2000).

Smith, P., *The Babi and Baha'i Religions* (Cambridge: Cambridge University Press, 1987).

Vaziri, M., *Iran as Imagined Nation* (New York: Paragon, 1993).

CONSTITUTIONAL PERIOD

Afary, J., *The Iranian Constitutional Revolution of 1906–1911* (NewYork: Columbia University Press, 1996).

Afshari, M., "The Historians of the Constitutional Movement," *International Journal of Middle East Studies*, Vol. 25, No. 3 (August 1993), pp. 477–94.

"The Pishivaran and Merchants in Precapitalist Iranian Society," *International Journal of Middle East Studies*, Vol. 15, No. 2 (May 1983), pp. 133–55.

Algar, H., *Mirza Malkum Khan* (Berkeley: University of California Press, 1973).

"The Oppositional Role of the Ulama's Power in Modern Iran," *Scholars, Saints and Sufis* (edited by N. Keddie) (Berkeley: University of California Press, 1972), pp. 211–30.

Religion and State in Iran, 1785–1906 (Berkeley: University of California Press, 1969).

Arjomand, S., "The Ulama's Traditionalist Opposition to Parliamentarianism: 1907–1909," *Middle Eastern Studies*, Vol. 17, No. 2 (April 1981), pp. 174–85.

Ashraf, A., "The Roots of Emerging Dual Class Structure in Nineteenth-Century Iran," *Iranian Studies*, Vol. 14, Nos. 1–2 (Winter–Spring 1981), pp. 5–28.

Bakhash, S., "Center–Periphery Relations in Nineteenth-Century Iran," *Iranian Studies*, Vol. 14, Nos. 1–2 (Winter–Spring 1981), pp. 29–52.

Balfour, H., *Recent Happenings in Persia* (London, 1922).

Bayat, M., *Iran's First Revolution* (Oxford: Oxford University Press, 1991).

Mysticism and Dissent: Socioreligious Thought in Qajar Iran (Syracuse University Press, 1982).

Berberian, H., *Armenians and the Iranian Constitutional Revolution of 1905–1911* (Boulder: Westview Press, 2001).

Browne, E., *The Persian Revolution of 1905–1909* (New York: Barnes and Noble, 1910).

Press and Poetry of Modern Persia (Cambridge: Cambridge University Press, 1914).

Fisher, J., *Curzon and British Imperialism in the Middle East* (London: Cass, 1999).

Gilbar, G., "The Opening of Qajar Iran," *Bulletin of the School of Oriental and African Studies*, Vol. 49, Part 1 (1986), pp. 76–89.

Gilmour, D., *Curzon* (London: Papermac, 1995).

Haeri, A., *Shi'ism and Constitutionalism in Iran* (Leiden: Brill, 1977).

Keddie, N., "Iranian Politics, 1900–1905: Background to Revolution," *Middle Eastern Studies*, Vol. 5, Nos. 1–3 (1969), pp. 3–31, 151–67, 234–50.

Qajar Iran and the Rise of Reza Shah (Costa Mesa: Mazda, 1966).

Religion and Rebellion in Iran: The Tobacco Protest of 1891–92 (London: Frank Cass, 1966).

Lambton, A., *Qajar Persia* (Austin: University of Texas Press, 1988).

Majd, M., *The Great Famine and Genocide in Persia, 1917–1919* (New York: University Press of America, 2003).

Martin, V., *Islam and Modernism: The Iranian Revolution of 1905* (Syracuse University Press, 1989).

Mozaffari, N. "Crafting Constitutionalism: Ali Akbar Dehkhoda and the Iranian Constitutional Revolution," PhD thesis, Harvard University (2001).

Najmabadi, A., *The Daughters of Quchan* (Syracuse: Syracuse University Press, 1998).

　Women with Mustaches and Men without Beards: Gender and Sexual Anxieties in Iranian Modernity (Berkeley: University of California Press, 2005).

Olson, W., *Anglo-Iranian Relations during World War I* (London: Cass, 1984).

Safiri, F., "The South Persian Rifles," PhD thesis, Edinburgh University (1976).

Sheikholeslami, R., *The Structure of Central Authority in Qajar Iran, 1871–96* (Atlanta: Scholars Press, 1997).

Shuster, M., *The Strangling of Persia* (New York, 1912).

Stanwood, F., *War, Revolution and British Imperialism in Central Asia* (London: Ithaca Press, 1983).

Tavakoli-Targhi, M., *Refashioning Iran: Orientalism, Occidentalism and Historiography* (New York: Palgrave, 2001).

PAHLAVI ERA

Akhavi, Sh., *Religion and Politics in Contemporary Iran* (Albany: State University of New York Press, 1980).

Amirsadeghi, H., *Twentieth Century Iran* (London: Heinemann, 1977).

Amuzegar, J., *The Dynamics of the Iranian Revolution: The Pahlavi Triumph and Tragedy* (Albany: State University of New York Press, 1991).

Ansari, A., *Modern Iran since 1921* (London: Longman, 2003).

Atabaki, T., *Azerbaijan: Ethnicity and Autonomy in Twentieth-Century Iran* (London: Tauris, 1993).

Azimi, F., *Iran: The Crisis of Democracy, 1941–1953* (New York: St. Martin's Press, 1989).

Banani, A., *Modernization of Iran* (Stanford: Stanford University Press, 1961).

Bayne, E., *Persian Kingship in Transition* (New York: American Universities Field Staff, 1968).

Binder, L., *Iran: Political Development in a Changing Society* (Berkeley: University of California Press, 1962).

Chehabi, H., "Staging the Emperor's New Clothes: Dress Codes and Nation-Building under Reza Shah," *Iranian Studies*, Vol. 26, Nos. 3–4 (Summer–Fall 1993), pp. 209–30.

Clawson, P., "Knitting Iran Together: The Land Transport Revolution," *Iranian Studies*, Vol. 26, Nos. 3–4 (Summer–Fall 1993), pp. 235–50.

Cronin, S. (ed.), *The Making of Modern Iran* (London: Tauris, 2003).

Dorman, W. and Farhang, M., *The US Press and Iran* (Berkeley: University of California Press, 1987).

Ehlers, E. and Floor, W., "Urban Change in Iran, 1920–1941," *Iranian Studies*, Vol. 26, Nos. 3–4 (Summer–Fall 1993), pp. 251–76.

Enayat, H., *Modern Islamic Political Thought* (London: Macmillan, 1982).

Ghani, C., *Iran and the Rise of Reza Shah* (London: Tauris, 1998).

Gheissari, A., *Iranian Intellectuals in the Twentieth Century* (Austin: University of Texas Press, 1998).

Hooglund, E., *Land and Revolution in Iran* (Austin: Texas University Press, 1980).

Jacvqz, J. (ed.), *Iran: Past, Present and Future* (New York: Aspen Institute, 1975).

Karshenas, M., *Oil, State and Industrialization in Iran* (Cambridge: Cambridge University Press, 1990).

Katouzian, H., *The Political Economy of Modern Iran* (New York: New York University Press, 1981).

Ladjevardi, H., *Labor Unions and Autocracy in Iran* (Syracuse: Syracuse University Press, 1985).

Lambton, A., *The Persian Land Reform* (Oxford: Clarendon Press, 1969).

Lenczowski, G. (ed.), *Iran under the Pahlavis* (Stanford: Hoover Institution, 1978).

Matthee, R., "Transforming Dangerous Nomads into Useful Artisans," *Iranian Studies*, Vol. 26, Nos. 3–4 (Summer–Fall 1993), pp. 313–36.

Menashri, D., *Education and the Making of Modern Iran* (Ithaca: Cornell University Press, 1992).

Milani, A., *The Persian Sphinx: Amir Abbas Hoveyda* (Washington, DC: Mage, 2000).

Millspaugh, A., *The American Task in Persia* (New York: Century, 1925).

Americans in Persia (Washington, DC: Brookings Institution Press, 1946).

Paidar, P., *Women and the Political Process in Twentieth-Century Iran* (Cambridge: Cambridge University Press, 1995).

Perry, J., "Language Reform in Turkey and Iran," *International Journal of Middle East Studies*, Vol. 17, No. 3 (August 1985), pp. 295–311.

Ramazani, R., *Iran's Foreign Policy, 1941–1973* (Charlottesville: Virginia University Press, 1975).

Rezun, M., *The Soviet Union and Iran* (London: Westview Press, 1988).

Upton, J., *The History of Modern Iran: An Interpretation* (Cambridge, Mass.: Harvard University Press, 1968).

Wilber, D., *Reza Shah Pahlavi* (New York: Exposition Press, 1975).

Yar-Shalter, E. (ed.), *Iran Faces the Seventies* (New York: Praeger, 1971).

Zonis, M., *Majestic Failure: The Fall of the Shah* (Chicago: University of Chicago Press, 1991).

THE ISLAMIC REVOLUTION AND REPUBLIC

Adelkhah, F., *Being Modern in Iran* (New York: Columbia University Press, 2000).

Afary, J. and Anderson, K., *Foucault and the Iranian Revolution* (Chicago: Chicago University Press, 2005).

Amuzegar, J., *Iran's Economy under the Islamic Republic* (London: Tauris, 1993).

Ansari, A., *Iran, Islam and Democracy* (London: Royal Institute of International Affairs, 2000).

Arjomand, S., *The Turban for the Crown* (New York: Oxford University Press, 1988).

Bakhash, S., *The Reign of the Ayatollahs* (New York: Basic Books, 1984).

Bakhtiari, B., *Parliamentary Politics in Revolutionary Iran* (Gainesville: University Press of Florida, 1996).

Bashuriyeh, H., *The State and Revolution in Iran* (London: Croom Helm, 1984).

Bayat, A., *Street Politics: Poor People's Movements in Iran* (New York: Columbia University Press, 1997).

   Workers and Revolution in Iran (London: Zed Books, 1987).

Behrooz, M., *Rebels with a Cause: Failure of the Left in Iran* (London: Tauris, 1999).

Bellaigue, C., *In the Rose Garden of the Martyrs: A Memoir of Iran* (New York: HarperCollins, 2005).

Boroujerdi, M., *Iranian Intellectuals and the West* (Syracuse: Syracuse University Press, 1996).

Brumberg, D., *Reinventing Khomeini* (Chicago: Chicago University Press, 2001).

Chehabi, H., *Iranian Politics and Religious Modernism* (New York: Cornell University Press, 1990).

Dabashi, H., *Iran: A People Interrupted* (New York: New Press, 2007).

   Theology of Discontent: The Ideological Foundation of the Islamic Revolution in Iran (New York: New York University Press, 1993).

Ebadi, S., *Iran Awakening: A Memoir of Revolution and Hope* (New York: Random House, 2006).

Ehteshami, A., *After Khomeini* (London: Routledge, 1995).

Farhi, F., *States and Urban-Based Revolutions* (Chicago: Illinois University Press, 1990).

Fischer, M., *Iran from Religious Dispute to Revolution* (Cambridge, Mass.: Harvard University Press, 1980).

Gheissari, A. and Nasr, V., *Democracy in Iran* (New York: Oxford University Press, 2006).

Green, J., *Revolution in Iran* (New York: Praeger, 1982).

Harney, D., *The Priest and the King: An Eyewitness Account of the Iranian Revolution* (London: Tauris, 1999).

Hooglund, E. (ed.), *Twenty Years of Islamic Revolution* (Syracuse: Syracuse University Press, 2002).

Howard, R., *Iran in Crisis?* (London: Zed Books, 2004).

Kazemi, F., *Poverty and Revolution in Iran* (New York: New York University Press, 1980).

Keddie, N., *Iran and the Muslim World* (London: Macmillan, 1995).

   Modern Iran: Roots and Results of Revolution (New Haven: Yale University Press, 2003).

Kurzman, C., *The Unthinkable Revolution in Iran* (Cambridge, Mass.: Harvard University Press, 2004).

Martin, V., *Creating an Islamic State* (London: Tauris, 2000).

Matin-asgari, A., *Iranian Student Opposition to the Shah* (Costa Mesa: Mazda, 2002).

Mir-Hosseini, Z., *Islam and Gender: The Religious Debate in Contemporary Iran* (Princeton: Princeton University Press, 1999).

Mirsepassi, A., *Intellectual Discourse and the Politics of Modernization* (Cambridge: Cambridge University Press, 2000).

Moaddel, M., *Class, Politics and Ideology in the Iranian Revolution* (New York: Columbia University Press, 1993).

Moin, B., *Khomeini* (London: Tauris, 1999).

Mottahedeh, R., *The Mantle of the Prophet: Religion and Politics in Iran* (New York: Simon and Schuster, 1983).

Mozaffari, N., *Strange Times, My Dear: The Pen Anthology of Contemporary Iranian Literature* (New York: Arcadia Press, 2005).

Nabavi, N., *Intellectuals and the State in Iran* (Gainesville: University Press of Florida, 2003).

Parsa, M., *Social Origins of the Iranian Revolution* (New Brunswick: Rutgers University Press, 1989).

Rahnema, A., *An Islamic Utopian: A Political Biography of Ali Shari'ati* (London: Tauris, 1998).

Rahnema, A. and Behdad, S. (eds.), *Iran after the Revolution* (London: Tauris, 1991).

Rahnema, A. and Nomani, F., *The Secular Miracle: Religion, Politics and Economic Policy in Iran* (London: Zed Books, 1990).

Richard, Y., *Shi'ite Islam* (Oxford: Blackwell, 1995).

Satrapi, M., *Persepolis: The Story of a Childhood* (New York: Pantheon, 2002).

Schirazi, A., *The Constitution of Iran* (London: Tauris, 1997).

   Islamic Development Policy: The Agrarian Question in Iran (London: Lynne Rienner, 1993).

Sciolino, E., *Persian Mirrors* (New York: Free Press, 2000).

Takeyh, R., *Hidden Iran: Paradox and Power in the Islamic Republic* (New York: Council on Foreign Relations, 2006).

Vahdat, F., *God and Juggernaut: Iran's Intellectual Encounter with Modernity* (Syracuse: Syracuse University Press, 2002).

Varzi, R., *Warring Souls: Youth, Media, and Martyrdom in Post-Revolution Iran* (London: Duke University Press, 2006).

Yaghmaian, B., *Social Change in Iran* (Albany: State University of New York Press, 2002).

Index